EXEGETICAL JOURNEYS IN BIBLICAL HEBREW

90 DAYS
of Guided Reading

H. H. HARDY II

Baker Academic

a division of Baker Publishing Group

Grand Rapids, Michigan

© 2025 by H. H. Hardy II

Published by Baker Academic
a division of Baker Publishing Group
Grand Rapids, Michigan
BakerAcademic.com

Library of Congress Cataloging-in-Publication Data
Names: Hardy, H. H., II, 1979– author.
Title: Exegetical journeys in Biblical Hebrew : 90 days of guided reading / H.H. Hardy, II.
Description: Grand Rapids, Michigan : Baker Academic, 2025. | Includes bibliographical references and index.
Identifiers: LCCN 2024030905 | ISBN 9781540965097 (paperback) | ISBN 9781540967756 (casebound) | ISBN 9781493446056 (ebook) | ISBN 9781493446063 (pdf)
Subjects: LCSH: Bible. Old Testament—Criticism, interpretation, etc. | Hebrew language—Grammar—Textbooks. | LCGFT: Textbooks.
Classification: LCC BS1171.3 .H38 2025 | DDC 221.6—dc23/eng/20240802
LC record available at https://lccn.loc.gov/2024030905

Unless otherwise indicated, Scripture translations are the author's own, and versification follows the Hebrew text.

Cover art of the Leningrad Codex: SuperStock, Pictures from History / Universal Images

Baker Publishing Group publications use paper produced from sustainable forestry practices and postconsumer waste whenever possible.

25   26   27   28   29   30   31   7   6   5   4   3   2   1

To Amy
and the journeys together

CONTENTS

ACKNOWLEDGMENTS

The idea for this volume was fashioned cooperatively with my fellow ex-egetical journeyer Ben Merkle of Southeastern Baptist Theological Seminary. His companion volume appears as *Exegetical Journeys in Biblical Greek* (Baker Academic, 2023). Bryan Dyer and the superb folks at Baker Publishing Group continue to be wonderful supporters and partners in developing high quality biblical language resources.

This volume was completed during the Michaelmas term of 2023 in Cambridge, England. I am grateful for the many fine people in the faculty of Asian and Middle Eastern studies for being such wonderful academic hosts, Tyndale House for the hospitable environment, Kirby Laing Center for Public Theology in Cambridge for the nurturing community, and Saint Andrew the Great for providing a spiritual home.

ABBREVIATIONS

General and Bibliographic

4Q424	Sarah J. Tanzer, "424. 4QInstruction-like Composition B," in *Qumran Cave 4*, vol. 26, *Cryptic Texts and Miscellanea*, part 1, *Miscellaneous Texts from Qumran*, ed. Stephen J. Pfann et al., Discoveries in the Judaean Desert 36 (Oxford: Clarendon, 2000), 333–46.
BH	Biblical Hebrew
cf.	compare
CSB	Christian Standard Bible
e.g.	*exempli gratia*, for example
ESV	English Standard Version
Gk.	Greek
KJV	King James Version
LXX	Septuagint/Old Greek
MT	Masoretic Text
NASB95	New American Standard Bible (1995)
NET	New English Translation
NIV	New International Version
NKJV	New King James Version
NLT	New Living Translation
NRSV	New Revised Standard Version
NT	New Testament
OT	Old Testament
Tanakh	JPS Tanakh: The Holy Scriptures
trans.	translation; translated by
v(v).	verse(s)

ABBREVIATIONS

Grammatical

1	first person	NEG	negative
2	second person	NP	noun phrase
3	third person	NUM	numeral
ABS	absolute state	Numb.	grammatical number
ACT PTCL	active participle	PASS PTCL	passive participle
ADJ	adjective	PC	prefix conjugation (or
ADV	adverb		imperfective, *yiqtol*)
CJ	conjunction	Pers.	person
Conj.	verb conjugation	PL	plural number
CP	common plural	PN	proper noun
CS	common singular	PP	prepositional phrase
CSTR	construct state	PREP	preposition
DEF ART	definite article	PRO	pronoun
DEM	demonstrative	PTC	particle
DU	dual number	PTCL	participle
F	feminine	REL	relative
FP	feminine plural	SC	suffix conjugation (or
FS	feminine singular		perfective, *qātal*)
Gend.	gender	SF	pronominal suffix
IMV	imperative	SG	singular number
INF ABS	infinitive absolute	VB	verb
INF CSTR	infinitive construct	*wayyiqtol*	consecutive preterite
INT	interrogative		(or *waw*-consecutive
JUSS	jussive		imperfect)
M	masculine	*wəqātal*	consecutive perfect
MP	masculine plural		(or *waw*-consecutive
MS	masculine singular		perfect)
N	noun		

Old Testament

Gen.	Genesis	2 Kings	2 Kings
Exod.	Exodus	1 Chron.	1 Chronicles
Lev.	Leviticus	2 Chron.	2 Chronicles
Num.	Numbers	Ezra	Ezra
Deut.	Deuteronomy	Neh.	Nehemiah
Josh.	Joshua	Esther	Esther
Judg.	Judges	Job	Job
Ruth	Ruth	Ps(s).	Psalm(s)
1 Sam.	1 Samuel	Prov.	Proverbs
2 Sam.	2 Samuel	Eccles.	Ecclesiastes
1 Kings	1 Kings	Song	Song of Songs

Isa.	Isaiah	Jon.	Jonah
Jer.	Jeremiah	Mic.	Micah
Lam.	Lamentations	Nah.	Nahum
Ezek.	Ezekiel	Hab.	Habakkuk
Dan.	Daniel	Zeph.	Zephaniah
Hosea	Hosea	Hag.	Haggai
Joel	Joel	Zech.	Zechariah
Amos	Amos	Mal.	Malachi
Obad.	Obadiah		

New Testament

Matt.	Matthew	1 Tim.	1 Timothy
Mark	Mark	2 Tim.	2 Timothy
Luke	Luke	Titus	Titus
John	John	Philem.	Philemon
Acts	Acts	Heb.	Hebrews
Rom.	Romans	James	James
1 Cor.	1 Corinthians	1 Pet.	1 Peter
2 Cor.	2 Corinthians	2 Pet.	2 Peter
Gal.	Galatians	1 John	1 John
Eph.	Ephesians	2 John	2 John
Phil.	Philippians	3 John	3 John
Col.	Colossians	Jude	Jude
1 Thess.	1 Thessalonians	Rev.	Revelation
2 Thess.	2 Thessalonians		

INTRODUCTION

Learning shares much in common with going on a journey. You begin in one place and end somewhere else. Sometimes a clear destination is in view. Other times it is about the exploration along the way. The allure of adventure and new experiences beckon travelers to set seemingly unattainable goals in search of undiscovered locations and distant heights.

The best journeys involve others. The wise traveler brings along an experienced guide, or at least a guidebook! Often the simple act of walking the route with someone else alleviates much of the burden. Veteran explorers convey indispensable travel tips. Harmful detours can be evaded. And being together can lead to knowing oneself and others better. In the end, the act of journeying changes your vantage point. You are not the same as when you left.

Learning to read Biblical Hebrew is a journey. From writing your first *aleph* to completing your first reading of the Torah, the trek is both transformative and challenging. But it can be arduous. It can be lonely. It can seem like the destination is too far off, or at times getting farther away. Yet, we set off with the goal to read Hebrew. This exegetical journey is worth the effort.

My hope is that this guidebook can provide some remedies for the weary Hebrew traveler. As someone who has walked with many, many others along the path, I want to encourage you by pointing out the glorious vistas and helping avoid hazards. Ultimately, my goal is that you will find the experience of the journey just as formative as the joy of arrival.

Who Can Benefit from This Book?

If you have completed a basic introduction to Biblical Hebrew grammar, this volume is written for you. Even if it's been a few (or many) years since your last encounter with Hebrew, you can benefit.

These exegetical journeys answer a question that I am asked at the completion of nearly every cycle of teaching Hebrew. *What's next?* I also hear a similar question from those more distant from their formal Hebrew schooling: *What can I do to pick back up with Hebrew or improve my comprehension?* Previously, I would point to various tools but encourage above all else: *Read the Bible!* A few verses at a time are all it takes. Find a biblical passage you want to know more about and read it. That is ostensibly the reason most students took Hebrew courses in the first place.

This advice is sound. And undoubtedly, many would try. Some may have even found their own way. The journey, as with all worthwhile journeys, is accomplished through small, incremental, and regular steps. But experience tells me that without further guidance, few create a pattern of regular engagement with the Hebrew Scriptures.

This volume is an attempt to provide better guidance. It is my way of walking together with you to read and journey through the Scriptures. I have attempted to assemble manageable, level-appropriate readings. Each increases in difficulty incrementally. And I try to point to the most salient details on the path and to provide encouragement along the way. Alongside my *Exegetical Gems from the Hebrew Old Testament: A Refreshing Guide to Grammar and Interpretation* (Baker Academic, 2019), this volume serves to build greater reading fluency, grammatical experience, and interpretive understanding.

My hope is that this shared journey becomes a lifelong adventure in reading the Scriptures in Hebrew and loving the God revealed therein.

How to Use This Book

The guided readings are divided into three month-long journeys consisting of twelve different routes. The thirty-day journeys progress in difficulty. Journey 1 is designed to ease most journeyers into their first month of exegetical reading. Journeys 2 and 3 continue and expand on the initial routes.

The twelve routes reflect a range of literary texts and genres. Some routes include as few as five verses. Others include an entire biblical chapter. The routes are split into manageable daily readings of between one and three verses.[1] Each day's reading can be completed in about

---

1. Wherever the chapter and verse divisions of the Hebrew text differ from the versification of modern English Bibles, only the Hebrew reference is given.

ten to fifteen minutes. Everything the reader needs is provided, including rare vocabulary, parsing, and descriptions of difficult grammar.[2] An appendix provides all forms and glosses of the most common Hebrew words occurring more than 200 times in the Hebrew Bible.

The first journey starts slow, and with each new route the reading progressively builds. It could be worthwhile to repeat a route as they become more challenging. By the end of each series, readers should feel confident to advance to the next route. If the readings become too difficult too quickly, head back to familiar ground. Return to the more challenging readings only after you have reviewed and mastered the earlier material.

Five steps organize each daily reading. This order follows a well-trodden pattern of exploring any biblical text.

1. **Read** aloud the text at least five times.

   Read the passage aloud. Try not to get stuck or glance ahead to the other steps. Read it again. Familiarize yourself with the sound of the words.[3] Then read it a third time. Take a deep breath, or a sip of coffee. Read it two more times.

2. **Parse** the verbs.

   Using a pencil or, for the daring, a pen, fill in the fundamental characteristics of each verb. The stem is recognized by the vowel patterns, lengthening, and affixes. The verbal stem gives nuance to the verb's meaning and how other elements (subject, object, etc.) are involved in the clause structure. The conjugation is further determined by various prefixes and suffixes.[4] The verbal conjugation provides a sense of the time, aspect, and modality of the action or event. When applicable, person, gender,

---

2. I attempt to use common grammatical descriptions so that the reader does not need to rely on additional resources. At times, referring to a beginning grammar may be helpful to refresh one's knowledge of basic Hebrew grammatical descriptions. In such cases, I have benefitted from Gary A. Long, *Grammatical Concepts 101 for Biblical Hebrew*, 2nd ed. (Grand Rapids: Baker Academic, 2013).

3. Traditional cantillation marks (accents) appear only in the Hebrew reading sections. Elsewhere, ʿōlê (ˋ) functions generically to mark any nonfinal accent to help with correct pronunciation (e.g., שְׂפָתֶ֫יךָ).

4. The terminology for BH verb forms varies widely among beginning textbooks and instructors. The names used in this volume are mostly descriptive and align with basic morphological features. Prefix conjugation (PC) describes what is elsewhere dubbed the imperfect(ive) or *yiqtol*. Suffix conjugation (SC) is used for the perfect(ive) or *qātal*. The corresponding *waw*-consecutive forms are labeled *wayyiqtol* and *wəqātal*, respectively.

and number detail the grammatical traits of the subject. The root is typically three letters. The verbal root provides a general notion of what the form means. Finally, a basic translation value or gloss is specified. All verb forms occurring less than 200 times in the Hebrew Bible are included. *The solutions are presented at the end of each day's reading.* Always check your work!

3. **Identify** the grammatical items.

Answer a few questions about the grammar of the reading. The point is to help you identify salient details that may otherwise be missed. The questions are examples of the kind of information that can be overlooked or missed in cursory readings or simply reading an English translation. By paying attention to these details, your Hebrew understanding and interpretation will improve. As you get used to these kinds of questions, you can listen for this information as you read other passages.[5] *The solutions are presented at the end of each day's reading.*

4. **Translate** the text.

Write an initial sketch of how you understand the reading. All vocabulary occurring less than 200 times is provided in the order of occurrence in the passage. At the end of the volume, a glossary includes all lexemes occurring more than 200 times in these passages. It is organized alphabetically by dictionary entry with grammatical descriptions for derived forms. *The author's English translation is presented at the end of each day's reading.*

5. **Notice** significant exegetical insights.

Consider some of the interesting and/or difficult issues in the passage. You may want to follow the references and look up additional information to understand the passage better.

Each reading ends with a section titled "For the Journey." This section provides a brief reflection on the broader exegetical realities of the passage. It is meant to foster greater connections between the daily reading and the Scriptures as a whole.

---

5. This step appears only for the first sixty days. At that point, readers should have progressed beyond the need for this repeated exercise.

Journey 1

BEGINNING

ROUTE 1

Genesis 1:1–5

DAY 1: GENESIS 1:1–3

STEP ONE: **Read** aloud the text at least five times.

בְּרֵאשִׁית בָּרָא אֱלֹהִים אֵת הַשָּׁמַיִם וְאֵת הָאָרֶץ: ²וְהָאָרֶץ
הָיְתָה תֹהוּ וָבֹהוּ וְחֹשֶׁךְ עַל־פְּנֵי תְהוֹם וְרוּחַ אֱלֹהִים מְרַחֶפֶת
עַל־פְּנֵי הַמָּיִם: ³וַיֹּאמֶר אֱלֹהִים יְהִי אוֹר וַיְהִי־אוֹר:

STEP TWO: **Parse** the following verbs.

	Stem	Conj.	Pers.	Gend.	Numb.	Root	Trans.
(1) בָּרָא	Qal	SC	3	M	S	ברא	create
(2) הָיְתָה							
(3) מְרַחֶפֶת							
(4) וַיֹּאמֶר							
(5) יְהִי							
(6) וַיְהִי							

STEP THREE: **Identify** the following.

A. What is the subject of בָּרָא? _____

B. What is אֵת in the first verse? _____

C. How is עַל־פְּנֵי functioning in the second verse? _____

7

STEP FOUR: **Translate** the text into understandable English.

> **VOCABULARY**
>
> רֵאשִׁית beginning, first (related to רֹאשׁ "head, top")
>
> בָּרָא Qal: create
>
> תֹהוּ וָבֹהוּ formless and void (see more below)
>
> חֹשֶׁךְ darkness
>
> תְּהוֹם the deep (waters)
>
> מְרַחֶפֶת hovering (from רחף)
>
> אוֹר light

STEP FIVE: **Notice** significant exegetical insights.

- בְּרֵאשִׁית: This prepositional phrase describes the setting of the creation account. An initial preposition is common in such situations and designates a temporal relationship ("when" or "in"). Some have understood רֵאשִׁית as a definite noun, but the article is missing (cf. Tiberian Hebrew בָּרֵאשִׁית). Another possible analysis understands the noun as in construct with the verb phrase (cf. Jer. 26:1). This would result in the entire first verse—not just the first word—being a temporal relation (see Hosea 1:2, תְּחִלַּת דִּבֶּר־יְהוָה בְּהוֹשֵׁעַ "when the LORD first spoke with Hosea").

- בָּרָא: This verb describes an originating action that only God does. Elsewhere, he creates (ברא) darkness (Isa. 45:7), wind (Amos 4:13), clouds of smoke and fire (Isa. 4:5), humankind (Gen. 5:1), male and female humans (Gen. 1:27), and all living creatures, winged birds, and the sea monsters (Gen. 1:21).

- אֵת הַשָּׁמַיִם וְאֵת הָאָרֶץ: The common hendiadys "the heavens and the land" depicts the entirety of the seen and unseen realm. It comprises everything. This word order is very consistent, so it is notable that the sequence is inverted in Gen. 2:4 (אֶרֶץ וְשָׁמָיִם "land and heaven"), completing the merism structure and signaling the end of this account.

- תֹהוּ וָבֹהוּ: This word pair represents the shapelessness and emptiness of the land (cf. Jer. 4:23). The unfolding narrative reveals God's purposes to form the cosmos (days 1–3) and fill it (days 4–6), depicted through the beautifully crafted account of the creation week.

- תְהוֹם . . . הַמָּיִם: In ancient cosmology, the watery abyss represents a chaotic realm, and "the watery deep" is the supreme antithesis of God. Dreadful beasts come from the sea (Dan. 7:3), but an end is coming for even the frightful sea (Rev. 21:1)!

- וַיֹּאמֶר אֱלֹהִים: God fashions the heavens and earth through creative speech acts. God speaks, and light breaks into darkness (v. 3). The content of his speech, יְהִי אוֹר "let there be light," comprises a jussive verb indicating an indirect command. It is followed by the narrative echo, "there was light" (וַיְהִי־אוֹר). The Word of God is active. The Word creates, forms, and accomplishes the divine purposes.

FOR THE JOURNEY

These opening words portray the purpose and intention of the Creator. Nothing is outside of his supreme reach or aims. Even the utter darkness and the dreadful waters are under the purview of divine authority, and they conform to his cosmic organization.

At the same time, God's Spirit (רוּחַ) and Word are manifest in this account displaying the agents of his originating activities. His Spirit moves the waters (Gen. 8:1; Exod. 15:10; Isa. 59:19), and ten divine speech acts form the entire cosmos (cf. Exod. 34:28, עֲשֶׂרֶת הַדְּבָרִים).

Later biblical texts expand on the mysterious nature of these first actors and identify their creative roles (Prov. 8:22–31; John 1; cf. Sirach 1).

ANSWER KEY

1. *Parse:* (1) בָּרָא (Qal sc 3ms ברא "create"). (2) הָיְתָה (Qal sc 3fs היה "be").
   (3) מְרַחֶפֶת (Piel ptcl fs רחף "hover"). (4) וַיֹּאמֶר (Qal *wayyiqtol* 3ms אמר
   "say"). (5) יְהִי (Qal juss 3ms היה "be"). (6) וַיְהִי (Qal *wayyiqtol* 3ms היה "be").

2. *Identify:* (A) אֱלֹהִים is the subject of בָּרָא even though it is indefinite and plural
   in form. (B) אֵת designates the definite direct object of the verb. (C) עַל־פְּנֵי is
   a prepositional phrase, meaning "upon the face of" or "above," functioning to
   indicate location.

3. *Translate:* "In the beginning when God created the whole cosmos and the
   world—at once the land was a muddled mess, dark covered the deep abyss,
   and the Spirit of God lingered expectantly upon the watery surface—God proclaimed, 'Let light be!' And light dawned."

10

DAY 2: GENESIS 1:4–5

STEP ONE: **Read** aloud the text at least five times.

וַיַּרְא אֱלֹהִים אֶת־הָאוֹר כִּי־טוֹב וַיַּבְדֵּל אֱלֹהִים בֵּין הָאוֹר וּבֵין
הַחֹשֶׁךְ: ⁵וַיִּקְרָא אֱלֹהִים | לָאוֹר יוֹם וְלַחֹשֶׁךְ קָרָא לָיְלָה
וַיְהִי־עֶרֶב וַיְהִי־בֹקֶר יוֹם אֶחָד:

STEP TWO: **Parse** the following verbs.

	Stem	Conj.	Pers.	Gend.	Numb.	Root	Trans.
(1) וַיַּרְא	Qal	*wayyiqtol*	3	M	S	רָאה	see
(2) וַיַּבְדֵּל							
(3) וַיִּקְרָא							
(4) קָרָא							
(5) וַיְהִי							

STEP THREE: **Identify** the following.

A. What is the object of וַיַּרְא in verse 4? _____

B. How does the sequence . . . וּבֵין . . . בֵּין function?

_____

C. In verse 5, the verb קרא is used with the preposition לְ to mean

_____ .

STEP FOUR: **Translate** the text into understandable English.

_____

_____

VOCABULARY

אוֹר   light
בדל   Hiphil: separate, divide
חֹשֶׁךְ   darkness
עֶרֶב   evening, sunset

11

STEP FIVE: **Notice** significant exegetical insights.

- הָאוֹר: The light is the focus of the first day of creation. But God does more than speak the light into existence. He observes (ראה), divides (בדל), and names (קרא). In each of these clauses, the word אוֹר takes different semantic roles. It is the object of God's observation. It is a part of a compound prepositional phrase, differentiating it from חֹשֶׁךְ, and it is given a name, *daylight* (יוֹם).

- אֶת־הָאוֹר כִּי־טוֹב: The syntax of this clause appears out of order in English but is normal in Hebrew (cf. Gen. 49:15; Ps. 25:19). The object of the verb (ראה) is the entity observed or perceived. The following כִּי indicates what is observed or perceived about the object (הָאוֹר).

- הָאוֹר . . . הַחֹשֶׁךְ: Perhaps surprisingly, God's creation of light does not utterly eradicate the existing darkness (v. 2). As with the waters in day 2 (v. 6), he orders and labels each, demonstrating his sovereignty and giving dark and light purpose.

- וַיְהִי־עֶרֶב וַיְהִי־בֹקֶר יוֹם אֶחָד: This narrative reframe ends the first six days of creation (vv. 5, 8, 13, 19, 23, 31). Evening precedes morning. Each daily cycle echoes day 1 as starting with darkness awaiting and anticipating God's creative light to dawn.

FOR THE JOURNEY

While many moderns ascribe unplanned futility to creation and the ancients supposed nefarious capriciousness, the biblical author declares that the created realms are purposefully good (טוֹב). God manifests favorable conditions that his ambassadors will inhabit (v. 14). He intends order in a world formerly portrayed as formless and void (v. 2).

Naming the light and darkness (v. 5) procures consequence and purpose. An entity is named to differentiate it from another (vv. 5, 10) or to separate between similar substances (v. 8). A name provides meaning as part of the identity of the named entity (Gen. 16:13), function (Gen. 3:20; Isa. 58:12), and/or promise (Gen. 2:19; 21:12). And often in this way the one doing the naming is exercising authority or ownership over the one named (Deut. 28:10; Isa. 4:1).

ANSWER KEY

1. *Parse:* (1) וַיַּרְא (Qal *wayyiqtol* 3MS רָאה "see"). (2) וַיַּבְדֵּל (Hiphil *wayyiqtol* 3MS בדל "separate"). (3) וַיִּקְרָא (Qal *wayyiqtol* 3MS קרא "call"). (4) קָרָא (Qal SC 3MS קרא "call"). (5) וַיְהִי (Qal *wayyiqtol* 3MS היה "be").

2. *Identify:* (A) The object of רָאה "see" is הָאוֹר "the light" created in verse 3. (B) The preposition sequence "between . . . and between . . . " is a standard way of describing separation between two spaces or entities. (C) The verb (קרא) with the preposition (לְ) occurs twice in verse 5. This verb and preposition combine to indicate the action of naming where the indirect object (לְ) is the named entity (הָאוֹר or הַחֹשֶׁךְ) and the direct object is its name (יוֹם or לַיְלָה).

3. *Translate:* "God saw that the light was good. God separated between the light and the darkness, and God named the light 'day,' but he named the darkness 'night.' Evening and morning transpired: day 1."

ROUTE 2

Genesis 1:26–2:4a

STEP ONE: **Read** aloud the text at least five times.

וַיֹּאמֶר אֱלֹהִים נַעֲשֶׂה אָדָם בְּצַלְמֵנוּ כִּדְמוּתֵנוּ וְיִרְדּוּ בִדְגַת הַיָּם וּבְעוֹף הַשָּׁמַיִם וּבַבְּהֵמָה וּבְכָל־הָאָרֶץ וּבְכָל־הָרֶמֶשׂ הָרֹמֵשׂ עַל־הָאָרֶץ:

STEP TWO: **Parse** the following verbs.

	Stem	Conj.	Pers.	Gend.	Numb.	Root	Trans.
(1) וַיֹּאמֶר	Qal	*wayyiqtol*	3	M	S	אמר	say
(2) נַעֲשֶׂה							
(3) וְיִרְדּוּ							
(4) הָרֹמֵשׂ							

STEP THREE: **Identify** the following.

A. What is the subject of נַעֲשֶׂה? _____

B. What is the meaning of the sequence of רדה with בְּ? _____

_____

C. How is the participle הָרֹמֵשׂ functioning? _____

STEP FOUR: **Translate** the text into understandable English.

VOCABULARY

צֶלֶם idol, image

דְּמוּת likeness; shape

רדה Qal: rule

דָּגָה fish

עוֹף birds; insects

בְּהֵמָה beast; cattle

רֶמֶשׂ creeping things

רמשׂ Qal: creep; move about

STEP FIVE: **Notice** significant exegetical insights.

- אָדָם: The object of the creative word is an indefinite noun. Elsewhere, אָדָם can refer to the named individual (e.g., Gen. 4:25). However, here the word refers to a group ("humanity; human beings") as evidenced by the plural verb that follows.

- בְּצַלְמֵנוּ כִּדְמוּתֵנוּ: The two prepositional phrases may describe either how humanity is made (an adverbial function) or the qualities of the preceding entity (an attributive function).

- וְיִרְדּוּ: The subject of the plural verb is אָדָם ("humanity; human beings"). The noun is singular in form, but it refers to the group of distinct entities.

- בִדְגַת הַיָּם וּבְעוֹף הַשָּׁמַיִם וּבַבְּהֵמָה וּבְכָל־הָאָרֶץ וּבְכָל־הָרֶמֶשׂ: Each of these ruled groups represents a previously discussed collection. Sea creatures and birds are created on day 5 (vv. 20–21), and land beasts and creepy-crawlies on day 6 (v. 24).

- וּבְכָל־הָאָרֶץ: The threefold assessment of creatures (vv. 24–25) leads some ancient and modern readings to assume the reference is to all land-dwelling life: "and over every living being of the land" (cf. Gen. 9:10, וּבְכָל־חַיַּת הָאָרֶץ).

FOR THE JOURNEY

Scholars debate the meaning of image and likeness in this final creative act of the first week. A few parallel uses are helpful to consider:

- *Image* (צֶלֶם) mostly refers to idols or images of worship (Num. 33:52; 2 Kings 11:18; Ezek. 7:20). Occasionally, it refers to a depiction of something else (1 Sam. 6:5; Ezek. 16:17).
- *Likeness* (דְּמוּת) is used for resemblances of shape (Ezek. 1:5, 10) or pattern (2 Kings 16:10). These resemblances can be embodied (Dan. 10:16) or engraved (2 Chron. 4:3). Broader similarities are sometimes expressed with this term (Ps. 58:5; Isa. 13:4).

The two words are used together only one other time (Gen. 5:1–3). This passage refers to God's creation of humanity and extends both the idea of *image* and *likeness* to Adam's son, Seth, and by extension all humanity.

Humanity holds a unique position in Scripture as the only authorized divine image (Exod. 20:4). The NT unexpectedly turns this idea upside down. The Son of God incarnates the divine image (Col. 1:15). Jesus reconciles humanity through his death (v. 21). He is the ruler over all (1 Cor. 15:26; Eph. 1:20–22). And knowing Christ creates God's likeness in truth, purity, and righteousness (Eph. 4:20–24).

ANSWER KEY

1. *Parse:* (1) וַיֹּאמֶר (Qal *wayyiqtol* 3MS אמר "say"). (2) נַעֲשֶׂה (Qal PC 1CP עשה "make"). (3) וְיִרְדּוּ (CJ + Qal PC 3MP רדה "rule"). (4) הָרֹמֶשׂ (DEF ART + Qal ACT PTCL MS רמש "creep").

2. *Identify:* (A) God is the subject of נַעֲשֶׂה even though some consider it to include the angelic beings on account of the plural form. (B) The preposition object (בְּ) designates the entity experiencing the verb רדה "rule (over)." (C) The participle הָרֹמֶשׂ functions as an attributive adjective describing רֶמֶשׂ "creepy-crawlies."

3. *Translate:* "God said: 'We shall make human beings in our image according to our likeness so that they will rule over the fish of the sea, the birds of the heavens, the animals along with everything on the land, and every creepy-crawly roving on the land.'"

DAY 4: GENESIS 1:27

STEP ONE: **Read** aloud the text at least five times.

וַיִּבְרָ֨א אֱלֹהִ֤ים ׀ אֶת־הָֽאָדָם֙ בְּצַלְמ֔וֹ בְּצֶ֥לֶם אֱלֹהִ֖ים בָּרָ֣א אֹת֑וֹ
זָכָ֥ר וּנְקֵבָ֖ה בָּרָ֥א אֹתָֽם:

STEP TWO: **Parse** the following verbs.

	Stem	Conj.	Pers.	Gend.	Numb.	Root	Trans.
(1) וַיִּבְרָא							
(2) בָּרָא							

STEP THREE: **Identify** the following.

A. What is the difference in meaning between וַיִּבְרָא and בָּרָא?

_____

B. What word marks the object of all three verbs?

_____

C. Why is אָדָם marked with the definite article?

_____

STEP FOUR: **Translate** the text into understandable English.

_____

_____

VOCABULARY

בְּרָא   Qal: create
צֶלֶם   idol, image
זָכָר   male
נְקֵבָה   female

17

STEP FIVE: **Notice** significant exegetical insights.

- **וַיִּבְרָא**: The previous narrative event ("God said," v. 26) is followed by this creative action of God. The verb **ברא** is used twice earlier (vv. 1, 21) and twice later (2:3–4) in this first account. Verse 27 contains three instances of the same root. These verbs do not represent separate actions but evoke the same creative event with deepening, expanding nuances.

- **בְּצַלְמוֹ**: The previous verse refers to "our image" (**בְּצַלְמֵנוּ**). With the singular masculine pronoun, the text signals a return to the narrator's portrayal of God and "his image."

- **בְּצֶלֶם אֱלֹהִים**: The second clause restates and reverses the order of the first clause. It begins rather than ends with the image of God.

- **זָכָר וּנְקֵבָה**: This doublet (or merism) is the common way of indicating an entity or group of entities irrespective of sex. The paired expression "male and female" is used to describe humans (Gen. 5:2; Lev. 12:7; 15:33) and animals (Gen. 6:19; 7:3, 9, 16; Lev. 3:1, 6). It specifies that God's image is a shared characteristic of all humans, regardless of biological distinction or cultural instantiation.

- **אֹתוֹ . . . אֹתָם**: In Hebrew, **אָדָם** can be grammatically singular, like English *humanity*, or plural, like *human beings*. Even though the pronominal suffix is singular in the first instance and plural in the second, **הָאָדָם** ("the human beings") are collectively created in God's image. Such grammatical variation is typical of Hebrew parallelism. And the plural reference clarifies God's creation of sexual difference.

FOR THE JOURNEY

One could say that the "Hymn of Creation" reaches fortissimo at the creation of humanity (vv. 26–31). The threefold repetition in verse 27 intones a crescendoing refrain. And the recurring chorus expresses that all human differences—the one and the many, the male and the female—resonate God's created image.

Hebrew exhibits complementary or matching features for a variety of semantic and pragmatic reasons. These features are commonly called *parallelism*. Some equate parallelism with poetry. Whereas it is a highly pronounced characteristic of Hebrew verse, the primary purpose of parallelism is not merely to distinguish a literary type or genre.[1] Parallelism is a way of thinking about relationships and communicating correspondences. Such expressions occur throughout the Bible in diverse literary contexts.

In this verse, the three short clauses use similar words and structures to enlarge and expound what is envisioned in this one creative act. The lyric echoes through time that every human has inherent dignity and divine value even in difference. This cadence declares the truth claim: *God created the human beings, male and female, in his image.*

ANSWER KEY

1. *Parse:* (1) וַיִּבְרָא (Qal *wayyiqtol* 3ms ברא "create"). (2) בָּרָא (Qal sc 3ms).

2. *Identify:* (A) The first verb form (וַיִּבְרָא) is the typical form used in narrative to indicate a sequence of events. The second and third forms (בָּרָא) convey a similar tense-aspect while signaling an explanative break in the narrative events. (B) The object marker is אֶת, which takes the form אֹת with certain pronominal suffixes. (C) The article indicates a known entity, and הָאָדָם was mentioned in the last verse—that is to say, "the humanity" previously mentioned.

3. *Translate:* "God created the human beings in his image—in God's image, he created humanity; he created them male and female."

---

1. Adele Berlin, *The Dynamics of Hebrew Parallelism*, rev. and exp. ed. (Grand Rapids: Eerdmans, 2008; orig. ed., 1985).

STEP ONE: **Read** aloud the text at least five times.

וַיְבָרֶךְ אֹתָם אֱלֹהִים וַיֹּאמֶר לָהֶם אֱלֹהִים פְּרוּ וּרְבוּ וּמִלְאוּ
אֶת־הָאָרֶץ וְכִבְשֻׁהָ וּרְדוּ בִּדְגַת הַיָּם וּבְעוֹף הַשָּׁמַיִם
וּבְכָל־חַיָּה הָרֹמֶשֶׂת עַל־הָאָרֶץ:

STEP TWO: **Parse** the following verbs.

	Stem	Conj.	Pers.	Gend.	Numb.	Root	Trans.
(1) וַיְבָרֶךְ							
(2) פְּרוּ							
(3) וּרְבוּ							
(4) וּמִלְאוּ							
(5) וְכִבְשֻׁהָ							
(6) וּרְדוּ							
(7) הָרֹמֶשֶׂת							

STEP THREE: **Identify** the following.

A. What is the referent of אֹתָם and לָהֶם?

B. What is the function of the pronominal suffix on וְכִבְשֻׁהָ?

C. What is the meaning of the sequence of רדה with בְּ (see v. 26)?

STEP FOUR: **Translate** the text into understandable English.

VOCABULARY

פרה   Qal: bear fruit, be fruitful

רבה   Qal: increase, be great

כבש   Qal: subdue

רדה   Qal: rule

דָּגָה   fish

עוֹף   birds; insects

חַיָּה   animal; living organism

רמשׂ   Qal: creep; move about

STEP FIVE: **Notice** significant exegetical insights.

- וַיְבָרֶךְ: Similar blessings are found on day 5 (v. 22) and day 7 (2:3). As with day 5, the blessing on day 6 entreats animate beings to multiply. But only here are the created beings directly addressed with the imperative (וַיֹּאמֶר לָהֶם).

- פְּרוּ וּרְבוּ וּמִלְאוּ . . . וְכִבְשֻׁהָ וּרְדוּ: Five commands are linked together with *waw*. The semantics of the first three are alike (see v. 22; 9:1; Exod. 1:7), and the final two overlap in meaning. The first two verbs do not have objects and may be considered statives (i.e., "be fruitful" and "be many"). The third and fourth verb share the same object (הָאָרֶץ). Only the final command is directly mentioned in the divine word of verse 26 and uniquely correlated to humanity.

- וּבְכָל־חַיָּה הָרֹמֶשֶׂת עַל־הָאָרֶץ: This expression appears to consolidate the land critters (cf. וּבַבְּהֵמָה וּבְכָל־הָאָרֶץ וּבְכָל־הָרֶמֶשׂ, v. 26; see day 2) into one collection as חַיָּה "living creatures" (vv. 25, 30). Elsewhere, the expression נֶפֶשׁ חַיָּה can refer to sea life as distinct from winged creatures (vv. 20–21) or generally to land beings (vv. 24, 30). Genesis 2:7 includes the ensouled man (נִשְׁמַת חַיִּים) as part of this latter group.

FOR THE JOURNEY

When considering the commands of God in verse 28, it is important to compare the similarities and differences with verse 26.

- The similarities involve the context of the divine image, the frame of divine speech, the same addressee in humanity, and the annexing of divine dominion (רדה ב).
- The primary difference includes the addition of the blessing language (v. 28). God's favor anticipates, among other things, fruitful multiplication that echoes the blessing of the fish and the birds (v. 22). In Exod. 1:7–14, a similarly worded divine blessing is pronounced on Israel, and it produces fear in the Egyptians, which results in their increased cruelty.

While commentators debate the details, it is interesting to note that the multiplication commands (v. 28) are absent in the earlier context of the image of God (v. 26). They follow only after the creation of "male and female" (v. 27). Engagement with the created realm is found in both places, however. The functional result of God's image is dominion. Joining these two notions together, the commands to fill and subjugate the land accompany the instruction to rule the animals.

ANSWER KEY

1. *Parse:* (1) וַיְבָרֶךְ (Piel *wayyiqtol* 3MS ברך "bless"). (2) פְּרוּ (Qal IMV MP פרה "bear fruit"). (3) וּרְבוּ (CJ + Qal IMV MP רבה "increase"). (4) וּמִלְאוּ (CJ + Qal IMV MP מלא "fill"). (5) וְכִבְשֻׁהָ (CJ + Qal IMV MP כבש "subdue" + 3FS SF). (6) וּרְדוּ (CJ + Qal IMV MP רדה "rule"). (7) הָרֹמֶשֶׂת (DEF ART + Qal ACT PTCL FS רמשׂ "creep").

2. *Identify:* (A) The 3MP pronominal suffixes refer to הָאָדָם "humanity; human beings" in verse 27. (B) The 3FS pronominal suffix points to הָאָרֶץ "the land," and it functions as the object of the verb. (C) The preposition object designates the entity experiencing the verb רדה "rule (over)."

3. *Translate:* "God blessed them, and God said to them: 'Bear fruit and increase, fill the land and subdue it, and rule over the fish of the sea, the birds of the sky, and every living creature moving on the land.'"

DAY 6: GENESIS 1:29

STEP ONE: **Read** aloud the text at least five times.

וַיֹּאמֶר אֱלֹהִים הִנֵּה נָתַתִּי לָכֶם אֶת־כָּל־עֵשֶׂב। זֹרֵעַ זֶרַע אֲשֶׁר
עַל־פְּנֵי כָל־הָאָרֶץ וְאֶת־כָּל־הָעֵץ אֲשֶׁר־בּוֹ פְרִי־עֵץ זֹרֵעַ זָרַע
לָכֶם יִהְיֶה לְאָכְלָה׃

STEP TWO: **Parse** the following verbs.

	Stem	Conj.	Pers.	Gend.	Numb.	Root	Trans.
(1) נָתַתִּי							
(2) זֹרֵעַ							
(3) יִהְיֶה							

STEP THREE: **Identify** the following.

A. Who is being spoken to in this passage? _____

B. How is the participle זֹרֵעַ functioning? _____

C. What is the best way to understand the sequence of היה ל- here?

_____

STEP FOUR: **Translate** the text into understandable English.

_____

_____

VOCABULARY

עֵשֶׂב　herbaceous plants

זרע　Qal: sow, seed

פְּרִי　fruit, produce

אָכְלָה　food

STEP FIVE: **Notice** significant exegetical insights.

- הִנֵּה: The first word of the divine speech is an attention-grabbing particle. It indicates a noteworthy or surprising piece of information.

- אֶת־כָּל־עֵשֶׂב . . . וְאֶת־כָּל־הָעֵץ: The direct-object marker is repeated to form a compound object specifying God's nutritional provision for humankind. Their diet includes seed-bearing herbs (including grains) and fruit trees.

- לָכֶם: Humans are the beneficiaries of God giving dietary substance as food (לְאָכְלָה). The second instance of לָכֶם before the verb (יִהְיֶה) places particular focus on the plural addressees and produces a contrast with the addressees of the following verse (v. 30).

FOR THE JOURNEY

God's provision for humanity is linked to his cultivation of various seed-bearing plants and fruit-bearing trees on the third day (vv. 11–12). The recursive productivity, "according to their kinds" (לְמִינֵהוּ, v. 12), establishes a divine endowment of sustenance for his image-bearers as part of the created order.

In the garden, Yahweh provides desirable and abundant food for the man and the woman (Gen. 2:9). They are commanded to eat freely from the fruit of the garden trees, excepting one (2:16–17). While disobedience leads to exile, food nevertheless grows, albeit borne by toil (3:17–19).

Today human beings feel the frustration of fruitless labor and exile—a world cursed by sin. But even in the wilderness, God looks after his people's need for provision (Exod. 16:15). He daily renews his gift of sustenance as we pray for bread (Luke 11:3) and anticipate the breaking of bread in the eternal kingdom (Rev. 19:9).

1. *Parse:* (1) נָתַתִּי (Qal sc 1cs נתן "give"). (2) זֹרֵעַ (Qal ACT PTCL MS זרע "seed").
   (3) יִהְיֶה (Qal PC 3MS היה "be[come]").

2. *Identify:* (A) God declares this provision לָכֶם "to you (MP)" (i.e., הָאָדָם "humanity; human beings," v. 27), continuing the plural pronominal reference from verse 28. (B) The participle זֹרֵעַ takes the cognate object זֶרַע ("seeding seed") and is attributive, describing כָּל־עֵשֶׂב "every herbaceous plant" as part of the object noun phrase. (C) The final three words make up a clause and ל- יהיה takes the sense of "be(come)," with the first prepositional phrase (לָכֶם) as the indirect object (beneficiary) and the second prepositional phrase (לְאָכְלָה) as the object (theme).

3. *Translate:* "God said: 'Notice: I give you every seed-bearing herbaceous plant on the entire land's surface and every seed-bearing fruit tree—it will be your food.'"

DAY 7: GENESIS 1:30

STEP ONE: **Read** aloud the text at least five times.

וּלְכָל־חַיַּת הָאָרֶץ וּלְכָל־עוֹף הַשָּׁמַיִם וּלְכֹל ׀ רוֹמֵשׂ עַל־הָאָרֶץ
אֲשֶׁר־בּוֹ נֶפֶשׁ חַיָּה אֶת־כָּל־יֶרֶק עֵשֶׂב לְאָכְלָה וַיְהִי־כֵן:

STEP TWO: **Parse** the following verbs.

	Stem	Conj.	Pers.	Gend.	Numb.	Root	Trans.
(1) רוֹמֵשׂ							
(2) וַיְהִי							

STEP THREE: **Identify** the following.

A. What verb can be assumed from the previous verse?

_____

B. How is the participle רוֹמֵשׂ functioning? _____

C. How is the ל preposition in לְאָכְלָה being used?

_____

STEP FOUR: **Translate** the text into understandable English.

_____

_____

VOCABULARY

חַיָּה   animal

עוֹף   birds

רמשׂ   Qal: creep; move about

חַי   living

יֶרֶק   green (grass)

עֵשֶׂב   herbaceous plants

אָכְלָה   food

STEP FIVE: **Notice** significant exegetical insights.

- **וּלְכָל־**: The series of three prepositional phrases indicates the compound indirect object (beneficiary) of the "give" verb, like נָתַתִּי לָכֶם in verse 29. This compound comprises similar creatures as in previous lists (vv. 26, 28) but excludes fish.

- **אֶת־כָּל־יֶרֶק עֵשֶׂב**: The verbal object is marked with the object marker. Unlike the seed-bearing herbaceous plants and the fruit trees, the green plants are given as food to the critters.

- **וַיְהִי־כֵן**: The narrative confirmation is the sixth and final echo. In each case, it affirms the outcome of a creative speech act (vv. 6–7, 9, 11, 14–15, 24, 29–30). Rather than reprise the divine command as in verse 3 (וַיְהִי־אוֹר), this short narrative phrase serves as shorthand: *then it was as he said it would be.*

FOR THE JOURNEY

God provides food for the animals, birds, and creepy-crawlies. Their diet consists of the green plants (יֶרֶק עֵשֶׂב) that began flourishing on the third day (vv. 11–12). These creatures receive special divine protection in the created order. They are to be subdued but not abused (vv. 26, 28). While eating meat is not explicitly forbidden, the principle of respecting animal life is implicit.

The post-flood allowance for carnivory does not overturn the creation mandate protecting animals (Gen. 9:2–3). The restriction of blood (9:4) is analogous to other doctrinal principles that constrain one element to demonstrate a lofty value. Consider, for example, the principle of offering the firstfruits as a reminder that all produce (Exod. 23:19) and all humanity (1 Cor. 15:20–23) belong to God.

In the messianic visions of the prophets, creation again returns to idyllic vegetarianism (Isa. 11:6–9), and bloodlust is vanquished (Hosea 2:18).

ANSWER KEY

1. *Parse:* (1) רֹמֵשׂ (Qal ACT PTCL MS רמשׂ "creep"). (2) וַיְהִי (Qal *wayyiqtol* 3MS היה "be").

2. *Identify:* (A) The verbal idea of God giving (נָתַתִּי) is continued from verse 29. (B) The participle רֹמֵשׂ functions as a substantive in the noun phrase with לְכֹל in parallel with the two preceding phrases (וּלְכָל־חַיַּת הָאָרֶץ וּלְכָל־עוֹף הַשָּׁמַיִם). (C) The prepositional phrase (לְאָכְלָה) indicates what the preceding clause object (אֶת־כָּל־יֶרֶק עֵשֶׂב) is given to be (i.e., sustenance to be consumed).

3. *Translate:* "'. . . but [I give] every green plant as food to every animal of the land, every bird of the heavens, and every creeper on the land which is a living creature.' Then it was so."

DAY 8: GENESIS 1:31

STEP ONE: **Read** aloud the text at least five times.

וַיַּרְא אֱלֹהִים אֶת־כָּל־אֲשֶׁר עָשָׂה וְהִנֵּה־טוֹב מְאֹד וַיְהִי־עֶרֶב
וַיְהִי־בֹקֶר יוֹם הַשִּׁשִּׁי:

STEP TWO: **Parse** the following verbs.

	Stem	Conj.	Pers.	Gend.	Numb.	Root	Trans.
(1) וַיַּרְא							
(2) עָשָׂה							

STEP THREE: **Identify** the following.

A. How is the object of the first verb וַיַּרְא marked?

B. How does וְהִנֵּה־טוֹב מְאֹד compare to previous descriptions?

STEP FOUR: **Translate** the text into understandable English.

> **VOCABULARY**
>
> עֶרֶב   evening, sunset
> שִׁשִּׁי   sixth

STEP FIVE: **Notice** significant exegetical insights.

- כָּל־אֲשֶׁר עָשָׂה: The object of the verb of sight (וַיַּרְא) is "everything he made." The relative delineates the totality (כֹּל) as those entities that God had made (עָשָׂה). This same verb is used to describe divine formation of the heavens (v. 7), the great lights (v. 16), the land animals (v. 25), humanity (v. 26), and his work in general (2:2).

29

- וְהִנֵּה טוֹב מְאֹד: The attention-grabbing particle is found this time as part of the narration. It indicates a noteworthy or significant piece of information for the audience.

FOR THE JOURNEY

This verse repeats and magnifies the observation of the goodness of God's creation. Verse 31 contains the seventh harmonious reverberation (טוֹב . . . וירא אלהים "God saw . . . good") in the first chapter (vv. 4, 10, 12, 18, 21, 25). Most of these examples assume the entity without mentioning the created thing in the formulation. The initial and final reports name explicitly that which is טוֹב (i.e., "light" in v. 4 and "everything he made" in v. 31). The adjective is customarily translated as simply "good," but it can elicit the ideals of goodness, pleasantness, harmony, abundance, and even congruence. In sum, God's completed work—the result of the creation week—is an unadulterated masterpiece.

This goodness comes into even sharper focus in sequence with the verb of seeing (ראה). Elsewhere in Genesis, a similar expression is used of human actors observing unforeseen favor (8:13; 22:13), unexpected visitors (18:2; 33:1), startling interactions (26:8), astonishing visions (31:10; 41:22), a surprise gift (42:27), and an ecstatic reunion (48:11). But in Gen. 6:12, God is the one who perceives a shocking reality. Creation is no longer "very pleasing," but the land is described as spoiled (נִשְׁחָתָה) and filled with violence (חָמָס). In just a few short chapters, God's pristine creative endeavor has become squalid and uninhabitable.

ANSWER KEY

1. *Parse:* (1) וַיַּרְא (Qal *wayyiqtol* 3MS ראה "see"). (2) עָשָׂה (Qal sc 3MS עשׂה "make, do").
2. *Identify:* (A) The complement of וַיַּרְא is marked with the object marker (אֶת־). (B) The previous six descriptions designate the creation as כִּי־טוֹב (vv. 4, 10, 12, 18, 21, 25).
3. *Translate:* "God saw all he made, and it was very fine indeed! Evening and morning transpired: the sixth day."

DAY 9: GENESIS 2:1–2

STEP ONE: Read aloud the text at least five times.

וַיְכֻלּוּ הַשָּׁמַיִם וְהָאָרֶץ וְכָל־צְבָאָם: ²וַיְכַל אֱלֹהִים בַּיּוֹם
הַשְּׁבִיעִי מְלַאכְתּוֹ אֲשֶׁר עָשָׂה וַיִּשְׁבֹּת בַּיּוֹם הַשְּׁבִיעִי
מִכָּל־מְלַאכְתּוֹ אֲשֶׁר עָשָׂה:

STEP TWO: Parse the following verbs.

	Stem	Conj.	Pers.	Gend.	Numb.	Root	Trans.
(1) וַיְכֻלּוּ							
(2) וַיְכַל							
(3) וַיִּשְׁבֹּת							

STEP THREE: Identify the following.

A. What is the subject of וַיְכֻלּוּ? _____

B. What is the subject of וַיְכַל? _____

C. How is the initial preposition מִן (with an assimilated final *nun*) in מִכָּל־מְלַאכְתּוֹ functioning in the last clause? _____

STEP FOUR: Translate the text into understandable English.

_____

_____

VOCABULARY

כלה   Piel: complete; Pual: be finished

צָבָא   host

שְׁבִיעִי   seventh

מְלָאכָה   work; occupation

שׁבת   Qal: stop, cease; rest

STEP FIVE: **Notice** significant exegetical insights.

- וַיְכַל . . . וַיְכֻלּוּ: The initial verbs in verses 1 and 2 contain the same verbal root (כלה). The first form is passive (Pual: "be finished"). The subject of the verb is the recipient of the action, and the agent is absent. This narrative summation completes the creative events begun in the first verse of chapter 1. The second form is active (Piel: "finish, complete"). God (the agent) is expressed as the subject, and the object is the work he finished.

- בַּיּוֹם הַשְּׁבִיעִי: The temporal expression occurs twice in the second verse. It denotes when God completed his work and rested. This day of completion is presented differently than the previous days. The concluding formula (וַיְהִי־עֶרֶב וַיְהִי־בֹקֶר יוֹם הַשְּׁבִיעִי) is missing. Instead, this final day is the object of God's blessing and sanctification (v. 3).

- מְלַאכְתּוֹ אֲשֶׁר עָשָׂה: This phrase is similar to "all he made" (כָּל־אֲשֶׁר עָשָׂה, 1:31).

FOR THE JOURNEY

In Gen. 2:1, the third element in the final punch list of completed projects seems peculiar. The compound phrase "heavens and earth" (הַשָּׁמַיִם וְהָאָרֶץ) echoes Gen. 1:1 (cf. 2:4a), but what does "all their host" (וְכָל־צְבָאָם) specify?

First, the term צָבָא has not been mentioned previously. It is related to but not identical with the heavens and the earth, which are the referent of the possessive pronoun suffix on צְבָאָם ("their host"). Second, the use of the totality word reminds the reader of the previous כֹל indicating the entirety of creation (1:31). Together, this phrase could refer to either the assorted assemblage that inhabits the heavens and the earth (i.e., the created entities filling those realms) or perhaps a previously unmentioned group.

It is tempting to assume the first option and move along. Before doing that, let us look at a few comparable texts. "All their host" could be associated with Micaiah's vision of Yahweh sitting enthroned and surrounded by "all the host of heaven" (כָּל־צְבָא הַשָּׁמַיִם; 1 Kings 22:19; 2 Chron. 18:18). Elsewhere, the Hallelujah Song of Creation recites a catalog describing those praising Yahweh (Ps. 148). Prior to enumerating the sun, moon, stars, heavens, and waters (vv. 3–5), Ps. 148 names two groups in parallel: "all his angels" (כָּל־מַלְאָכָיו) and "all his host(s)" (כָּל־צְבָאָו). And the litany of blessing includes the heavenly armies (כָּל־צְבָאָיו, Ps. 103:21). These similar phrases elicit the idea of the heavenly beings (see also Dan. 8:10; Luke 2:13).

While either option is credible, these texts suggest that reflections on the creation story excited other authors with the idea that God fashioned more than the material world in the first six days. He made both the seen and the unseen world and all their inhabitants!

ANSWER KEY

1. *Parse:* (1) וַיְכֻלּוּ (Pual *wayyiqtol* 3MP כלה "be finished"). (2) וַיְכַל (Piel *wayyiqtol* 3MS כלה "finish, complete"). (3) וַיִּשְׁבֹּת (Qal *wayyiqtol* 3MS שבת "cease").

2. *Identify:* (A) The subject of וַיְכֻלּוּ is the compound NP (הַשָּׁמַיִם וְהָאָרֶץ וְכָל־צְבָאָם). (B) The subject of וַיְכַל is "God" (אֱלֹהִים). (C) The preposition (מִן) describes a privative relationship designating the element missing or removed (i.e., God's creating work).

3. *Translate:* "The heavens, the earth, and all their entourage were finished. On the seventh day, God finished his work that he had made, and on the seventh day he rested from all his work that he had made."

DAY 10: GENESIS 2:3–4A

STEP ONE: **Read** aloud the text at least five times.

וַיְבָ֤רֶךְ אֱלֹהִים֙ אֶת־י֣וֹם הַשְּׁבִיעִ֔י וַיְקַדֵּ֖שׁ אֹת֑וֹ כִּ֣י ב֤וֹ שָׁבַת֙
מִכָּל־מְלַאכְתּ֔וֹ אֲשֶׁר־בָּרָ֥א אֱלֹהִ֖ים לַעֲשֽׂוֹת׃ ⁴אֵ֣לֶּה תוֹלְד֧וֹת
הַשָּׁמַ֛יִם וְהָאָ֖רֶץ בְּהִבָּֽרְאָ֑ם

STEP TWO: **Parse** the following verbs.

	Stem	Conj.	Pers.	Gend.	Numb.	Root	Trans.
(1) וַיְבָ֤רֶךְ							
(2) וַיְקַדֵּ֖שׁ							
(3) שָׁבַת							
(4) בָּרָ֥א							
(5) לַעֲשֽׂוֹת							
(6) בְּהִבָּֽרְאָ֑ם							

STEP THREE: **Identify** the following.

A. What is the referent of the 3MS suffix with אֹתוֹ and בוֹ?

B. How is אֵלֶּה functioning syntactically?

C. Is the 3MP pronominal suffix (בְּהִבָּרְאָם) serving as the subject or object of the infinitive construct?

STEP FOUR: **Translate** the text into understandable English.

VOCABULARY

שְׁבִיעִי   seventh

קָדַשׁ   Piel: set apart, dedicate, sanctify, honor

שָׁבַת   Qal: stop, cease; rest

מְלָאכָה   work, occupation

בָּרָא   Qal: create; Niphal: be created

תּוֹלְדוֹת   generations

STEP FIVE: **Notice** significant exegetical insights.

- מִכָּל־מְלַאכְתּוֹ אֲשֶׁר־בָּרָא אֱלֹהִים לַעֲשׂוֹת: This expression is nearly identical to the last clause of the previous verse (מִכָּל־מְלַאכְתּוֹ אֲשֶׁר עָשָׂה, Gen. 2:2). The relative clause repeats the verb "make" (עשׂה) and adds the verb for "create" (ברא). These verbs link the first and seventh day of the narrative and coalesce to complete God's creative acts.

- בְּהִבָּרְאָם: The temporal expression connects this phrase to the initial statement of this creation story (Gen. 1:1).

FOR THE JOURNEY

Repeating the genealogical digest (תּוֹלְדוֹת) provides an inherent ten-fold structure to the book of Genesis. Genesis 2:4 contains the first of these accounts at the termination of the initial creation narrative. The others expound the ancestral lines of Adam (5:1), Noah (6:9), the sons of Noah (10:1, 32), Shem (11:10), Terah (11:27), Ishmael (25:12, 13), and Esau (36:1, 9). Two examples initiate stories about the troubled patriarchal descendants: Isaac (25:19) and Jacob (37:2). Other biblical books use the same generational trope to elaborate the Levitical lineage (Num. 3:1; also Exod. 6:16), explicate David's pedigree (Ruth 4:18), and revisit Abraham's descendants (1 Chron. 1:29).

This literary device recounts the outworking of the initial divine command. Each occurrence registers God's faithfulness to the creative and missional directive to be fruitful and multiply (Gen. 1:22, 28; 8:17; 9:1, 7; 17:6, 20; 26:22; 28:3; 35:11; 41:52; 47:27; 48:4). God fills the cosmos, and God's people are numerous (Ps. 105:24). While the faithful remnant awaits the future and final fulfillment of creation's capacity, God's promise is sure (Ezek. 36:11; Jer. 23:3). God is filling the earth with salvation and increasing righteousness from the heavens (Isa. 45:8).

ANSWER KEY

1. *Parse:* (1) וַיְבָרֶךְ (Piel *wayyiqtol* 3MS בָּרַךְ "bless"). (2) וַיְקַדֵּשׁ (Piel *wayyiqtol* 3MS קָדַשׁ "honor"). (3) שָׁבַת (Qal SC 3MS שׁבת "cease"). (4) בָּרָא (Qal SC 3MS ברא "create"). (5) לַעֲשׂוֹת (PREP + Qal INF CSTR עשׂה "make"). (6) בְּהִבָּרְאָם (PREP + Niphal INF CSTR ברא "be created" + 3MP SF).

2. *Identify:* (A) The referent of the 3MS suffix (אֹתוֹ and בוֹ) is the seventh day (יוֹם הַשְּׁבִיעִי). (B) The demonstrative (אֵלֶּה "these") is the subject of a verbless clause; the following NP is the predicate. (C) The 3MP pronominal suffix refers to the heavens and earth, serving as the subject of the passive verb ("were created").

3. *Translate:* "God blessed the seventh day and honored it because on it he rested from all his work that he created to make. These were the generations of the heavens and the earth when they were created."

ROUTE 3

Deuteronomy 6:1–9

STEP ONE: **Read** aloud the text at least five times.

וְזֹאת הַמִּצְוָה הַחֻקִּים וְהַמִּשְׁפָּטִים אֲשֶׁר צִוָּה יְהוָה אֱלֹהֵיכֶם
לְלַמֵּד אֶתְכֶם לַעֲשׂוֹת בָּאָרֶץ אֲשֶׁר אַתֶּם עֹבְרִים שָׁמָּה
לְרִשְׁתָּהּ׃

STEP TWO: **Parse** the following verbs.

	Stem	Conj.	Pers.	Gend.	Numb.	Root	Trans.
(1) צִוָּה							
(2) לְלַמֵּד							
(3) לַעֲשׂוֹת							
(4) עֹבְרִים							
(5) לְרִשְׁתָּהּ							

STEP THREE: **Identify** the following.

   A. How is זֹאת functioning syntactically? _____

   B. What kind of suffix is on שָׁמָּה? _____

STEP FOUR: **Translate** the text into understandable English.

> VOCABULARY
>
> מִצְוָה   commandment
>
> חֹק   ordinance, regulation (PL חֻקִּים)
>
> לׇמַד   Piel: teach

STEP FIVE: **Notice** significant exegetical insights.

- וְזֹאת הַמִּצְוָה הַחֻקִּים וְהַמִּשְׁפָּטִים: The FS demonstrative is connected to the predicate "the commandment" (הַמִּצְוָה) as an identification clause. The following two words are MP and seem to be appositional to the predicate, expounding the directive.

- אֲשֶׁר . . . אֲשֶׁר: The relative particle typically occurs as close as possible after the modified element (i.e., its head). The first describes the directive (הַמִּצְוָה). The land (הָאָרֶץ) is qualified by the second.

- אֲשֶׁר אַתֶּם עֹבְרִים שָׁמָּה לְרִשְׁתָּהּ: The relative clause uses a resumptive pronoun (FS) on the last word to locate the head word (הָאָרֶץ) as a syntactic element in the embedded clause, "to possess it (i.e., the land)" (לְרִשְׁתָּהּ).

FOR THE JOURNEY

The demonstrative and the definite noun, "this is the commandment" (וְזֹאת הַמִּצְוָה), suggests a singular instruction is in view. Yet the three-fold cluster of the commandment, the decrees, and the regulations reprises Moses's first-person account of God's expanded direction at the end of the previous chapter (Deut. 5:31). The same grouping is repeated a chapter later (7:11). Altogether this repetition trains the hearer to recognize *the* crucial charge in chapter 6 along with its elaboration.

This directive is traditionally called the *Shema* (6:4–9). Its theological importance is unmatched in the Hebrew Bible and expands through the Scriptures. The *Shema* serves as the paradigm of faithfulness to God. Israel's observance of every aspect of this commandment (כָּל־הַמִּצְוָה הַזֹּאת) is considered their righteousness (צְדָקָה, 6:25). In reflecting on the history of the sons of Jacob, the book of Kings includes this very trivium alongside the concept of "covenant" (בְּרִית, 2 Kings 17:34–39) and again with "the law" (הַתּוֹרָה, v. 37) to expose Samaria's enduring idolatry.

In the NT, Jesus refers to this command as the foremost (πρώτη, Mark 12:29–30). This attribution could refer to the *Shema*'s status as the first in order (Eph. 6:2) or the first in prominence (Matt. 22:38; Mark 12:28). The second (δευτέρα) command (Mark 12:31) is, of course, found later in the Torah (Lev. 19:18, 34).

ANSWER KEY

1. *Parse:* (1) צִוָּה (Piel sc 3ms צוה "command"). (2) לְלַמֵּד (PREP + Piel INF CSTR למד "teach"). (3) לַעֲשׂוֹת (PREP + Qal INF CSTR עשׂה "do, make"). (4) עֹבְרִים (Qal ACT PTCL MP עבר "cross [over]"). (5) לְרִשְׁתָּהּ (PREP + Qal INF CSTR ירשׁ "possess" + 3FS SF).

2. *Identify:* (A) Syntactically, the FS demonstrative (זֹאת "this") is the subject of the verbless clause. (B) The unaccented locative-*heh* suffix indicates the spatial direction to a place ("to there").

3. *Translate:* "This is the commandment, accompanied by the decrees and the regulations, that Yahweh your God commanded to teach you [what] to do in the land that you are crossing into to possess."

DAY 12: DEUTERONOMY 6:2

STEP ONE: Read aloud the text at least five times.

לְמַׁעַן תִּירָא אֶת־יְהוָה אֱלֹהֶיךָ לִשְׁמֹר אֶת־כָּל־חֻקֹּתָיו וּמִצְוֺתָיו
אֲשֶׁר אָנֹכִי מְצַוְּךָ אַתָּה וּבִנְךָ וּבֶן־בִּנְךָ כֹּל יְמֵי חַיֶּיךָ וּלְמַעַן
יַאֲרִכֻן יָמֶיךָ:

STEP TWO: Parse the following verbs.

	Stem	Conj.	Pers.	Gend.	Numb.	Root	Trans.
(1) תִּירָא							
(2) לִשְׁמֹר							
(3) מְצַוְּךָ							
(4) יַאֲרִכֻן							

STEP THREE: Identify the following.

A. How is לְמַעַן functioning semantically? Are both instances similar?

B. Who is the subject of the first verb (תִּירָא)?

C. What is the subject of יַאֲרִכֻן?

STEP FOUR: Translate the text into understandable English.

VOCABULARY

חֹק   ordinance, regulation (PL + 3MS SF חֻקֹּתָיו)

מִצְוָה   commandment (PL + 3MS SF מִצְוֺתָיו)

ארך   Hiphil: prolong; endure

40

STEP FIVE: **Notice** significant exegetical insights.

- אַתָּה וּבִנְךָ וּבֶן־בִּנְךָ: The verbal object focuses on a directly addressed individual (אָנֹכִי מְצַוְּךָ), a male progenitor. The following threefold expression expands the command to three generations. As such, the direction focuses on the father but has implications for the entire household (בֵּית־אָב).

- כֹּל יְמֵי חַיֶּיךָ: The adverbial noun phrase "for all your living days" can be understood as setting the time frame for the fearing of Yahweh (תִּירָא), the keeping the instructions (שְׁמֹר), or the commanding (מְצַוְּךָ). The semantic correspondence with יָמֶיךָ ("your days") in the following clause likely links it to the principal verbal idea of fearing God and secondarily keeping his commands.

FOR THE JOURNEY

Yahweh incorporates every member of the household into his covenant family. Parents are responsible to guard their relationship with Yahweh and fear and teach. Children honor father and mother (Deut. 5:16). And rebellion has tragic domestic consequences (5:9).

The great commandment anticipates intergenerational accountability and transgenerational reverberations. These words are to be repeated to the children (6:7). When they ask what these decrees mean (6:20), the mighty acts of God are to be remembered and extolled (6:21–23). Know and believe: Yahweh delivers his people! Therefore, follow his commands. The promises are for us today. Continued prosperity and righteousness are intertwined (6:24–25). Long life in the land for the adherent and his family is the result (6:2).

The children's obedience results in an analogous outcome (5:16). They too participate in the covenant obligations and promises. The honoring of father and mother contains a similar promise (Eph. 6:1–3).

ANSWER KEY

1. *Parse:* (1) תִּירָא (Qal PC 2MS ירא "fear"). (2) לִשְׁמֹר (PREP + Qal INF CSTR שמר "keep, guard"). (3) מְצַוְּךָ (Piel PTCL MS צוה "command" + 2MS SF). (4) יַאֲרִכֻן (Hiphil PC 3MP ארך "prolong"; the final *nun* is described as paragogic, a vestige of an older form of יַאֲרִיכוּ).

2. *Identify:* (A) The conjunction (לְמַעַן) designates result in both clauses. (B) The 2MS subject of תִּירָא designates the male head of the household. The representative nature of the Israelite father is clarified in the relative clause with "you (MS), your son, and your grandson" (אַתָּה וּבִנְךָ וּבֶן־בִּנְךָ). (C) The 3MP subject of יַאֲרִכֻן is "your days" (יָמֶיךָ), referring to the father's lifetime.

3. *Translate:* ". . . so that you will fear Yahweh your God all your lifetime by observing his decrees and commandments that he commanded you, your child, and your grandchild, and so that your life will endure."

DAY 13: DEUTERONOMY 6:3

STEP ONE: Read aloud the text at least five times.

וְשָׁמַעְתָּ יִשְׂרָאֵל וְשָׁמַרְתָּ לַעֲשׂוֹת אֲשֶׁר יִיטַב לְךָ וַאֲשֶׁר
תִּרְבּוּן מְאֹד כַּאֲשֶׁר דִּבֶּר יְהוָה אֱלֹהֵי אֲבֹתֶיךָ לָךְ אֶרֶץ זָבַת
חָלָב וּדְבָשׁ:

STEP TWO: Parse the following verbs.

	Stem	Conj.	Pers.	Gend.	Numb.	Root	Trans.
(1) וְשָׁמַעְתָּ							
(2) וְשָׁמַרְתָּ							
(3) יִיטַב							
(4) תִּרְבּוּן							
(5) דִּבֶּר							
(6) זָבַת							

STEP THREE: Identify the following.

A. What is the syntactic role of יִשְׂרָאֵל?

B. How is the phrase אֶרֶץ זָבַת חָלָב וּדְבָשׁ functioning?

C. Describe the relationship of the participle זָבַת to the following
nouns (חָלָב וּדְבָשׁ)?

STEP FOUR: Translate the text into understandable English.

VOCABULARY

יטב	Qal: be good; go well	חָלָב	milk
רבה	Qal: increase; be great	דְּבַשׁ	honey
זוב	Qal: flow		

43

STEP FIVE: **Notice** significant exegetical insights.

- וְשָׁמַרְתָּ . . . וְשָׁמַעְתָּ: The *weqātal* verbs continue the volitional notion of the previous verse (לְמַעַן תִּירָא "so that you will fear . . . [and then you will listen and carefully observe]").

- וְשָׁמַרְתָּ לַעֲשׂוֹת: The sequence of these two verbs is a common collocation (Deut. 4:6; 5:1, 32; 6:25; 7:12; 8:1; 11:22, 32; 12:1; 13:1; 15:5; 16:12; 17:10, 19; 19:9; 23:24; 24:8; 26:16; 28:1, 15, 58; 29:8; 31:12; 32:46). This combination ("guard to do") can convey a sense of vigilance, similar to "keep doing" or even "be careful to do."

- אֲשֶׁר . . . וַאֲשֶׁר: The sequenced relative clauses signal the compounded result of Israel's obedience.

FOR THE JOURNEY

Israel is promised a good and abundant life in a land flowing with milk and honey. This lavish vision recapitulates God's promise enacted at the burning bush and repeated throughout Exodus (3:8, 17; 13:5; 33:3). The twelve scouts report the land's bounty using this same description of plentiful cream and nectar (Num. 13:27; 14:8; 16:13, 14). Using the same image, the prophet Jeremiah reminds his contemporaries of the connection between God's oath to give them a prosperous land and their obedience to the life-giving words of the covenant (Jer. 11:2–5).

This promised land coalesces with the promise given to their forebears (Gen. 15:16; also, Jer. 32:22). The bountiful land before these Egyptian captives is the very land pledged to Abraham and his progeny as their future inheritance (Gen. 17:8).

The NT extends these promises along two horizons. First, the land includes not just Canaan but the entire world (κόσμος, Rom. 4:13). Second, Abraham's progeny includes all those characterized by like faith in God, not just Israel (Rom. 4:16–25).

ANSWER KEY

1. *Parse:* (1) וְשָׁמַעְתָּ (Qal *wəqātal* 2ms שמע "listen"). (2) וְשָׁמַרְתָּ (Qal *wəqātal* 2ms שמר "keep"). (3) יִיטַב (Qal PC 3ms יטב "be good"). (4) תִּרְבּוּן (Qal PC 2mp רבה "multiply"; the final *nun* is described as paragogic, a vestige of an older form of תִּרְבּוּ). (5) דִּבֶּר (Piel sc 3ms דבר "speak"). (6) זָבַת (Qal ACT PTCL FS זוב "flow").

2. *Identify:* (A) The name יִשְׂרָאֵל is appositional to the MS subject of the imperative (i.e., vocative). (B) The NP אֶרֶץ זָבַת חָלָב וּדְבַשׁ describes the location where the result of obedience to the commandment takes place. (C) The participle זָבַת describes the land (אֶרֶץ) and is in construct with the compound NP (חָלָב וּדְבַשׁ), which specifies the object undergoing the action.

3. *Translate:* "Listen, Israel, and carefully observe [the commandment] so that it may go well for you and so that you may greatly increase in a land flowing with milk and honey, as Yahweh the God of your fathers spoke to you."

DAY 14: DEUTERONOMY 6:4–6

STEP ONE: **Read** aloud the text at least five times.

שְׁמַע יִשְׂרָאֵל יְהוָה אֱלֹהֵינוּ יְהוָה| אֶחָד: ⁵וְאָהַבְתָּ אֵת יְהוָה
אֱלֹהֶיךָ בְּכָל־לְבָבְךָ וּבְכָל־נַפְשְׁךָ וּבְכָל־מְאֹדֶךָ: ⁶וְהָיוּ הַדְּבָרִים
הָאֵלֶּה אֲשֶׁר אָנֹכִי מְצַוְּךָ הַיּוֹם עַל־לְבָבֶךָ:

STEP TWO: **Parse** the following verbs.

	Stem	Conj.	Pers.	Gend.	Numb.	Root	Trans.
(1) שְׁמַע							
(2) וְאָהַבְתָּ							
(3) וְהָיוּ							
(4) מְצַוְּךָ							

STEP THREE: **Identify** the following.

A. What kind of word is אֶחָד and how is it functioning?

B. What is the typical function of מְאֹד?

STEP FOUR: **Translate** the text into understandable English.

> VOCABULARY
>
> אהב   Qal: love, show fidelity

STEP FIVE: **Notice** significant exegetical insights.

- יהוה אֱלֹהֵינוּ יהוה אֶחָד: These four words present several syntactic dilemmas. Primary is whether it represents one verbless clause of four words or two clauses with two words each. Depending on one's preferred solution, the Shema may be understood as extolling

Yahweh's identity as Israel's God (2 Chron. 13:10), his exclusivity (Deut. 4:35, 39; Zech. 14:9), or his unity (Matt. 11:27; John 10:30).

- הַיּוֹם עַל־לְבָבֶךָ: These final words function adverbially in two separate clauses. The former ("today") describes the time frame of the relative clause (אָנֹכִי מְצַוְּךָ הַיּוֹם). The latter serves as part of the predicate of the main clause (וְהָיוּ הַדְּבָרִים הָאֵלֶּה . . . עַל־לְבָבֶךָ), indicating the location ("upon your heart/mind") where the vital instruction should be inscribed (Jer. 31:33).

FOR THE JOURNEY

The command to love is the whole of the Scriptures (Matt. 22:37–40; Rom. 13:8–10; Gal. 5:14; James 2:8).

Deuteronomy 6:4–6 states that fidelity (אהב) is Yahweh's central edict. Love involves a keen awareness of who the object of devotion is: Yahweh. He is our God. Yahweh alone deserves our devoted love.

Exclusive loyalty to Yahweh requires all-encompassing dedication. The common word pair "heart and soul" (Deut. 4:29; 10:12; 11:13; 13:4; 26:16; 30:2, 6, 10) is expanded here to include a third element (בְּכָל־מְאֹדֶךָ; repeated only at 2 Kings 23:25). Traditionally, this addition is understood as "might, strength" (see δύναμις [LXX] and ἰσχύς [Luke 10:27]). The Hebrew term appears to be more extensive, detailing one's external capacities, surplus, and even possessions (see Gen. 17:2, 6, 20; Ezek. 16:13).

One's whole self, entire existence, and all attendant realities should express faithful love for God.

ANSWER KEY

1. *Parse:* (1) שְׁמַע (Qal ɪᴍᴠ ᴍs שמע "listen"). (2) וְאָהַבְתָּ (Qal *wəqāṭal* 2ᴍs אהב "love"). (3) וְהָיוּ (Qal *wəqāṭal* 3ᴍᴘ היה "be"). (4) מְצַוְּךָ (Piel ᴘᴛᴄʟ ᴍs צוה "command" + 2ᴍs sғ).

2. *Identify:* (A) The word אֶחָד is a numeral and is functioning like an adjective. (B) The word מְאֹד is typically an adverb of degree that indicates a gradable characteristic of an adjective or another adverb. In this context, it is a noun, probably denoting strength, greatness, or property.

3. *Translate:* "Listen, Israel: Yahweh is our God—Yahweh alone. Love Yahweh your God with all your awareness, all your being, and all your capacity, and let these words that I am commanding you today be on your mind."

DAY 15: DEUTERONOMY 6:7–9

STEP ONE: **Read** aloud the text at least five times.

וְשִׁנַּנְתָּם לְבָנֶ֫יךָ וְדִבַּרְתָּ בָּם בְּשִׁבְתְּךָ בְּבֵיתֶ֫ךָ וּבְלֶכְתְּךָ בַדֶּ֫רֶךְ
וּֽבְשָׁכְבְּךָ וּבְקוּמֶֽךָ: ⁸וּקְשַׁרְתָּם לְא֖וֹת עַל־יָדֶ֑ךָ וְהָי֥וּ לְטֹטָפֹ֖ת בֵּ֥ין
עֵינֶֽיךָ: ⁹וּכְתַבְתָּם עַל־מְזוּזֹ֥ת בֵּיתֶ֖ךָ וּבִשְׁעָרֶֽיךָ:

STEP TWO: **Parse** the following verbs.

	Stem	Conj.	Pers.	Gend.	Numb.	Root	Trans.
(1) וְשִׁנַּנְתָּם							
(2) וְדִבַּרְתָּ							
(3) בְּשִׁבְתְּךָ							
(4) וּבְלֶכְתְּךָ							
(5) וּֽבְשָׁכְבְּךָ							
(6) וּבְקוּמֶ֫ךָ							
(7) וּקְשַׁרְתָּם							
(8) וְהָיוּ							
(9) וּכְתַבְתָּם							

STEP THREE: **Identify** the following.

A. What is the referent of the 3MP suffix with וְשִׁנַּנְתָּם and בָּם?

B. Identify the semantics of the preposition with . . . בְּשִׁבְתְּךָ
וּבְלֶכְתְּךָ . . . וּֽבְשָׁכְבְּךָ וּבְקוּמֶ֫ךָ.

C. What is the syntactic function of the 2MS suffix with the infinitives (בְּשִׁבְתְּךָ, etc.)?

STEP FOUR: **Translate** the text into understandable English.

VOCABULARY

שנן Piel: repeat

קשר Qal: bind

אות sign

טוֹטָפֹת phylacteries

מְזוּזָה doorpost

STEP FIVE: **Notice** significant exegetical insights.

- בְּשִׁבְתְּךָ בְּבֵיתֶךָ וּבְלֶכְתְּךָ בַדֶּרֶךְ וּבְשָׁכְבְּךָ וּבְקוּמֶךָ: The second half of verse 7 contains four temporal designations constituting two pairs. Each paired merism involves life's essential activities: *stay/ go* and *recline/rise*. Further, the phrases ("in your house"/"along the way") specify the whereabouts for discussing God's words, and these locations entail both private and public audiences—one's family and one's community. Every encounter, every place, and every activity is an opportunity to engage with God and love him with one's whole existence!

- עַל־יָדֶךָ . . . בֵּין עֵינֶיךָ: The location of the physical signs include one's body parts—"hand" and "eyes." The engagement with God is a physical activity. It does not occur with one's thoughts alone but with corporeal participation. The adornments on one's person and the activities of one's body constitute a sign of one's loyalty to God.

- עַל־מְזוּזֹת בֵּיתֶךָ וּבִשְׁעָרֶיךָ: The location of the physical signs also enmeshes the totality of one's localities. Yahweh's words are written on the doorpost of one's house and one's gates. The latter commonly refers to the entrance to a city or a temple but can be the outer entrance of a residence. These written symbols create permanent opportunities for the remembrance of Yahweh. And they signal the liminal space connecting public and private devotion.

FOR THE JOURNEY

How can one remain faithfully committed to God on life's journey?

Verses 7–9 embody allegiance and attention to Yahweh's words with three practices: speech, symbol, and inscription. First, repeat God's word aloud and declare it in every aspect of life at all times. Second, bind it on one's person as a visible reminder to oneself and to those you meet. Third, imprint it on one's domicile to mark your comings and goings as belonging to God. This ancient exposition of the greatest commandment requires attentiveness, meditation, and physicality.

Yahweh's words are meant to be proclaimed vocally and tangibly, and they are to inhabit the believer's entire existence! Later, in Deut. 11:18–25, these same physical signs are connected to spiritual devotion and a prosperous life. The meditative life is oriented by regular, physical engagement with Scripture as the embodiment of a flourishing existence (Josh. 1:8). The psalmist describes the blessed person as one who walks the path of all-inclusive devotion through habitual recitation and daily living of God's word (Ps. 1).

ANSWER KEY

1. *Parse:* (1) וְשִׁנַּנְתָּם (Piel *waqātal* 2MS שׁנן "repeat, recount" + 3MP SF). (2) וְדִבַּרְתָּ (Piel *waqātal* 2MS דבר "speak"). (3) בְּשִׁבְתְּךָ (PREP + Qal INF CSTR ישׁב "stay" + 2MS SF). (4) וּבְלֶכְתְּךָ (CJ + PREP + Qal INF CSTR הלך "go" + 2MS SF). (5) וּבְשָׁכְבְּךָ (CJ + PREP + Qal INF CSTR שׁכב "lie down" + 2MS SF). (6) וּבְקוּמֶךָ (CJ + PREP + Qal INF CSTR קום "arise" + 2MS SF). (7) וּקְשַׁרְתָּם (Qal *waqātal* 2MS קשׁר "bind" + 3MP SF). (8) וְהָיוּ (Qal *waqātal* 3MP היה "be"). (9) וּכְתַבְתָּם (Qal *waqātal* 3MP כתב "write" + 3MP SF).

2. *Identify:* (A) The 3MP referent of the suffixes (וּקְשַׁרְתָּם, בָּם, וְשִׁנַּנְתָּם, and וּכְתַבְתָּם) and the subject of the verb (וְהָיוּ) is הַדְּבָרִים הָאֵלֶּה in the previous verse (v. 6). (B) The *bet* preposition with each infinitive functions as a temporal expression, like English *when*. The same preposition with the nouns (בְּבֵיתֶךָ, וּבִשְׁעָרֶיךָ, בַדֶּרֶךְ) is spatial or locative (English *in, on*). (C) The 2MS suffix with the infinitives (וּבְקוּמֶךָ, וּבְשָׁכְבְּךָ, וּבְלֶכְתְּךָ, בְּשִׁבְתְּךָ) serves as the agent of each action ("when you stay [ישׁב]," "and when you go [הלך]," "and when you lie down [שׁכב]," "and when you get up [קום]").

3. *Translate:* "Recount [these words] to your children and speak about them when you stay in your house and you go along the way and whenever you recline and you rise. Tie them to your hand as a sign. Let them become an adornment [Gk. φυλακτήριον] between your eyes. And write them on the doorposts of your house and on your gates."

ROUTE 4

Exodus 20:1–17

STEP ONE: **Read** aloud the text at least five times.

וַיְדַבֵּר אֱלֹהִים אֵת כָּל־הַדְּבָרִים הָאֵלֶּה לֵאמֹר: ²אָנֹכִי יְהוָה
אֱלֹהֶיךָ אֲשֶׁר הוֹצֵאתִיךָ מֵאֶרֶץ מִצְרַיִם מִבֵּית עֲבָדִים: ³לֹא
יִהְיֶה־לְךָ אֱלֹהִים אֲחֵרִים עַל־פָּנָיַ:

STEP TWO: **Parse** the following verbs.

	Stem	Conj.	Pers.	Gend.	Numb.	Root	Trans.
(1) וַיְדַבֵּר							
(2) הוֹצֵאתִיךָ							
(3) יִהְיֶה							

STEP THREE: **Identify** the following.

A. What does לֵאמֹר indicate comes next? _____

B. What is the relationship between מֵאֶרֶץ מִצְרַיִם and מִבֵּית עֲבָדִים? _____

C. The adjective אֲחֵרִים corresponds grammatically to the _____,
_____, and _____ of the noun it modifies (אֱלֹהִים).

51

STEP FOUR: **Translate** the text into understandable English.

> ### VOCABULARY
>
> אֲחֵרִים   (an)other (MP)

STEP FIVE: **Notice** significant exegetical insights.

- אֱלֹהִים (v. 1): The indefinite plural noun functions like a proper noun or title for Yahweh. It is the subject of the clause, even though the verb is singular. Notice the contrast with the plural NP אֱלֹהִים אֲחֵרִים "other gods; another God" in verse 3.

- אָנֹכִי יְהוָה אֱלֹהֶיךָ: Starting in the second verse, two sets of cantillation marks indicate the variant ways that the Decalogue was read. One option (עֶבְדִּים) understands verse 2 as only the first half of a unit, while the second option (עֲבָדִים) sees it as the completion of the first statement. Verse 3 either ends the first unit with the pausal reading עַל־פָּנָי, or עַל־פְּנֵי begins the next statement ending with לָאָרֶץ in verse 4. The combination of these different traditions explains the orthographic hybrid עַל־פָּנָי.

- יִהְיֶה־לְךָ: The verb-particle construction הָיָה לְ indicates possession, where the preposition's object is a possessor (e.g., וַיְהִי־לוֹ צֹאן־וּבָקָר "He (i.e., Abram) *had* sheep and cattle," Gen. 12:16).

- לֹא יִהְיֶה־לְךָ: The negation לֹא with the prefix conjugation is atypical for a negative command. Such a command more commonly employs the negative אַל with a jussive verb: אַל־יְהִי (e.g., Ps. 69:26; Jer. 50:29). The negated PC forms an absolute prohibition and is found elsewhere in the Ten Words (vv. 4–5, 7, 10, 13–17).

- עַל־פְּנֵי: This prepositional phrase typically indicates a location, *upon (the face/surface of)* or *in the presence of* the object of the preposition (e.g., Gen. 1:2; 7:18; Num. 3:4). In some instances, it can denote priority, *over* (Deut. 21:16). It is not the same as the exclusionary relation זוּלָתִי ("except me," Isa. 45:21) or the temporal relation לְפָנַי ("before me," Isa. 43:10).

FOR THE JOURNEY

The metaphor of God's "face" (פָּנִים) signifies the divine characteristics of imminence and intimacy. His presence comforts and brings grace (Gen. 33:10). Rebuke and calamity result when God turns his face away (Jer. 18:17). Yahweh is near to the brokenhearted (Ps. 34:19), those who call on him (Deut. 4:7; Ps. 145:18), and those who seek his face (Isa. 55:6).

God's nearness with Israel requires exclusive reverence. He redeems the enslaved, and only he may be present with his rescued people. He alone upholds the covenant (Exod. 20:1–3). The prophet Isaiah further declares that only Yahweh is truly God, and there is no other like him (Isa. 45:5–6). Even the foreign nations will acknowledge his preeminence (45:14). No other deity answers prayer and saves those who turn to him (45:20–22). Idols are worthless, and Yahweh is unequaled (46:1–13).

ANSWER KEY

1. *Parse:* (1) וַיְדַבֵּר (Piel *wayyiqtol* 3ms דבר "speak"). (2) הוֹצֵאתִיךָ (Hiphil sc 1cs יצא "bring out" + 2ms sf). (3) יִהְיֶה (Qal pc 3ms היה "be").

2. *Identify:* (A) The construction לֵאמֹר marks direct speech, much like quotation marks. (B) Syntactically, מֵאֶרֶץ מִצְרַיִם and מִבֵּית עֲבָדִים are appositional, indicating a twofold description of the location from which Yahweh rescued his people. (C) The adjective (אֲחֵרִים) corresponds grammatically to the *gender* (m), *number* (p), and *definiteness* (indefinite) of the noun it modifies (אֱלֹהִים).

3. *Translate:* "God spoke all these words: 'I am Yahweh, your God, who brought you out from the land of Egypt, the house of slavery. You shall not have another deity in my presence.'"

DAY 17: EXODUS 20:4

STEP ONE: **Read** aloud the text at least five times.

לֹא תַעֲשֶׂה־לְךָ פֶסֶל֙ וְכָל־תְּמוּנָ֔ה אֲשֶׁ֤ר בַּשָּׁמַ֙יִם֙ מִמַּ֔עַל
וַאֲשֶׁר֙ בָּאָ֣רֶץ מִתַּ֔חַת וַאֲשֶׁ֥ר בַּמַּ֖יִם מִתַּ֥חַת לָאָֽרֶץ׃

STEP TWO: **Parse** the following verb.

	Stem	Conj.	Pers.	Gend.	Numb.	Root	Trans.
(1) תַעֲשֶׂה							

STEP THREE: **Identify** the following.

A. Describe the verbal sense of לֹא תַעֲשֶׂה.

B. What is the prepositional phrase לְךָ doing?

C. How are the attributives מִמַּעַל and מִתַּחַת functioning?

STEP FOUR: **Translate** the text into understandable English.

VOCABULARY

פֶסֶל idol, image

תְּמוּנָה likeness, form

מִמַּעַל from above (מִן + מַעַל)

מִתַּחַת from under (מִן + תַּחַת)

STEP FIVE: **Notice** significant exegetical insights.

- פֶסֶל . . . תְּמוּנָה: This word pair is repeated several times in Deuteronomy (4:16, 23, 25), prohibiting the construction and worship of various sorts of idolatry (4:16–19). It covers all forms of idol- and image-making. Other related terms in the Torah include סֶמֶל "statue" (4:16), תַּבְנִית "image" (4:16), תַּבְנִית "depiction"

(4:16–18), מַסֵּכָה "cast idol" (27:15), and אֱלִיל "worthless [idol]" and מַשְׂכִּית "carving" (Lev 26:1). God is not a creature and therefore cannot be represented with creaturely images (Deut. 4:10–12, 39).

• אֲשֶׁר בַּשָּׁמַיִם מִמַּעַל וַאֲשֶׁר בָּאָרֶץ מִתַּחַת וַאֲשֶׁר בַּמַּיִם מִתַּחַת לָאָרֶץ: Three relative clauses combine to describe the all-encompassing extent of the restricted images (כָל־תְּמוּנָה "any representation"). The threefold realms (*above, below, beneath*) correlate to days 1 through 3 of creation (Gen. 1:1–13), and these realms are filled by creatures in days 4 through 6 (1:14–31). All three created realms (*heavens, earth, waters*) and their embodied entities are proscribed from representing God. This verse prohibits making (and by extension worshiping) an idol (פֶּסֶל) or representation (תְּמוּנָה) of any created being. Yet God makes humanity in the divine image (צֶלֶם) and likeness (דְּמוּת; see the readings for days 3 and 4 above).

FOR THE JOURNEY

Yahweh redeemed Israel to be his and serve him truly. Not only does God require exclusive worship (Exod. 20:3), but he also prohibits material and artistic depictions of himself (v. 4). Nothing in the natural order or supernatural realm can be used to represent the Creator. He is not to be confused with any created being, because he made everything. Accordingly, Israel's worship must be exclusive and aniconic.

In Exod. 32, Israel's request for an image brings dire consequences to the community whose allegiance to God wavered in Moses's absence. The people foolishly instructed Aaron: "Make us gods that will lead us" (עֲשֵׂה־לָנוּ אֱלֹהִים אֲשֶׁר יֵלְכוּ לְפָנֵינוּ, v. 1). The result was "a cast idol [in the form of] a calf" (עֵגֶל מַסֵּכָה, v. 4; see also Deut. 9:16). They imagined that their rescuer from Egypt could be embodied as a golden calf (אֵלֶּה אֱלֹהֶיךָ יִשְׂרָאֵל אֲשֶׁר הֶעֱלוּךָ מֵאֶרֶץ מִצְרָיִם "These are your gods, Israel, which brought you up from the land of Egypt," Exod. 32:4, 8). The people thought of God in much the same way as their Egyptian enslavers did. Their faith and theology demanded a physical depiction. These unorthodox beliefs and practices were addressed in the very covenant document that Moses shattered in response to Israel's disloyalty.

ANSWER KEY

1. *Parse:* (1) תַעֲשֶׂה (Qal PC 2MS עשׂה "do, make").

2. *Identify:* (A) The negation and prefix conjugation (לֹא תַעֲשֶׂה) serve as a negative imperative ("Do not . . ."). (B) The prepositional phrase (לְךָ) is often described as an ethical dative, meaning that it expresses the action as for the benefit of the object. (C) The attributives מִמַּעַל and מִתַּחַת function as adverbs of location, "above" and "below."

3. *Translate:* "Do not make yourself an image or representation of anything in the heavens above, the earth below, or the waters beneath the earth."

DAY 18: EXODUS 20:5–6

STEP ONE: **Read** aloud the text at least five times.

לֹא־תִשְׁתַּחֲוֶה לָהֶם וְלֹא תָעָבְדֵם כִּי אָנֹכִי יְהוָה אֱלֹהֶיךָ
אֵל קַנָּא פֹּקֵד עֲוֹן אָבֹת עַל־בָּנִים עַל־שִׁלֵּשִׁים וְעַל־רִבֵּעִים
לְשֹׂנְאָי: ⁶וְעֹשֶׂה חֶסֶד לַאֲלָפִים לְאֹהֲבַי וּלְשֹׁמְרֵי מִצְוֹתָי:

STEP TWO: **Parse** the following verbs.

	Stem	Conj.	Pers.	Gend.	Numb.	Root	Trans.
(1) תִשְׁתַּחֲוֶה							
(2) תָעָבְדֵם							
(3) לְשֹׂנְאָי							
(4) לְאֹהֲבַי							

STEP THREE: **Identify** the following.

A. What is the referent of the 3MP suffix (לָהֶם and תָעָבְדֵם)?
_____

B. How is the 1CS suffix serving with שֹׂנְאָי? _____

C. Are the participles (שֹׁמְרֵי ,אֹהֲבַי ,שֹׂנְאָי) functioning like main verbs, attributives, or substantives? _____

STEP FOUR: **Translate** the text into understandable English.

_____

_____

> **VOCABULARY**
>
> חוה   Hishtaphel: bow down, worship
> קַנָּא   jealous
> שִׁלֵּשִׁים   third [generation]
> רִבֵּעִים   fourth [generation]
> שׂנא   Qal: hate
> מִצְוָה   commandment

STEP FIVE: **Notice** significant exegetical insights.

- לֹא־תִשְׁתַּחְוֶה לָהֶם וְלֹא תָעָבְדֵם: This twofold proscription limits all kinds of idolatrous cultic activities. Spiritual and religious devotion is restricted to Yahweh. The following כִּי clause explains the reason for exclusive submission.

- יְהוָה אֱלֹהֶיךָ אֵל קַנָּא: The predicate includes a three-part apposition. Yahweh speaks and identifies himself by name (יְהוָה), by title (אֱלֹהֶיךָ), and by description (אֵל קַנָּא). The name connects the deliverance of the people from Egypt with the promises given to the patriarchs (Exod. 3:12–18; 6:2–8). The second element identifies Yahweh's role as *their* God—he is not someone else's god. And the third designation is associated with the proscription of worshiping other gods alongside Yahweh (Exod. 34:14; Deut. 4:23–24) and the punishment of idolatry (Deut. 6:14–15).

- פֹּקֵד עֲוֹן אָבֹת . . . וְעֹשֶׂה חֶסֶד: The participle phrases are attributive, elaborating the nature of Yahweh's actions in response to those who reject his ways and those who accept his ways. The first response is negative, and the second positive. For those who are not loyal to him (i.e., שֹׂנְאָי), their waywardness is punished. For those who are loyal to him and his commandments (i.e., אֹהֲבַי), he dispenses his faithful love without limit.

FOR THE JOURNEY

Two disparities occur in these verses. The first transfers the punishment for a father's iniquity (עֲוֹן אָבֹת) to three successive generations (עַל־בָּנִים עַל־שִׁלֵּשִׁים וְעַל־רִבֵּעִים). Transgenerational retribution seems unduly punitive as it potentially punishes uninvolved or yet-to-be progeny.

It is important to note that the disloyalty in view centers on the head of an Israelite household (בֵּית אָב), who is responsible for a multigenerational family unit. Yahweh's commandments archetypally obligate the paterfamilias in his conduct vis-à-vis the other family members (Exod. 20:5). A father's faith can benefit future generations (Gen. 26:24), and his faithlessness is directly detrimental to those under his care (Josh. 7:24–26). In the ancient world, each person in the household did not have the same accountability, ability, or obligation to act with autonomy.

Individual iniquity could bring collective injury. Yet this communal culpability is not unremitting or unending. In Exod. 20:5–6, the by-product of disloyalty is constrained to four generations, perhaps to be understood as all those alive at the time of the male progenitor's iniquity.

The second disparity involves Yahweh's extravagant provision of his covenant faithfulness (חֶ֫סֶד). This profuse devotion represents an exponential inversion of the father's guilt. Thousands (אֲלָפִים) experience his fidelity! These are not, however, constrained to one's bloodline. They include all those following Yahweh in faithful obedience and love. His mercy is wide-reaching, even as transgenerational punishment is restricted.

ANSWER KEY

1. *Parse:* (1) תִשְׁתַּחֲוֶה (Hishtaphel PC 2MS חוה "bow down"). (2) תָעָבְדֵם (Hophal PC 2MS עבד "be led to serve" + 3MP SF). (3) לְשֹׂנְאַי (PREP + Qal ACT PTCL MP שׂנא "hate" + 1CS SF). (4) לְאֹהֲבַי (PREP + Qal ACT PTCL MP אהב "love" + 1CS SF).

2. *Identify:* (A) The 3MP pronominal suffixes (לָהֶם and תָעָבְדֵם) refer to the idols (פֶּסֶל וְכָל־תְּמוּנָה) in verse 4. (B) The 1CS pronominal suffix serves as the object of the participle, "those hating me" (שֹׂנְאַי). (C) These three participles are functioning as substantives and as the objects of the prepositions, e.g., "to those loving me and to those keeping my commandments" (לְאֹהֲבַי וּלְשֹׁמְרֵי מִצְוֹתָי).

3. *Translate:* "Do not bow down to them or be led to serve them, for I am Yahweh, your God—a jealous God, who punishes familial iniquity upon the children up to the third and fourth [generations] to those hating me but who gives faithful love to thousands to those loving me and keeping my commandments."

STEP ONE: Read aloud the text at least five times.

לֹא תִשָּׂא אֶת־שֵׁם־יְהוָה אֱלֹהֶיךָ לַשָּׁוְא כִּי לֹא יְנַקֶּה יְהוָה אֵת
אֲשֶׁר־יִשָּׂא אֶת־שְׁמוֹ לַשָּׁוְא׃

STEP TWO: Parse the following verbs.

	Stem	Conj.	Pers.	Gend.	Numb.	Root	Trans.
(1) תִשָּׂא							
(2) יְנַקֶּה							

STEP THREE: Identify the following.

A. How are the nouns שֵׁם־יְהוָה אֱלֹהֶיךָ related grammatically?

B. What is the syntactic function of the sequence: אֵת אֲשֶׁר?

C. What is the referent of the 3MS suffix שְׁמוֹ?

STEP FOUR: Translate the text into understandable English.

VOCABULARY

שָׁוְא   emptiness, vanity

נקה   Piel: free; acquit

STEP FIVE: Notice significant exegetical insights.

- כִּי: The conjunction indicates cause or explanation (*for, because*). The previous restriction (v. 5) employed a similar construction to highlight Yahweh's character and his response to those ignoring and those heeding his words. In contrast, the present description only pledges punishment to the defiant.

- לַשָּׁוְא: The prepositional phrase functions adverbially. It can serve to indicate the vanity or emptiness of an individual (Job 11:11; Ps. 26:4), of an activity (Ps. 127:1), or of idol worship (Jer. 18:15; Zech. 10:2). Elsewhere it involves speaking (Exod. 23:1; Ps. 144:8, 11; Isa. 59:4; Ezek. 13:8) or walking (Job 31:5) in a false or deceitful way.

FOR THE JOURNEY

The expression "do not bear" (לֹא תִשָּׂא) uses the embodied metaphor of lifting and carrying something. In Exod. 20:7, Yahweh's name is the thing that is elevated. It is tempting to assume that "not lifting a name" proscribes a simple speech act (Exod. 23:1; Ps. 12:3). The divine name should not be invoked in a vain or false way. So, keep from dishonoring his name with deceitful swearing (Ps. 24:4) or wicked intent (Ps. 139:20).

Another more far-reaching understanding may be in view here. What if bearing the name has more to do with a life characterized by truth than simply avoiding verbal taboos and vanities?

Those who bear Yahweh's name are to be fully devoted to him.[1] Their existence is embossed with his character, authority, and reputation. They may even carry his insignia on their person, particularly their hand (Isa. 44:5) and their head (Exod. 28:36–38; Ezek. 9:4). Devotion involves whatever one sets their hand and their head to do. Using a similar expression, Aaron is said to bear the names of the tribes on the high-priestly garments (Exod. 28:12, 29). The jewels on the ephod shoulders (vv. 11–12) and breastplate (v. 21) were engraved with the names of the tribes. These inscriptions served as a reminder of who the high priest represented, and this practice is called a memorial (זִכָּרוֹן) for the sons of Israel (v. 12) and before Yahweh (v. 29).

Just as a priest would not bear such holy regalia in mundane circumstances, so too must followers of Yahweh not bear his name for untoward purposes.

---

1. Carmen Joy Imes, *Bearing Yhwh's Name at Sinai: A Reexamination of the Name Command of the Decalogue*, Bulletin for Biblical Research Supplement 19 (University Park, PA: Eisenbrauns, 2018).

ANSWER KEY

1. *Parse:* (1) תִשָּׂא (Qal PC 2MS נשא "lift, carry"). (2) יְנַקֶּה (Piel PC 3MS נקה "free; acquit").

2. *Identify:* (A) The first two nouns, שֵׁם־יהוה, form a construct phrase ("Yahweh's name"), and the second and third nouns, יהוה אֱלֹהֶיךָ, are in apposition ("Yahweh, your God"). (B) The first word, אֶת, designates the object of the verb (יְנַקֶּה), and the second, אֲשֶׁר, indicates that the object is the forthcoming nominalized clause (אֲשֶׁר־יִשָּׂא אֶת־שְׁמוֹ לַשָּׁוְא). (C) The 3MS possessive suffix (שְׁמוֹ) replaces "Yahweh, your God" in the parallel noun phrase (שֵׁם־יהוה אֱלֹהֶיךָ).

3. *Translate:* "Do not bear the name of Yahweh your God deceitfully, for Yahweh does not acquit the one who bears his name deceitfully."

DAY 20: EXODUS 20:8–10

STEP ONE: **Read** aloud the text at least five times.

זָכוֹר֩ אֶת־י֨וֹם הַשַּׁבָּ֜ת לְקַדְּשׁ֗וֹ: ⁹שֵׁ֤שֶׁת יָמִים֙ תַּֽעֲבֹד֔ וְעָשִׂ֖יתָ
כָּל־מְלַאכְתֶּֽךָ֒: ¹⁰וְי֙וֹם֙ הַשְּׁבִיעִ֗י שַׁבָּ֣ת ׀ לַיהוָ֖ה אֱלֹהֶ֑יךָ
לֹֽא־תַעֲשֶׂ֣ה כָל־מְלָאכָ֡ה אַתָּ֣ה ׀ וּבִנְךָֽ־וּבִתֶּ֣ךָ עַבְדְּךָ֤ וַאֲמָֽתְךָ֙
וּבְהֶמְתֶּ֔ךָ וְגֵרְךָ֖ אֲשֶׁ֥ר בִּשְׁעָרֶֽיךָ:

STEP TWO: **Parse** the following verbs.

	Stem	Conj.	Pers.	Gend.	Numb.	Root	Trans.
(1) זָכוֹר֩							
(2) לְקַדְּשׁ֗וֹ							
(3) וְעָשִׂ֖יתָ							

STEP THREE: **Identify** the following.

A. What is the referent of the 3MS suffix with לְקַדְּשׁ֗וֹ?

B. What is the noun phrase שֵׁ֤שֶׁת יָמִים doing in the clause?

STEP FOUR: **Translate** the text into understandable English.

VOCABULARY

שַׁבָּת   sabbath

קדש   Piel: sanctify, honor, set apart, dedicate

מְלָאכָה   work, occupation

שְׁבִיעִי   seventh

אָמָה   maidservant; female slave

בְּהֵמָה   beast; cattle

גֵּר   sojourner, immigrant

STEP FIVE: **Notice** significant exegetical insights.

- זָכוֹר: In verse 8 and again in verse 12, the infinitive absolute acts like a command. These are the only positive directives in the Decalogue, and just like the rare negative command form (e.g., לֹא־תַעֲשֶׂה "do not do," v. 10), they are not the typical imperative form (זְכֹר "remember").

- זָכוֹר or שָׁמוֹר: The parallel passage in Deut. 5:12–15 employs a different verb (שָׁמוֹר "keep," v. 12; also, Exod. 31:16) and an alternate reason for sabbath observance focusing on the cessation of household labor. Israel must remember (וְזָכַרְתָּ Deut. 5:15) that Yahweh freed them from Egyptian enslavement as another motive to honor the sabbath.

- לְקַדְּשׁוֹ: Israel's remembrance is enacted in the complete cessation of work on the seventh day. The sabbath is sanctified as Israel memorializes the final day of the week. In this way, the seventh day correlates with the creation week in which God consecrated his own work (וַיְבָרֶךְ אֱלֹהִים אֶת־יוֹם הַשְּׁבִיעִי וַיְקַדֵּשׁ אֹתוֹ כִּי בוֹ שָׁבַת מִכָּל־מְלַאכְתּוֹ Gen. 2:3). Just as God completed all his work in six days, so too the Israelites should perform all their weekly tasks (כָּל־מְלַאכְתֶּךָ Exod. 20:9) in six days and rest on the seventh.

- אַתָּה וּבִנְךָ־וּבִתֶּךָ עַבְדְּךָ וַאֲמָתְךָ וּבְהֶמְתֶּךָ וְגֵרְךָ אֲשֶׁר בִּשְׁעָרֶיךָ: This phrase specifies seven representative groups of humans and animals that are commanded to cease their work on the seventh day. Notice that the primary addressee (אַתָּה "you" and לֹא־תַעֲשֶׂה "do not do," both 2MS) is the head of the family. The father is responsible to ensure the proper observance of the sabbath among all members of his household.

FOR THE JOURNEY

The six-plus-one pattern is established in the creation week (Gen. 1:1–2:4). A similar seven-day routine is followed with the provision of the manna in the wilderness (Exod. 16:5, 22, 26, 29) and the weekly sabbath (Lev. 23:3). The Feast of Unleavened Bread (Exod. 13:6–7; 23:15; Lev. 23:5–8) and Sukkot (i.e., the Feast of Booths, Num. 29:12–38) also mirror this arrangement. The sabbatical year brings cessation (שַׁבָּתוֹן) of normal agricultural activity every seventh year (Lev. 25:1–7), and the

Jubilee (יוֹבֵל) promises economic autonomy to the subjugated after the seventh sabbatical year (Lev. 25:8–22).

The passion week culminating in the resurrection orients to this six-plus-one cycle. Jesus's death on Friday (John 19:31) completes the work of his kingdom (Acts 13:29). He rests in the grave on the sabbath (Luke 23:53–56; John 19:42). On the first day of the week (Mark 16:1–2), his resurrection initiates a new pattern (Rom. 6:5). And it produces a sabbath rest for God's people in a new way (Heb. 4:8–11).

ANSWER KEY

1. *Parse:* (1) זָכוֹר (Qal INF ABS זכר "remember"). (2) לְקַדְּשׁוֹ (PREP + Piel INF CSTR קדשׁ "honor" + 3MS SF). (3) וְעָשִׂיתָ (Qal *wǝqātal* 2MS עשׂה "do, make").

2. *Identify:* (A) The 3MS suffix on לְקַדְּשׁוֹ refers to יוֹם הַשַּׁבָּת "the sabbath day." (B) The noun phrase שֵׁשֶׁת יָמִים functions as a temporal adverb, "[for] six days."

3. *Translate:* "Remember the sabbath day to honor it. You shall work for six days and do all your work, but the seventh day is a sabbath for Yahweh your God. Do not do any work—you, your son or daughter, your male or female servant, or your cattle or immigrant in your gates."

DAY 21: EXODUS 20:11

STEP ONE: **Read** aloud the text at least five times.

כִּי שֵׁשֶׁת־יָמִים עָשָׂה יְהוָה אֶת־הַשָּׁמַיִם וְאֶת־הָאָרֶץ אֶת־הַיָּם
וְאֶת־כָּל־אֲשֶׁר־בָּם וַיָּנַח בַּיּוֹם הַשְּׁבִיעִי עַל־כֵּן בֵּרַךְ יְהוָה
אֶת־יוֹם הַשַּׁבָּת וַיְקַדְּשֵׁהוּ׃

STEP TWO: **Parse** the following verbs.

	Stem	Conj.	Pers.	Gend.	Numb.	Root	Trans.
(1) וַיָּנַח							
(2) בֵּרַךְ							
(3) וַיְקַדְּשֵׁהוּ							

STEP THREE: **Identify** the following.

A. What is the referent of the 3MP suffix (בָּם)? _____

B. What is the subject of וַיָּנַח? _____

C. What is the referent of the 3MS suffix (וַיְקַדְּשֵׁהוּ)?

_____

STEP FOUR: **Translate** the text into understandable English.

_____

_____

VOCABULARY

נוח   Qal: rest, repose

שְׁבִיעִי   seventh

שַׁבָּת   sabbath

קדשׁ   Piel: set apart, dedicate, sanctify, honor

STEP FIVE: **Notice** significant exegetical insights.

- שֵׁשֶׁת־יָמִים: This temporal expression echoes verse 9. It correlates the weekly labors of humans (תַּעֲבֹד וְעָשִׂיתָ, v. 9) with the creative work of God (עָשָׂה, v. 11; see Gen. 2:3–4).

- אֶת־הַשָּׁמַיִם וְאֶת־הָאָרֶץ אֶת־הַיָּם וְאֶת־כָּל־אֲשֶׁר־בָּם: This fourfold sequence is a way of discussing all of God's creation. It is especially common in the Psalms (146:6; also, 69:35; 96:11) and other Israelite prayers (Neh. 9:6). These passages extol the mighty acts of Yahweh in creation and his worthiness to be praised, which are central themes in the sabbath day hymn (Ps. 92).

- יוֹם הַשַּׁבָּת: The object of blessing and honor matches the blessing of the seventh day in Gen. 2:3. "The seventh day" (יוֹם הַשְּׁבִיעִי, Gen. 2:3; בַּיּוֹם הַשְּׁבִיעִי, Exod. 20:11) is renamed "the sabbath day" (Exod. 20:11), as identified in verses 8 and 10 (also Exod. 31:15), linking the hebdomadal cycle and the pursuit of cessation.

FOR THE JOURNEY

The Hebrew notions of שַׁבָּת "sabbath" and נוּח "rest" are mostly distinct in the Torah. The former centers on a particular day (or year) and the activity of stopping work as a perpetual covenantal sign (e.g., Exod. 31:12–17). The latter involves Israel's peaceful habitation of the promised land (Deut. 3:18–20; 25:19). Divine rest (מְנוּחָה) is both a place and a time that is to be anticipated (Deut. 12:9–14). Only in the rationale of the weekly sabbath do the verbal notions merge. On the day of cessation, God rests (נוּח; Exod. 20:11), and laborers should be allowed to rest (נוּח; Deut. 5:14).

Drawing on the warning against disobedience of Ps. 95:7–11, the book of Hebrews combines the sabbath and the yet-to-be resting place (3:7–4:11). Bringing together the temporal concept of שַׁבָּת and the physical concept of מְנוּחָה, the author proclaims that today (הַיּוֹם or σήμερον) is the promised time to enter God's rest. Both ideas are expressed with the Greek terms καταπαύω/κατάπαυσις (Heb. 4:1–11). Rest remains for those who hear in faith and are not disobedient to God's word (Ps. 95:7–8, 11). Just as God rested at the foundation of the world (Gen. 2:2; Heb. 4:3–4), God's people may now enter divine repose (Heb. 4:10–11).

ANSWER KEY

1. *Parse:* (1) וַיָּנַח (Qal *wayyiqtol* 3MS נוח "rest"). (2) בֵּרַךְ (Piel SC 3MS ברך "bless"). (3) וַיְקַדְּשֵׁהוּ (Piel *wayyiqtol* 3MS קדשׁ "honor" + 3MS SF).

2. *Identify:* (A) The 3MP suffix (בָּם) refers to the compound direct object expressed as אֶת־הַשָּׁמַיִם וְאֶת־הָאָרֶץ אֶת־הַיָּם וְאֶת־כָּל־אֲשֶׁר־בָּם. (B) The subject of וַיָּנַח is the same as the expressed agent of the previous clause (יהוה). (C) The 3MS suffix (וַיְקַדְּשֵׁהוּ) refers to the object of the preceding clause: יוֹם הַשַּׁבָּת "the sabbath day."

3. *Translate:* "For in six days Yahweh made the heavens, the earth, and the sea as well as everything in them, and he rested on the seventh day. Consequently, Yahweh blessed the sabbath day and honored it."

DAY 22: EXODUS 20:12–15

STEP ONE: **Read** aloud the text at least five times.

כַּבֵּד אֶת־אָבִיךָ וְאֶת־אִמֶּךָ לְמַעַן יַאֲרִכוּן יָמֶיךָ עַל הָאֲדָמָה
אֲשֶׁר־יְהוָה אֱלֹהֶיךָ נֹתֵן לָךְ: ¹³ לֹא תִּרְצָח: ¹⁴ לֹא תִּנְאָף:
¹⁵ לֹא תִּגְנֹב:

STEP TWO: **Parse** the following verbs.

	Stem	Conj.	Pers.	Gend.	Numb.	Root	Trans.
(1) כַּבֵּד							
(2) יַאֲרִכוּן							
(3) תִּרְצָח							
(4) תִּנְאָף							
(5) תִּגְנֹב							

STEP THREE: **Identify** the following.

A. What is the 3MP subject of יַאֲרִכוּן? _____

B. What is the relative clause beginning with אֲשֶׁר describing?

_____

STEP FOUR: **Translate** the text into understandable English.

_____

_____

VOCABULARY

כבד   Piel: make heavy; honor, glorify, respect

ארך   Hiphil: prolong; endure

רצח   Qal: kill, slay, murder

נאף   Qal: commit adultery

גנב   Qal: steal

STEP FIVE: **Notice** significant exegetical insights.

- יַאֲרִכוּן יָמֶיךָ: The subject of the Hiphil stem of אֲרַךְ may participate in the action as the causer or the affected semantic role. The subject is the causer, and the object is the affected in 1 Kings 3:14: וְהַאֲרַכְתִּי אֶת־יָמֶיךָ "I [i.e., Yahweh] will lengthen your days." Elsewhere, as in Exod. 20:13 (and Deut. 5:16), the subject is the affected with no causer expressed: וּלְמַעַן יַאֲרִכֻן יָמֶיךָ "so that your days may endure" (Deut. 6:2). The causer is unstated even when the source is known.

- לֹא תִּרְצָ֥ח: The line above the first letter of this verb is called *rafe*. In the Tiberian tradition, it is found on all *begad-kephat* letters without a *dagesh lene*, but in most printed editions, *rafe* is not used. This marking is used here to show two different traditions of intoning the text. In verses 13–15, the *rafe* corresponds to the conjunctive cantillation (לֹא תִּרְצָ֥ח), and the *dagesh lene* corresponds to the disjunctive (לֹא תִּרְצָח). While this reading dissimilarity is straightforward, little semantic difference appears to accompany the disparity.

- תִּרְצָח: The meaning of this verb is not easily isolated to a lone English word. It can be understood as "kill," "slay," or even "murder." The situation may be seen to parallel the legal classifications of voluntary and involuntary manslaughter. In Num. 35, רצח represents the taking of someone's life inadvertently (vv. 11–19) or without malice (vv. 20–21). In either case, the label הָרֹצֵחַ is used (vv. 22–25), and the credible accused, or even a convict, could avail himself of the city of refuge (vv. 26–32; also, Deut. 4:42; 19:3–6; Josh. 20:3–6). A few situations (1 Kings 21:19; Job 24:14) describe premeditated killing, and the legal retribution itself is called רצח (Num. 35:27, 30). Generally, the act of homicide may be the most fitting modern comparison.

- תִּרְצָח . . . תִּנְאָף . . . תִּגְנֹב: This series of moral constraints is found as part of various expanded lists. Hosea 4:2 presents these three alongside cursing, lying, and bloodshed. Jeremiah 7:9 continues the list with swearing falsely, false worship, and following other gods. Job 24:13–17 describes individuals who subvert God's wisdom, starting with a murderer (רוֹצֵחַ), a thief (גַּנָּב), and an adulterer (נֹאֵף; vv. 14–15).

FOR THE JOURNEY

The Decalogue establishes Yahweh's ethical framework for the Israelite community. Perhaps to the surprise of the modern audience, none of these provisions demand one's own rights or freedoms. They outline communal obligations rather than personal liberties. Each is focused on a particular responsibility of the community—particularly the male leader of the household (notice the 2ms verbal forms)—to protect others.

The initial commands safeguard Yahweh: his claim to exclusive allegiance, to define his own image, and to reverence. But the people of God are also responsible to each other. The duty of the individual is to defend the rights of others. The subsequent command restricts the ability of the patriarch to demand unending work (Exod. 20:8–11; Deut. 5:12–15). Exodus 20:12–15 safeguards the members of one's household and community by instituting the privileges of parental respect, innocent life, marital purity, and ownership of property.

These "tablets" establish love of God and love of neighbor. Jesus's response identifying the greatest commandment depicts this twofold truth. Love seeks to place others above oneself and to protect their rights. In sum, the law of Moses is ultimately about loving God and neighbor (Matt. 22:36–40).

ANSWER KEY

1. *Parse:* (1) כַּבֵּד (Piel INF ABS [or IMV MS] כבד "honor"). (2) יַאֲרִכוּן (Hiphil PC 3MP ארך "prolong"; the final *nun* is described as paragogic, a vestige of an older form of יַאֲרִיכוּ). (3) תִּרְצָח (Qal PC 2MS רצח "murder"). (4) תִּנְאָף (Qal PC 2MS נאף "commit adultery"). (5) תִּגְנֹב (Qal PC 2MS גנב "steal").

2. *Identify:* (A) The 3MP subject of יַאֲרִכוּן is יָמֶיךָ "your days." (B) The relative clause beginning with אֲשֶׁר expands the attributes of the noun immediately preceding it, הָאֲדָמָה "the ground."

3. *Translate:* "Respect your father and mother so that your days will be lengthened on the ground that Yahweh your God is giving you. Do not murder. Do not commit adultery. Do not steal."

DAY 23: EXODUS 20:16–17

STEP ONE: **Read** aloud the text at least five times.

לֹא־תַעֲנֶה בְרֵעֲךָ עֵד שָׁקֶר: ¹⁷לֹא תַחְמֹד בֵּית רֵעֶךָ לֹא־תַחְמֹד
אֵשֶׁת רֵעֶךָ וְעַבְדּוֹ וַאֲמָתוֹ וְשׁוֹרוֹ וַחֲמֹרוֹ וְכֹל אֲשֶׁר לְרֵעֶךָ:

STEP TWO: **Parse** the following verbs.

	Stem	Conj.	Pers.	Gend.	Numb.	Root	Trans.
(1) תַעֲנֶה							
(2) תַחְמֹד							

STEP THREE: **Identify** the following.

A. What meaning works best to describe the preposition with בְרֵעֲךָ? _____

B. How many times is "your neighbor" referenced?

_____

STEP FOUR: **Translate** the text into understandable English.

_____

_____

VOCABULARY

רֵעַ   companion, neighbor, friend

עֵד   witness

שֶׁקֶר   deception, deceit

חמד   Qal: desire, take (pleasure in)

אָמָה   maidservant; female slave

שׁוֹר   ox, bovine; cattle

חֲמוֹר   male donkey

STEP FIVE: **Notice** significant exegetical insights.

- תַעֲנֶה . . . עֵד שָׁקֶר: "Giving a false testimony" connotes more than simply lying, being dishonest, or acting deceitfully. This expression has legal ramifications, akin to swearing to "give the whole truth and nothing but the truth" (Deut. 19:18). False testimony is likened to a deadly weapon (Prov. 25:18).

- לֹא־תַחְמֹד . . . לֹא תַחְמֹד: The repetition of the same negative command functions like apposition. The first object, בֵּית רֵעֶךָ ("your neighbor's household"), is itemized with the following verb's compound object, which includes all people and things associated with his household: "your neighbor's wife, servant, maidservant, cattle, donkey, and possessions" (אֵשֶׁת רֵעֶךָ וְעַבְדּוֹ וַאֲמָתוֹ וְשׁוֹרוֹ וַחֲמֹרוֹ וְכֹל אֲשֶׁר לְרֵעֶךָ).

- וְכֹל אֲשֶׁר לְרֵעֶךָ: The relative clause describes everything else belonging to your neighbor. The preposition לְ can designate possession where the object is the possessor (i.e., "object *x* belongs to [someone]").

FOR THE JOURNEY

The interpersonal ethical focus continues in these two verses.

- The first negative command promotes judicial credibility. Witnesses are told to report iniquity (Lev. 5:1) and warned not to join evildoers in a false report (Exod. 23:1). Trustworthiness is essential in society and legal proceedings. After all, the sentence of death can be issued only on the shared testimony of two or three witnesses (עֵדִים, Num. 35:30; Deut. 17:2–7). And a false testimony carries the equivalent verdict on the one giving a deceitful statement (Deut. 19:15–19).

- The second instruction safeguards a neighbor's basic right to security. The English verb "covet" seems appropriate for חמד since it conveys the notions of "craving" and "acquiring" something. This action enmeshes conceited seeing and illicit consuming (Gen. 3:6; Josh. 7:21). Securing pleasure at the expense of another is the opposite of royal love (James 2:8).

Loving one's neighbor means seeking to protect the reputation and security of others. Accordingly, 1 John 3:16–18 instructs Christians to act in truth and not to withhold compassion. As Jesus laid down his life, so too should we seek the welfare of others, even at great personal cost.

ANSWER KEY

1. *Parse:* (1) תַּעֲנֶה (Qal PC 2MS ענה "reply, testify"). (2) תַחְמֹד (Qal PC 2MS חמד "desire").

2. *Identify:* (A) The adversative meaning of the prepositional phrase, בְרֵעֶךָ ("against your neighbor"), describes the negative implication of the giving of a false testimony. (B) "Your neighbor" is referenced eight times in these three clauses: בְרֵעֶךָ "against your neighbor," בֵּית רֵעֶךָ "your neighbor's house," אֵשֶׁת רֵעֶךָ "your neighbor's wife," וְעַבְדּוֹ "his [i.e., your neighbor's] slave," וַאֲמָתוֹ "his female slave," וְשׁוֹרוֹ "his ox," וַחֲמֹרוֹ "his donkey," and וְכֹל אֲשֶׁר לְרֵעֶךָ "your neighbor's possessions."

3. *Translate:* "Do not give a false testimony against your neighbor. Do not desire your neighbor's household. Do not desire your neighbor's wife, his slave, his female slave, his ox, his donkey, or anything that belongs to your neighbor."

ROUTE 5

2 Samuel 7:4–17

STEP ONE: **Read** aloud the text at least five times.

וַיְהִי בַּלַּיְלָה הַהֻוא וַיְהִי דְּבַר־יְהוָֹה אֶל־נָתָן לֵאמֹר: ⁵לֵךְ
וְאָמַרְתָּ אֶל־עַבְדִּי אֶל־דָּוִד כֹּה אָמַר יְהוָה הַאַתָּה תִּבְנֶה־לִּי
בַיִת לְשִׁבְתִּי:

STEP TWO: **Parse** the following verbs.

	Stem	Conj.	Pers.	Gend.	Numb.	Root	Trans.
(1) לֵךְ							
(2) וְאָמַרְתָּ							
(3) תִּבְנֶה							
(4) לְשִׁבְתִּי							

STEP THREE: **Identify** the following.

A. What does לֵאמֹר signal? _____

B. What is the initial הַ morpheme found with הַאַתָּה? _____

C. What is the semantic function of the 1cs suffix with לְשִׁבְתִּי? _____

75

STEP FOUR: **Translate** the text into understandable English.

VOCABULARY

נָתָן   Nathan

STEP FIVE: **Notice** significant exegetical insights.

- לֵךְ וְאָמַרְתָּ: The series of an imperative and *wəqātal* verb indicates a volitive sequence. The verbs are understood progressively: first *go*, and then *say*. Such sequences are analogous to *wayyiqtol* narrative series. A string of sequential imperative verbs (e.g., לֵךְ עֲשֵׂה "Go do," 2 Sam. 7:3), in contrast, does not necessarily elicit a sequence of discrete actions; they may be undifferentiated, simultaneous, and/or consecutive.

- כֹּה אָמַר יְהוָה: This expression is a common trope in prophetic speech. It serves as an authenticating figure of speech both in prophetic narratives (e.g., Exod. 4:22; Josh. 7:13; 1 Sam. 2:27) and prophetic oracles (e.g., Isa. 7:7; Jer. 2:2; Ezek. 21:3).

- הַאַתָּה תִּבְנֶה־לִּי: The 2MS independent pronoun is pleonastic on account of the finite verb and contrasts with the 1CS pronominal suffix as the divine reference. "Will *YOU* build for *me*?"

FOR THE JOURNEY

Concerning his desire to build God a permanent dwelling place, the prophet initially directs the king to do all that he wants (כֹּל אֲשֶׁר בִּלְבָבְךָ לֵךְ עֲשֵׂה, v. 3). That night Nathan receives a contravening instruction. The prophetic vision challenges both the prophet's established prudence and the king's prerogative as builder of God's house. A central question emerges: Who can really build a lasting house for whom (v. 5)? While the king and prophet assume that they would erect a temple for God, Yahweh declares that he, not David, is the true house builder. He promises David a royal house (v. 11) that will surpass anything the king can imagine!

It might be easy to rush over verse 4, but it deserves a closer look. The narrator uses a specialized frame to introduce the divine response to the previous interchange (vv. 2–3). Yahweh's word is portrayed as a moveable agent (וַיְהִי דְּבַר־יְהוָה אֶל־נָתָן, v. 4). The same expression is used to authenticate utterances to prophets (e.g., to Abram, Gen. 15:1; to Samuel, 1 Sam. 15:10; to Elijah, 1 Kings 21:17; to Isaiah, Isa. 38:4). God's word is on the move. It acts in the world. Such encounters bring disruptive words of comfort and commission to God's people.

ANSWER KEY

1. *Parse:* (1) לֵךְ (Qal IMV MS הלך "go"). (2) וְאָמַרְתָּ (Qal *waqātal* 2MS אמר "say"). (3) תִּבְנֶה (Qal PC 2MS בנה "build"). (4) לְשִׁבְתִּי (PREP + Qal INF CSTR ישב "dwell" + 1CS SF).

2. *Identify:* (A) The form לֵאמֹר signals direct speech, comparable to quotation marks in English. (B) The initial morpheme with הַאַתָּה is the interrogative particle הַ, indicating a yes-no question. (C) The 1CS suffix (שִׁבְתִּי) functions as a subjective agent, designating the one doing the action ("my dwelling" ≈ "I will dwell").

3. *Translate:* "That very night, Yahweh's word came to Nathan, 'Go and say to my servant David: "Thus says Yahweh, will you build me a house for me to dwell?"'"

DAY 25: 2 SAMUEL 7:6–7

STEP ONE: **Read** aloud the text at least five times.

כִּי לֹא יָשַׁבְתִּי בְּבַיִת לְמִיּוֹם הַעֲלֹתִי אֶת־בְּנֵי יִשְׂרָאֵל מִמִּצְרַיִם
וְעַד הַיּוֹם הַזֶּה וָאֶהְיֶה מִתְהַלֵּךְ בְּאֹהֶל וּבְמִשְׁכָּן: ⁷בְּכֹל
אֲשֶׁר־הִתְהַלַּכְתִּי בְּכָל־בְּנֵי יִשְׂרָאֵל הֲדָבָר דִּבַּרְתִּי אֶת־אַחַד
שִׁבְטֵי יִשְׂרָאֵל אֲשֶׁר צִוִּיתִי לִרְעוֹת אֶת־עַמִּי אֶת־יִשְׂרָאֵל
לֵאמֹר לָמָּה לֹא־בְנִיתֶם לִי בֵּית אֲרָזִים:

STEP TWO: **Parse** the following verbs.

	Stem	Conj.	Pers.	Gend.	Numb.	Root	Trans.
(1) הַעֲלֹתִי							
(2) מִתְהַלֵּךְ							
(3) הִתְהַלַּכְתִּי							
(4) לִרְעוֹת							
(5) בְנִיתֶם							

STEP THREE: **Identify** the following.

A. Who is the first-person speaker of יָשַׁבְתִּי . . . וָאֶהְיֶה?

B. What is the initial הֲ morpheme found with הֲדָבָר?

C. What element does לֵאמֹר expand?

STEP FOUR: **Translate** the text into understandable English.

VOCABULARY

מִשְׁכָּן   abode, dwelling place

שֵׁבֶט   rod, scepter; tribe, tribal leader (PL CSTR שִׁבְטֵי)

רעה   Qal: shepherd, graze; pasture; feed

אֶרֶז   cedar

STEP FIVE: **Notice** significant exegetical insights.

- לְמִיּוֹם הֶעֱלֹתִי . . . וְעַד הַיּוֹם הַזֶּה: This sequence of temporal prepositions relates a beginning (לְמִיּוֹם) and an ending point (וְעַד). In this case, the end is the moment of speaking (i.e., "today"), and the start is Yahweh's deliverance of Israel from Egypt.

- בְּאֹהֶל וּבְמִשְׁכָּן: The former term may be a shortened version of "tent of meeting" (אֹהֶל מוֹעֵד) as the place of divine oracles and theophany outside the camp (Exod. 33:7–11). The latter often refers to the place of sacrifice as Yahweh's dwelling, patterned on the heavenly tabernacle (Exod. 25:8–9; 26:30). These two concepts are allied in various passages (particularly, Exod. 39:32–40:35).

- בְּכֹל אֲשֶׁר־הִתְהַלַּכְתִּי: The prepositional phrase may describe the locations ("in every [place]," KJV, ESV, Tanakh) or the occasions ("in every [time]," NIV, NRSV) in which God visited his people. The notion of place describes the location where God could have demanded a permanent structure (דִּבַּרְתִּי, v. 7b). The notion of time, on the other hand, could specify either God's travel itinerary (וָאֶהְיֶה מִתְהַלֵּךְ, v. 6b) or the time frame of the hypothetical request (v. 7b).

FOR THE JOURNEY

David's comparison of his and God's accommodations (v. 2) may seem inconsequential upon first thought. Would God really care about this housing inequality? Why focus on one structural style or building material over another?

The description "house of cedar" (בֵּית אֲרָזִים) is not simply a material description. It conveys the concept of permanence as compared with God's residence "among the curtains" (בְּתוֹךְ הַיְרִיעָה, v. 2). David

---

identifies the disparity between his resilient palace and God's provisional tent. The difference involved not just prestige but security. As king, David wanted to secure an enduring abode for his God. Such a lasting structure would ensure Yahweh's presence and his favor.

Three ironies are instructive. First, David's residence was not permanent. No physical building (even one made of cedar!) can be secure without God providing rest (v. 1). Second, the future of David's household was anything but assured. Only God's faithfulness could safeguard the longevity of David's lineage (v. 11). Third, God's dwelling endures because it exists in heaven and not on earth (1 Kings 8:27). Actual security would only be guaranteed by Yahweh's promise, and his favor assured only by fidelity to him.

ANSWER KEY

1. *Parse:* (1) הֶעֱלֹתִי (Hiphil INF CSTR עלה "bring up" + 1CS SF). (2) מִתְהַלֵּךְ (Hitpael PTCL MS הלך "travel about"). (3) הִתְהַלַּכְתִּי (Hitpael SC 1CS הלך "travel about"). (4) לִרְעוֹת (PREP + Qal INF CSTR רעה "shepherd"). (5) בְּנִיתֶם (Qal SC 2MP בנה "build").

2. *Identify:* (A) The first-person speaker of the verbal sequence יָשַׁבְתִּי . . . וָאֶהְיֶה is Yahweh, continuing the speech from verse 5. (B) The initial morpheme with הֲדָבָר is the interrogative particle, indicating a yes-no question.[1] (C) The form לֵאמֹר signals direct speech, functionally comparable to quotation marks in English, and describes what the purported הַדָּבָר would have been.

3. *Translate:* "For I have not inhabited a house from the time I brought the Israelites out of Egypt until this very day. I used to move about in a tent and a tabernacle. Wherever I traveled with all the Israelites, did I ever mention to one of the Israelite leaders whom I commanded to shepherd my people Israel, saying, 'Why don't you build me a cedar house?'"

1. The default vocalization of the prefixed interrogative particle is *hatef patach* (הֲ). A full *patach* is used when it precedes a letter with a *sheva* or a guttural letter (see, e.g., the discussion of הַאַתָּה on day 24, 2 Sam. 7:5). A *segol* is found when the guttural letter is followed by the vowel *qamets*.

DAY 26: 2 SAMUEL 7:8–9

STEP ONE: **Read** aloud the text at least five times.

וְעַתָּ֡ה כֹּֽה־תֹאמַ֣ר לְעַבְדִּ֣י לְדָוִ֗ד כֹּ֤ה אָמַר֙ יְהוָ֣ה צְבָא֔וֹת אֲנִ֤י
לְקַחְתִּ֙יךָ֙ מִן־הַנָּוֶ֔ה מֵאַחַ֖ר הַצֹּ֑אן לִֽהְי֣וֹת נָגִ֔יד עַל־עַמִּ֖י עַל־
יִשְׂרָאֵֽל: ⁹וָאֶהְיֶ֣ה עִמְּךָ֗ בְּכֹל֙ אֲשֶׁ֣ר הָלַ֔כְתָּ וָאַכְרִ֥תָה
אֶת־כָּל־אֹיְבֶ֖יךָ מִפָּנֶ֑יךָ וְעָשִׂ֧תִי לְךָ֛ שֵׁ֥ם גָּד֖וֹל כְּשֵׁ֥ם הַגְּדֹלִ֖ים
אֲשֶׁ֥ר בָּאָֽרֶץ:

STEP TWO: **Parse** the following verbs.

	Stem	Conj.	Pers.	Gend.	Numb.	Root	Trans.
(1) לְקַחְתִּ֙יךָ֙							
(2) וָאֶהְיֶ֣ה							
(3) הָלַ֔כְתָּ							
(4) וָאַכְרִ֥תָה							
(5) וְעָשִׂ֧תִי							

STEP THREE: **Identify** the following.

A. What is the relationship between the two prepositional phrases, עַל־עַמִּ֖י and עַל־יִשְׂרָאֵֽל? _____

B. How is the adjective הַגְּדֹלִ֖ים being used? _____

STEP FOUR: **Translate** the text into understandable English.

_____

_____

VOCABULARY

נָוֶה   meadow, grazing place

נָגִיד   leader, ruler

STEP FIVE: **Notice** significant exegetical insights.

- וְעַתָּה: This particle is more than a temporal marker ("and now"). It functions to mark a major transition or inferential statement in a discourse (see also 2 Sam. 7:25).

- מֵאַחַר הַצֹּאן: A similar expression connects this passage to Amos 7:15 and the prophet's claim to divine authorization of his mission.

- וְאֶהְיֶה . . . וָאַכְרִתָה . . . וְעָשִׂיתִי: The sequence of the *wayyiqtol* (וָאֶהְיֶה) and the *wayyiqtol*/cohortative (וָאַכְרִתָה) indicates the result or consequence of the previous narrative claim ("so that"). The outcome of Yahweh being with David was that no enemy could stand before the king. The final *wəqātal* (וְעָשִׂיתִי) shifts to a future promise.

FOR THE JOURNEY

The Hebrew term שֵׁם ("name") refers to much more than a distinct designation of an individual. It includes the notions of reputation and remembrance. First Chronicles 14:17 portrays "David's name" (שֵׁם־דָּוִיד) as going out into the lands surrounding Judah and bringing fear to the nations. In modern terms, we would describe such a concept as David's fame or repute. His military successes were formidable, and his name carried a fearsome reputation to those he had yet to encounter.

David's renown involves a comparison with other illustrious individuals. Genesis 6:4 describes the infamous progeny as "men of name" (אַנְשֵׁי הַשֵּׁם). Similar descriptions are given to Israel's ancestral leadership (Num. 16:2) and the valiant warriors of Manasseh (1 Chron. 5:24) and Ephraim (12:31). Ultimately, Yahweh's promise to procure for David a great name is more than notoriety among other famous people (שֵׁם גָּדוֹל כְּשֵׁם הַגְּדֹלִים). Second Samuel 7:9 identifies the renown of David and his lineage with the great name of God (Josh. 7:9; 1 Sam. 12:22; 1 Kings 8:42). Such an association prompts notions of divine power, rescue, and promise.

1. *Parse:* (1) לְקַחְתִּ֫יךָ (Qal sc 1cs לקח "take" + 2ms sf). (2) וָאֶהְיֶה (Qal *wayyiqtol* 1cs היה "be"). (3) הָלַ֫כְתָּ (Qal sc 2ms הלך "go"). (4) וָאַכְרִתָה (Hiphil *wayyiqtol*/cohortative 1cs כרת "cut off"). (5) וְעָשִׂ֫יתִי (Qal *waqātal* 1cs עשה "do, make").

2. *Identify:* (A) The two prepositional phrases עַל־עַמִּי עַל־יִשְׂרָאֵל are appositional: they both describe the group over which David was appointed as a ruler. (B) The adjective הַגְּדֹלִים is being used as a substantive/noun.

3. *Translate:* "So now you shall say to my servant David: Thus Yahweh of Armies says: I took you from the grazing place following the sheep to be a ruler over my people Israel. I was with you wherever you went, and consequently I removed all your enemies before you. I will make for you a great name like that of the mighty men on the earth."

DAY 27: 2 SAMUEL 7:10–11A

STEP ONE: **Read** aloud the text at least five times.

וְשַׂמְתִּ֣י מָק֠וֹם לְעַמִּ֨י לְיִשְׂרָאֵ֤ל וּנְטַעְתִּיו֙ וְשָׁכַ֣ן תַּחְתָּ֔יו וְלֹ֥א יִרְגַּ֖ז
ע֑וֹד וְלֹֽא־יֹסִ֤יפוּ בְנֵי־עַוְלָה֙ לְעַנּוֹת֔וֹ כַּאֲשֶׁ֖ר בָּרִאשׁוֹנָֽה׃
¹¹וּלְמִן־הַיּ֗וֹם אֲשֶׁ֨ר צִוִּ֤יתִי שֹׁפְטִים֙ עַל־עַמִּ֣י יִשְׂרָאֵ֔ל וַהֲנִיחֹ֥תִי
לְךָ֖ מִכָּל־אֹיְבֶֽיךָ

STEP TWO: **Parse** the following verbs.

	Stem	Conj.	Pers.	Gend.	Numb.	Root	Trans.
(1) וְשַׂמְתִּ֣י							
(2) וּנְטַעְתִּיו							
(3) יֹסִ֤יפוּ							
(4) לְעַנּוֹתוֹ							
(5) צִוִּ֤יתִי							
(6) וַהֲנִיחֹ֥תִי							

STEP THREE: **Identify** the following.

A. What is the pronominal referent of וּנְטַעְתִּיו?

B. How should the verb יֹסִ֤יפוּ be understood with the following infinitive construct?

STEP FOUR: **Translate** the text into understandable English.

> VOCABULARY
>
> נטע   Qal: plant
> שכן   Qal: dwell
> רגז   Qal: tremble; quake; excite
> עַוְלָה   injustice; wrong; unrighteousness
> ענה   Piel: humble; afflict
> רִאשׁוֹן   first; beginning
> נוח   Hiphil: give rest; satisfy; leave

STEP FIVE: **Notice** significant exegetical insights.

- וְשַׂמְתִּי מָקוֹם לְעַמִּי לְיִשְׂרָאֵל וּנְטַעְתִּיו . . . וַהֲנִיחֹתִי: The *wəqātal* verbs continue the sequence of prophetic pronouncements from the previous verse. The land promise connects to the patriarchal covenant (Gen. 15:7; 48:4) and the assurance of the established place of rest (Deut. 6:10–11; Josh. 24:13).

- וְשָׁכַן . . . וְלֹא יִרְגַּז עוֹד וְלֹא־יֹסִיפוּ: The next clause continues the *wəqātal* sequence but shifts the topic to Israel. The result of God planting his people is that Israel will be settled. The following two negative clauses interrupt the promise sequence and elaborate the last positive statement (וְשָׁכַן). Israel's dwelling is to be characterized as free from trouble, harassment, and oppression.

- כַּאֲשֶׁר בָּרִאשׁוֹנָה וּלְמִן־הַיּוֹם: The verse break here is unfortunate, splitting the temporal phrase. The circumstantial setting incorporates two coordinated phases: Israel's experience of oppression began at its beginning and persisted through the time of the judges.

FOR THE JOURNEY

The memory of past harm and difficulties motivates much of this part of the promise. One can image that holding on to God's promise may have become wearisome to even the most faithful Israelite. They had suffered at the hand of the Egyptians, they wandered in the wilderness, they fought internal and external threats once they reached the land, and now the divinely ordained king found himself embattled with enemies without and even within his family. How good is the promised land if it is always under threat?

Yahweh, through the prophet, reiterates the promise and elaborates its reality. Peace would be part of the promise, and good would come. Much of this section is echoed in Ps. 89, with the added emphasis on God's power strengthening David (vv. 20–22). Verse 23 reiterates the real threat of both enemies (אֹיֵב) and wrongdoers (וּבֶן־עַוְלָה). Yet they will be defeated and the king exalted (vv. 24–25).

ANSWER KEY

1. *Parse:* (1) וְשַׂמְתִּי (Qal *wəqātal* 1cs שׂים "put, place"). (2) וּנְטַעְתִּיו (Qal *wəqātal* 1cs נטע "plant" + 3ms sf). (3) יֹסִיפוּ (Qal pc 3mp יסף "add"). (4) לְעַנּוֹתוֹ (prep + Piel inf cstr ענה "afflict" + 3ms sf). (5) צִוִּיתִי (Piel sc 1cs צוה "command"). (6) וַהֲנִיחֹתִי (Hiphil *wəqātal* 1cs נוח "give rest").

2. *Identify:* (A) The 3ms pronoun with וּנְטַעְתִּיו refers to "my people, Israel" in the previous clause (לְעַמִּי לְיִשְׂרָאֵל). (B) The verb יֹסִיפוּ functions like the auxiliary "continue to do" with the infinitive construct (לְעַנּוֹתוֹ) describing the core verbal action.

3. *Translate:* "I will designate a place for my people Israel, and I will plant them. Then they will settle there—they will no longer be unsettled, and wrongdoers will not keep subjugating them as at the beginning and since the time that I appointed judges over my people Israel. And I will give you rest from all your enemies."

DAY 28: 2 SAMUEL 7:11B–13

STEP ONE: Read aloud the text at least five times.

וְהִגִּיד לְךָ֙ יְהוָ֔ה כִּי־בַ֖יִת יַעֲשֶׂה־לְּךָ֥ יְהוָֽה: ¹²כִּ֣י ׀ יִמְלְא֣וּ יָמֶ֗יךָ
וְשָׁכַבְתָּ֙ אֶת־אֲבֹתֶ֔יךָ וַהֲקִימֹתִ֤י אֶֽת־זַרְעֲךָ֙ אַחֲרֶ֔יךָ אֲשֶׁ֥ר יֵצֵ֖א
מִמֵּעֶ֑יךָ וַהֲכִינֹתִ֖י אֶת־מַמְלַכְתּֽוֹ: ¹³ה֚וּא יִבְנֶה־בַּ֖יִת לִשְׁמִ֑י
וְכֹנַנְתִּ֛י אֶת־כִּסֵּ֥א מַמְלַכְתּ֖וֹ עַד־עוֹלָֽם:

STEP TWO: Parse the following verbs.

	Stem	Conj.	Pers.	Gend.	Numb.	Root	Trans.
(1) וְהִגִּיד							
(2) יִמְלְאוּ							
(3) וַהֲקִימֹתִי							
(4) וַהֲכִינֹתִי							
(5) וְכֹנַנְתִּי							

STEP THREE: Identify the following.

A. Explain the word order בַּ֖יִת יַעֲשֶׂה־לְּךָ֥ יְהוָֽה.

B. How is כִּי functioning in verse 12?

STEP FOUR: Translate the text into understandable English.

VOCABULARY

מֵעֶה   internal parts, loins

מַמְלָכָה   kingdom, dominion; sovereignty; reign

STEP FIVE: **Notice** significant exegetical insights.

- וְהִגִּיד לְךָ יְהוָה: The declaration formula appears to be extraneous. The entire discourse began with the notification that Yahweh was speaking (v. 8). This reiteration serves to underscore the following statement and give it particular prominence in the divine discourse. Don't miss the point: "Yahweh will make a *house* for you" (בַּיִת !וְיַעֲשֶׂה־לְךָ יְהוָה)

- אֲשֶׁר יֵצֵא מִמֵּעֶיךָ: This description of David's offspring may seem superfluous, but it produces a strong textual link with another of Yahweh's covenant partners. In response to Abram's uncertainty about his progeny, God unequivocally assigns his lineage to one from his own stock, using an identical relative clause (Gen. 15:4).

FOR THE JOURNEY

The double meaning of the Hebrew term בַּיִת is exploited to drive home Yahweh's promise. The term "house" has been used five times so far in this chapter (vv. 1, 2, 5, 6, 7). Each of these instances denotes a physical structure that serves as one's abode. This meaning is reinforced by the structure materials (אֲרָזִים, vv. 2, 7), construction activities (בנה, vv. 5, 7), and dwelling terms (ישב, vv. 1, 2, 5, 6).

In verse 11, Yahweh upends David's and the reader's expectations. The previous meaning of the term is reoriented (כִּי־בַיִת יַעֲשֶׂה־לְּךָ יְהוָה). First, בַּיִת no longer refers to a physical place but to a family unit, a household. Second, the "house" is not built but made (עשה). Third, David is the recipient of the house and not the builder. Fourth, Yahweh fulfills his promise and makes it a reality. Fifth, David's desire to build a house for Yahweh's name is not forgotten but will be accomplished through David's posterity (הוּא יִבְנֶה־בַּיִת לִשְׁמִי, v. 13) as a proof and extension of God's faithfulness in establishing David's household and kingdom.

The contrastive statements of verses 11 and 13 are instructive. Yahweh is in ultimate control. He is faithful to his promises. God does not work according to the limitations and expectations of even his covenant partners.

ANSWER KEY

1. *Parse:* (1) וְהִגִּיד (Hiphil *wəqātal* 3ms נגד "declare"). (2) יִמְלְאוּ (Qal pc 3mp מלא "be full"). (3) וַהֲקִימֹתִי (Hiphil *wəqātal* 1cs קום "raise"). (4) וַהֲכִינֹתִי (Hiphil *wəqātal* 1cs כון "prepare, accomplish"). (5) וְכֹנַנְתִּי (Polel *wəqātal* 1cs כון "establish, make firm").

2. *Identify:* (A) The object (בַּיִת) is fronted in the clause to express its prominence. (B) The first word in verse 12 initiates a compound subordinate clause describing the temporal circumstances of the following assertion ("when").

3. *Translate:* "Yahweh declares to you that Yahweh will make a house for you. When your days are complete and you lie down with your fathers, I will raise up after you your progeny, who will come from your stock, and I will prepare his kingdom. He will build a house for my name, and I will establish the throne of his kingdom forever."

DAY 29: 2 SAMUEL 7:14–15

STEP ONE: **Read** aloud the text at least five times.

אֲנִי֙ אֶֽהְיֶה־לּ֣וֹ לְאָ֔ב וְה֖וּא יִהְיֶה־לִּ֣י לְבֵ֑ן אֲשֶׁר֙ בְּהַ֣עֲוֺת֔וֹ
וְהֹֽכַחְתִּיו֙ בְּשֵׁ֣בֶט אֲנָשִׁ֔ים וּבְנִגְעֵ֖י בְּנֵ֥י אָדָֽם׃ ¹⁵ וְחַסְדִּ֖י לֹא־יָס֣וּר
מִמֶּ֑נּוּ כַּאֲשֶׁ֤ר הֲסִרֹ֙תִי֙ מֵעִ֣ם שָׁא֔וּל אֲשֶׁ֥ר הֲסִרֹ֖תִי מִלְּפָנֶֽיךָ׃

STEP TWO: **Parse** the following verbs.

	Stem	Conj.	Pers.	Gend.	Numb.	Root	Trans.
(1) בְּהַעֲוֺתוֹ							
(2) וְהֹכַחְתִּיו							
(3) הֲסִרֹתִי							

STEP THREE: **Identify** the following.

A. Who is the referent of הוּא?

B. What is the object of the first instance of הֲסִרֹתִי?

C. What is the object of the second instance of הֲסִרֹתִי?

STEP FOUR: **Translate** the text into understandable English.

VOCABULARY

עוה Hiphil: commit iniquity, do wrong
יכח Hiphil: reprove; judge; discipline
שֵׁבֶט rod, staff, scepter; tribe
נֶגַע illness; plague; wound (PL CSTR נִגְעֵי)
סור Qal: turn aside, depart; neglect; Hiphil: divert, remove

90

STEP FIVE: **Notice** significant exegetical insights.

- אֲשֶׁר בְּהַעֲוֹתוֹ: This sequence introduces a circumstantial phrase ("whenever") connecting to the following main clause. The pronominal suffix is subjective, and the infinitive construct serves as the action, "he does wrong" (עוה).

- בְּשֵׁבֶט אֲנָשִׁים וּבְנִגְעֵי בְּנֵי אָדָם: The prepositional phrases introduce a compound modification of the main verb (וְהֹכַחְתִּיו). The preposition בְּ likely either describes how (means/manner) or with what (instrument) God promises to discipline David's seed. The parallel terms אֲנָשִׁים and בְּנֵי אָדָם suggest understanding the initial lexemes, שֵׁבֶט and נֶגַע, with corresponding semantics.

- וְחַסְדִּי לֹא־יָסוּר מִמֶּנּוּ: The subject-initial clause syntax draws a contrast with the previous clause. God limits the extent of his punishment of iniquity.

FOR THE JOURNEY

Few statements in the English-speaking world are as recognizable as "I pronounce that they bee man and wyfe together." This brief statement comes from the *Book of Common Prayer* of 1549. As part of the marriage covenant, this pronouncement serves both to acknowledge a reality and initiate it. In this way, uttering these words performs an action. They sanction the marriage covenant.

In the same way, the scriptural proclamation "I will be your X, and you will be my Y" enacts a covenant between two parties (e.g., Jer. 7:23). A truncated version conveys Ruth's commitment to her mother-in-law. She declares: "Your people will be my people, and your God will be my God" (עַמֵּךְ עַמִּי וֵאלֹהַיִךְ אֱלֹהָי, Ruth 1:16). Ruth claims Naomi's people and God as her own. This proclamation reidentifies their relationship status.

An astounding revelation is ratified in the Davidic covenant. Yahweh defines his relationship with David's progeny as one of a father and son. Previously, divine sonship seems to be reserved for the nation as a whole: "Israel is my son, my firstborn" (בְּנִי בְכֹרִי יִשְׂרָאֵל, Exod. 4:22–23; see also Hosea 11:1). In like manner, God is referred to as Israel's father (e.g., Deut. 32:6; Isa. 63:16; 64:7; Jer. 31:9). Yet Yahweh declares in 2 Sam. 7:14 that David's seed is his own son! And David is

Yahweh's firstborn, who calls Yahweh father (Ps. 89:27–28). Yahweh proclaims David's adoptive status as an irrevocable and sure promise.

ANSWER KEY

1. *Parse:* (1) בְּהַעֲוֹתוֹ (PREP + Hiphil INF CSTR עוה "do wrong" + 3MS SF).
   (2) וְהֹכַחְתִּיו (Hiphil *wəqātal* 1CS יכח "reprove" + 3MS SF). (3) הֲסִרֹתִי (Hiphil SC 1CS סור "remove").

2. *Identify:* (A) The pronoun הוּא refers to David's "seed" (זֶרַע) in verse 12.
   (B) The object of the first instance of הֲסִרֹתִי is "my loving-kindness" (חַסְדִּי), inferred from the previous clause. (C) The object of the second instance of הֲסִרֹתִי is Saul (שָׁאוּל).

3. *Translate:* "I will be his father, and he will be my son. Whenever he commits iniquity, I will reprove him with the discipline of men and with the afflictions of humanity. However, my loving-kindness will not depart from him as I removed [it] from Saul whom I removed before you."

DAY 30: 2 SAMUEL 7:16–17

STEP ONE: **Read** aloud the text at least five times.

וְנֶאְמַ֨ן בֵּיתְךָ֤ וּמַֽמְלַכְתְּךָ֙ עַד־עוֹלָ֖ם לְפָנֶ֑יךָ כִּסְאֲךָ֕ יִהְיֶ֥ה נָכ֖וֹן
עַד־עוֹלָֽם: ¹⁷כְּכֹל֙ הַדְּבָרִ֣ים הָאֵ֔לֶּה וּכְכֹ֖ל הַחִזָּי֣וֹן הַזֶּ֑ה כֵּ֥ן דִּבֶּ֖ר
נָתָ֖ן אֶל־דָּוִֽד:

STEP TWO: **Parse** the following verbs.

	Stem	Conj.	Pers.	Gend.	Numb.	Root	Trans.
(1) וְנֶאְמַן							
(2) נָכוֹן							

STEP THREE: **Identify** the following.

A. What is the subject of וְנֶאְמַן? _____

B. What are the semantics of היה followed by a participle (יִהְיֶה נָכוֹן)? _____

C. What is the initial morpheme of עַד־עוֹלָם? _____

STEP FOUR: **Translate** the text into understandable English.

_____

_____

VOCABULARY

אמן   Niphal: be faithful; be established, firm

מַמְלָכָה   kingdom, dominion; sovereignty; reign

כִּסֵּא   seat; throne

חִזָּיוֹן   vision; oracle, prophecy

נָתָן   Nathan

STEP FIVE: **Notice** significant exegetical insights.

- וְנֶאְמַן: The initial clause connects to the previous verb sequence: וְהֹכַחְתִּיו . . . וְחַסְדִּי לֹא־יָסוּר . . . וְנֶאְמַן "I will reprove him . . . however, my loving-kindness will not depart . . . and then it will be established." Together this series outlines the promise: even in reproof Yahweh will be faithful to establish David's household and kingdom.

- יִהְיֶה נָכוֹן: The second clause in verse 16 expands the enduring promise to David's throne. The nonsequential prefix conjugation does not introduce a new series but provides an epexegetical expansion in parallel to the first clause of the verse.

- כְּכֹל הַדְּבָרִים הָאֵלֶּה וּכְכֹל הַחִזָּיוֹן הַזֶּה: Verse 17 connects the end of the divine vision to the beginning of the narrative (v. 4) that framed Nathan's night vision as "That very night, Yahweh's word came to Nathan" (וַיְהִי בַּלַּיְלָה הַהוּא וַיְהִי דְּבַר־יְהוָה אֶל־נָתָן).

FOR THE JOURNEY

The divine vision in 2 Sam. 7 culminates in the promise to David of an enduring throne. What is implied in this assurance? Central is the concept of authority and sovereignty. It is embodied in the metonym "throne" (כִּסֵּא), which serves as a significant keyword throughout the Scriptures.

Already in verse 13, an established and enduring "throne" was pledged to David's descendant. This promise becomes a crucial theme in Solomon's ascendency (1 Kings 1:13, 17, 20, 24, 27, 30, 35, 37, 46, 47, 48; 2:4, 12, 19, 24, 33, 45; 3:6). Its fulfillment is merged with Solomon's construction of the temple (1 Kings 5:19; 8:25; 9:5). And the Queen of Sheba blesses Yahweh because of his wise choice of Solomon as king (1 Kings 10:9).

The illimitable aspects of the promise persist beyond the time of Solomon. Focusing on the expansiveness of the kingdom, the prophet Isaiah envisions the throne of David as unending, with immeasurable dominion and enduring peace (Isa. 9:6; see also Ps. 132:11–12; Jer. 33:14–17). The angel Gabriel refers to the eternality of the promised kingdom. He tells Mary that her son will occupy the throne of David

(Luke 1:32–33). Finally, Peter proclaims that the fulfillment of this promise is found in the resurrected Messiah as the one who occupies the heavenly throne (Acts 2:30–33).

ANSWER KEY

1. *Parse:* (1) וְנֶאְמַן (Niphal *wəqātal* 3ms אמן "be established"). (2) נָכוֹן (Niphal PTCL MS כון "be firm").

2. *Identify:* (A) The subject of וְנֶאְמַן is the compound phrase בֵּיתְךָ וּמַמְלַכְתְּךָ "your house and your kingdom." (B) The periphrastic construction with the finite verb היה and participle (יִהְיֶה נָכוֹן) denotes a non-past progression: "it is being established." (C) The initial morpheme of עַד־עוֹלָם is either the noun ("perpetuity") or the preposition ("unto")—both analyses indicate future permanence (i.e., for a long time to come).

3. *Translate:* "'Then your house and kingdom will endure into perpetuity before you—your throne will be secure forever.' According to all these words and all this vision, thus Nathan spoke to David."

Journey 2

CONTINUING

ROUTE 6

Joshua 24:14–28

STEP ONE: **Read** aloud the text at least five times.

וְעַתָּ֞ה יְר֧אוּ אֶת־יְהוָ֛ה וְעִבְד֥וּ אֹת֖וֹ בְּתָמִ֣ים וּבֶאֱמֶ֑ת וְהָסִ֣ירוּ
אֶת־אֱלֹהִ֗ים אֲשֶׁר֩ עָבְד֨וּ אֲבוֹתֵיכֶ֜ם בְּעֵ֤בֶר הַנָּהָר֙ וּבְמִצְרַ֔יִם
וְעִבְד֖וּ אֶת־יְהוָֽה׃

STEP TWO: **Parse** the following verbs.

	Stem	Conj.	Pers.	Gend.	Numb.	Root	Trans.
(1) יְראוּ							
(2) וְעִבְדוּ							
(3) וְהָסִ֣ירוּ							
(4) עָבְדוּ							

STEP THREE: **Identify** the following.

A. Who is the speaker, and who is the audience?

B. What does וְעַתָּה signal?

99

STEP FOUR: **Translate** the text into understandable English.

> ### VOCABULARY
>
> תָּמִים   complete, sound
>
> אֱמֶת   truth; faithfulness
>
> עֵבֶר   opposite side (of a body of water)
>
> נָהָר   river

STEP FIVE: **Notice** significant exegetical insights.

- יִרְאוּ אֶת־יְהוָה: The semantics of "fear" involves awe motivating appropriate reverence of Yahweh. This type of fear entails a response of faith and not merely fright, alarm, or distress.

- וְעִבְדוּ אֹתוֹ . . . אֲשֶׁר עָבְדוּ אֲבוֹתֵיכֶם . . . וְעִבְדוּ אֶת־יְהוָה: The contrast between the imperative forms and suffix conjugation of the same root (עבד) is striking. Joshua commands the Israelites to serve and worship Yahweh rather than returning to the gods whom their fathers served in the past!

- בְּעֵבֶר הַנָּהָר: The idiom "Beyond the River" serves like a name. It is the location from which Abram's family emigrated (Josh. 24:3). The region is on the opposite side of the Euphrates River from Palestine, what is commonly known as Mesopotamia.

FOR THE JOURNEY

The two locations—"Beyond the [Euphrates] River" and "Egypt"— bring to mind the unfaithfulness of the previous generations. Their Mesopotamian ancestors included Terah and his sons Abram and Nahor, who "worshiped other gods" (וַיַּעַבְדוּ אֱלֹהִים אֲחֵרִים, Josh. 24:2). Despite Abram's idolatry, Yahweh rescued him and brought him into the land. And he promised to multiply his descendants and make them a great nation.

In Egypt, God similarly responded to the Israelites' disbelief. As the Hebrews multiplied, the Egyptians forced the people into harsh service (Exod. 1:12–14). Freedom to serve Yahweh was supposed to be a sign of God's faithfulness (3:12). And idol worship was prohibited (20:4–5). Yet Israel continued to fear the Egyptians more than Yahweh (14:12–14). Even still, Yahweh was faithful. He delivered the people (Josh. 24:5–7), and he gave them the land of the promise (24:13).

ANSWER KEY

1. *Parse:* (1) יְרָאוּ (Qal IMV MP יְרָא "fear"). (2) וְעִבְדוּ (CJ + Qal IMV MP עבד "serve; worship"). (3) וְהָסִירוּ (CJ + Hiphil IMV MP סור "remove, discard"). (4) עָבְדוּ (Qal SC 3MP עבד "serve; worship").

2. *Identify:* (A) The speaker is Joshua, and the audience includes all the tribes of Israel, along with the leadership, who are gathered at Shechem (see Josh. 24:1–2). (B) The initial element of verse 14 (וְעַתָּה) signals a logical transition from the description of Yahweh's faithfulness to Israel in the past and Israel's expected response to Yahweh in the future.

3. *Translate:* "So consequently, revere Yahweh and serve him completely and steadfastly, remove the gods that your ancestors served beyond the [Euphrates] River and in Egypt, and serve Yahweh."

DAY 32: JOSHUA 24:15

STEP ONE: **Read** aloud the text at least five times.

וְאִם֩ רַ֨ע בְּעֵֽינֵיכֶ֜ם לַעֲבֹ֣ד אֶת־יְהוָ֗ה בַּחֲר֨וּ לָכֶ֤ם הַיּוֹם֙ אֶת־מִ֣י
תַעֲבֹד֒וּן אִ֣ם אֶת־אֱלֹהִ֞ים אֲשֶׁר־עָבְד֣וּ אֲבֽוֹתֵיכֶ֗ם אֲשֶׁר֙ בְּעֵ֣בֶר
הַנָּהָ֔ר וְאִם֙ אֶת־אֱלֹהֵ֣י הָאֱמֹרִ֔י אֲשֶׁ֥ר אַתֶּ֖ם יֹשְׁבִ֣ים בְּאַרְצָ֑ם
וְאָנֹכִ֣י וּבֵיתִ֔י נַעֲבֹ֖ד אֶת־יְהוָֽה׃

STEP TWO: **Parse** the following verbs.

	Stem	Conj.	Pers.	Gend.	Numb.	Root	Trans.
(1) בַּחֲרוּ							
(2) תַעֲבֹדוּן							
(3) יֹשְׁבִים							
(4) נַעֲבֹד							

STEP THREE: **Identify** the following.

   A. What is the object of the verb בַּחֲרוּ? _____

   B. How many "serve" (עבד) verbs are found in this verse?

STEP FOUR: **Translate** the text into understandable English.

_____

_____

VOCABULARY

בחר   Qal: choose

עֵבֶר   opposite side (of a body of water)

נָהָר   stream, river

אֱמֹרִי   Amorite

STEP FIVE: **Notice** significant exegetical insights.

- וְאִם רַע בְּעֵינֵיכֶם לַעֲבֹד אֶת־יְהוָה: The verse begins with a contrastive conditional statement: "But if it is bad in your eyes to serve Yahweh . . ." This hypothetical sets up a choice contrary to the plea to serve Yahweh (v. 14). The following apodosis (*then*-clause) begins with the command to "choose" (בַּחֲרוּ) an alternative.

- אִם אֶת־אֱלֹהִים . . . וְאִם אֶת־אֱלֹהֵי הָאֱמֹרִי: The correlating sequence of אִם . . . וְאִם provides two options for the people to serve instead of Yahweh. These possibilities are presented as the referent of אֶת־מִי ("the ones whom") and repeat the object marker (אֶת) before the word for deity. These choices correspond to the gods of their ancestors (vv. 2–3) and those from whom Yahweh had previously delivered the people (vv. 8–13).

- וְאָנֹכִי וּבֵיתִי: The fronted compound subject contrasts with those being addressed who view the service of Yahweh as not good (רַע).

FOR THE JOURNEY

The statement of allegiance to Yahweh (נַעֲבֹד אֶת־יְהוָה "we will serve Yahweh") may seem somewhat mundane at this point in Joshua's speech. After all, it is the seventh occurrence of the verb "serve" (עבד) in just the first two verses of his appeal (vv. 14–15). But his affirmation is central to the initiation of the covenant ceremony starting in verse 25.

Three times the people echo this declaration as a response to Joshua's challenge (vv. 18–24). Each reprisal includes a slight variation or clarification. They build toward verse 24 and culminate with the promise to heed Yahweh's voice (וּבְקוֹלוֹ נִשְׁמָע). The people first reiterate Joshua's pledge with the addition of the reason for their devotion: "for he is *our God*" (כִּי־הוּא אֱלֹהֵינוּ, v. 18). The second reverberation moves the object before the verb to the initial position of the clause: "*Yahweh* we will serve" (אֶת־יְהוָה נַעֲבֹד, v. 21). The final instance combines these previous statements and clarifies Yahweh's unique description, "Yahweh *our God* we will serve" (v. 24).

This threefold response matches the people's endorsement of the Decalogue. In the Sinai narrative, the people respond to Moses. Three times they swear covenant fidelity: כֹּל אֲשֶׁר־דִּבֶּר יְהוָה נַעֲשֶׂה "All [the words] that Yahweh has spoken, we will do" (Exod. 19:8; 24:3, 7). And with these words, the covenant is ratified.

ANSWER KEY

1. *Parse:* (1) בַּחֲרוּ (Qal IMV MP בחר "choose"). (2) תַעֲבֹדוּן (Qal PC 2MP עבד "serve; worship"; the final *nun* is described as paragogic, a vestige of an older form of תַּעַבְדוּ). (3) יֹשְׁבִים (Qal ACT PTCL MP ישׁב "sit, live"). (4) נַעֲבֹד (Qal PC 1CP עבד "serve; worship").

2. *Identify:* (A) The object of the verb בַּחֲרוּ is the embedded clause marked with the direct-object marker (אֶת־מִי תַעֲבֹדוּן "the one(s) whom you will serve"). (B) Forms of the verb "serve" (עבד) occur four times in this verse.

3. *Translate:* "If it does not seem good in your eyes to serve Yahweh, then choose today for yourselves whom you will serve—whether the gods your fathers served beyond the river or the gods of the Amorites in whose land you are dwelling—regardless, I and my household will serve Yahweh."

DAY 33: JOSHUA 24:16–17A

STEP ONE: **Read** aloud the text at least five times.

וַיַּעַן הָעָם וַיֹּאמֶר חָלִילָה לָּנוּ מֵעֲזֹב אֶת־יְהוָה לַעֲבֹד אֱלֹהִים
אֲחֵרִים: ¹⁷ כִּי יְהוָה אֱלֹהֵינוּ הוּא הַמַּעֲלֶה אֹתָנוּ וְאֶת־אֲבוֹתֵינוּ
מֵאֶרֶץ מִצְרַיִם מִבֵּית עֲבָדִים

STEP TWO: **Parse** the following verb.

	Stem	Conj.	Pers.	Gend.	Numb.	Root	Trans.
(1) הַמַּעֲלֶה							

STEP THREE: **Identify** the following.

A. What is the form and function of מֵעֲזֹב? _____

B. How do the phrases מֵאֶרֶץ מִצְרַיִם and מִבֵּית עֲבָדִים relate to each other? _____

STEP FOUR: **Translate** the text into understandable English.

_____

_____

VOCABULARY

חָלִיל   far be it, may it not be

אַחֵר   (an)other; later

STEP FIVE: **Notice** significant exegetical insights.

- וַיַּעַן הָעָם וַיֹּאמֶר: The narrative forms (*wayyiqtol*) resume and provide the people's response to Joshua's address that started in verse 2 (וַיֹּאמֶר יְהוֹשֻׁעַ אֶל־כָּל־הָעָם). The people's affirmation continues until verse 18. Joshua replies to the people in verse 19.

- כִּי: The people give several reasons for their promised allegiance to Yahweh. The first follows the causal conjunction: Yahweh rescued them from slavery in Egypt.

FOR THE JOURNEY

The people avow their allegiance to Yahweh based on his past redemptive actions on their behalf. The place from which they were rescued is described as the land of Egypt, the house of slavery. This expression is identical to the end of Yahweh's self-presentation in the Decalogue: "I am Yahweh, your God, who brought you out from the land of Egypt, the house of slavery" (אָנֹכִי יְהוָה אֱלֹהֶיךָ אֲשֶׁר הוֹצֵאתִיךָ מֵאֶרֶץ מִצְרַיִם מִבֵּית עֲבָדִים:, Exod. 20:2, day 16). It is the basis on which Yahweh requires sole fidelity from "other gods" (אֱלֹהִים אֲחֵרִים, Exod. 20:3).

How does one remain loyal to God? The frequent biblical exhortation is to remember one's previous condition and meditate on Yahweh's gracious redemption of his people.

Deuteronomy employs this trope to encourage the people to faithfulness in times of temptation. Do not forget what Yahweh has done when you are safe and content in your grand cities and homes (Deut. 6:12). Do not become proud and forget Yahweh in great prosperity (8:14). Do not turn to false worship even though your neighbors entice you (13:11).

ANSWER KEY

1. *Parse:* (1) הַמַּעֲלֶה (DEF ART + Hiphil PTCL MS עלה "bring up").

2. *Identify:* (A) The form מֵעֲזֹב combines the preposition מִן with an infinitive construct (עֲזֹב). The infinitive construct functions as a gerund, like English "abandoning," and the preposition can be understood as a privative which inverts the sense (i.e., "from abandoning" ≈ "we will *not* abandon"). (B) The phrases מֵאֶרֶץ מִצְרַיִם and מִבֵּית עֲבָדִים are in apposition.

3. *Translate:* "The people answered and said: 'Far be it from us to abandon Yahweh to serve other gods! For Yahweh our God is the one who brought us and our fathers up from Egypt, the house of slavery.'"

DAY 34: JOSHUA 24:17B–18

STEP ONE: Read aloud the text at least five times.

וַאֲשֶׁ֣ר עָשָׂ֣ה לְעֵינֵ֗ינוּ אֶת־הָאֹתֹ֤ות הַגְּדֹלֹות֙ הָאֵ֔לֶּה וַֽיִּשְׁמְרֵ֗נוּ
בְּכָל־הַדֶּ֙רֶךְ֙ אֲשֶׁ֣ר הָלַ֣כְנוּ בָ֔הּ וּבְכֹל֙ הָֽעַמִּ֔ים אֲשֶׁ֥ר עָבַ֖רְנוּ
בְּקִרְבָּֽם׃ ¹⁸וַיְגָ֨רֶשׁ יְהוָ֜ה אֶת־כָּל־הָעַמִּ֗ים וְאֶת־הָאֱמֹרִ֛י יֹשֵׁ֥ב
הָאָ֖רֶץ מִפָּנֵ֑ינוּ גַּם־אֲנַ֙חְנוּ֙ נַעֲבֹ֣ד אֶת־יְהוָ֔ה כִּי־ה֖וּא אֱלֹהֵֽינוּ׃

STEP TWO: Parse the following verbs.

	Stem	Conj.	Pers.	Gend.	Numb.	Root	Trans.
(1) וַֽיִּשְׁמְרֵ֗נוּ							
(2) הָלַ֣כְנוּ							
(3) וַיְגָ֨רֶשׁ							
(4) נַעֲבֹ֣ד							

STEP THREE: Identify the following.

A. What is the best way to understand and translate לְעֵינֵ֗ינוּ?

B. What is the function of אֲנַ֙חְנוּ֙ in the last clause?

STEP FOUR: Translate the text into understandable English.

VOCABULARY

אֹות   sign, omen, miracle

גרש   Piel: cast out, expel

אֱמֹרִי   Amorite

אֲנַ֙חְנוּ   we

STEP FIVE: **Notice** significant exegetical insights.

- וַאֲשֶׁר . . . כִּי: Yahweh doing miraculous signs (הָאֹתוֹת הַגְּדֹלוֹת
הָאֵלֶּה) provides another basis for covenant fidelity, connecting to
verse 17. The following *wayyiqtol* sequence expounds his mar-
velous actions: וַיִּשְׁמְרֵנוּ . . . וַיְגָרֶשׁ "he protected us . . . and he
expelled . . ." (vv. 17b–18).

- בְּכָל־הַדֶּרֶךְ . . . וּבְכֹל הָעַמִּים: Yahweh's protection extended to
Israel's journey through many different places and nations. The
people recognize his faithfulness to keep them safe during the perils
of their movement (הלך) and their crossing over (עבר) on the way
to the promised land.

FOR THE JOURNEY

Part of the historic summary of God's miraculous acts includes the
expulsion of the nations (Acts 7:45). The most famous are the two
kings of the Amorites (Num. 21:21–35; Deut. 3:8; Josh. 2:10; 9:10;
etc.) and the coalition of Amorite peoples west of the Jordan (Josh.
10). The former were mentioned earlier in Joshua's description (24:8,
12), and the latter occur in a list of Canaanite foes after the inhabitants
of Jericho (v. 11).

In verses 15 and 18, the Amorites receive exclusive reference as the
people dwelling in the promised land. Their presence in the land challenged more than Israel's physical relocation to Canaan. Owing to their
proximity, their religious practices represented the greatest threat to
Israel's covenant fidelity to Yahweh (24:15). Israel would be tempted
to adapt to the worship of their neighbors and to lose their distinctive-
ness. Yet God would be faithful to expel these enticements (as he had
previously) if Israel proves loyal to Yahweh.

ANSWER KEY

1. *Parse:* (1) וַיִּשְׁמְרֵנוּ (Qal *wayyiqtol* 3MS שמר "guard" + 1CP SF). (2) הָלַכְנוּ (Qal SC 1CP הלך "walk"). (3) וַיְגָרֶשׁ (Piel *wayyiqtol* 3MS גרשׁ "expel"). (4) נַעֲבֹד (Qal PC 1CP עבד "serve").

2. *Identify:* (A) The adverbial expression "to (i.e., before) our eyes" (לְעֵינֵינוּ) explains Yahweh's public performance (עשׂה) of these great signs. (B) The subject pronoun functions to provide additional weightiness on the agent of the action: אֲנַחְנוּ נַעֲבֹד אֶת־יְהוָה "*We* will serve Yahweh." The same people (1CP) who experienced Yahweh's miracles are those committing to serve him exclusively.

3. *Translate:* "And before our eyes he did these great miracles: he safeguarded us along every path on which we traveled and through all the nations in whose midst we traversed, and Yahweh expelled all the nations from before us—even the Amorites living in the land. Therefore, we will serve Yahweh, for he is our God."

DAY 35: JOSHUA 24:19–20

STEP ONE: **Read** aloud the text at least five times.

וַיֹּ֨אמֶר יְהוֹשֻׁ֜עַ אֶל־הָעָ֗ם לֹ֤א תֽוּכְלוּ֙ לַעֲבֹ֣ד אֶת־יְהוָ֔ה
כִּֽי־אֱלֹהִ֥ים קְדֹשִׁ֖ים ה֑וּא אֵל־קַנּ֣וֹא ה֗וּא לֹֽא־יִשָּׂ֛א לְפִשְׁעֲכֶ֖ם
וּלְחַטֹּאותֵיכֶֽם: ²⁰כִּ֤י תַֽעַזְבוּ֙ אֶת־יְהוָ֔ה וַעֲבַדְתֶּ֖ם אֱלֹהֵ֣י נֵכָ֑ר
וְשָׁ֨ב וְהֵרַ֤ע לָכֶם֙ וְכִלָּ֣ה אֶתְכֶ֔ם אַחֲרֵ֖י אֲשֶׁר־הֵיטִ֥יב לָכֶֽם:

STEP TWO: **Parse** the following verbs.

	Stem	Conj.	Pers.	Gend.	Numb.	Root	Trans.
(1) תֽוּכְלוּ֙							
(2) תַֽעַזְבוּ֙							
(3) וַעֲבַדְתֶּ֖ם							
(4) וְשָׁ֨ב							
(5) וְהֵרַ֤ע							
(6) וְכִלָּ֣ה							
(7) הֵיטִ֥יב							

STEP THREE: **Identify** the following.

A. How does כִּי function in verses 19 and 20? _____

B. What are the subject and object(s) of לֹֽא־יִשָּׂ֛א? _____

STEP FOUR: **Translate** the text into understandable English.

_____

_____

יכל   Qal: be able; endure

קָדוֹשׁ   sacred, holy

קַנּוֹא   jealous

פֶּשַׁע   transgression; crime (+ 2MP SF פִּשְׁעֲכֶם)

נֵכָר   foreignness; foreigner

רעע   Hiphil: treat badly; bring misfortune

יטב   Hiphil: deal well with; bring fortune

STEP FIVE: Notice significant exegetical insights.

- **לֹא תוּכְלוּ . . . כִּי תַעַזְבוּ**: Joshua's response to the people begins with a negative consequence. This incapability does not need to be read as an inescapable or inevitable reality, but it is an assured outcome of the situation presented in verse 20. In this way, the כִּי of verse 20 presents a conditional clause. It underscores the need for exclusive loyalty to Yahweh: he cannot be worshiped alongside other gods, and he will not forgive Israel such idolatrous rebellion.

- **תַעַזְבוּ . . . וַעֲבַדְתֶּם . . . וְשָׁב וְהֵרַע**: The series of verbs changes agents from second-person plural (i.e., הָעָם) to third-person singular (יהוה). The shift indicates how Yahweh responds to those abandoning him to serve foreign gods.

- **וְכִלָּה אֶתְכֶם אַחֲרֵי אֲשֶׁר־הֵיטִיב לָכֶם**: Perhaps one of the most terrifying realities of Joshua's warning is that the past favor of Yahweh is not a guarantee of his future grace. Because of God's character (v. 19; see "For the Journey" below), he calls his children to conform to his character (1 Pet. 1:14–16). Presuming on God's goodness is not a mark of devoted worship and covenant loyalty.

FOR THE JOURNEY

Forgiveness of wrongdoing is central to the ethics of the Bible. At his brothers' request, Joseph pardons their attempt on his life and his ensuing decades of enslavement. Refusing to exact revenge, he chooses instead to extend clemency and seeks their welfare (Gen. 50:15–21).

Jesus's disciples are exhorted to exculpate even the most harmful action and intent. He condemns the servant forgiven his debts who refuses to show mercy to another (Matt. 18:21–35).

How then can God refuse to forgive his people? Doesn't he promise abundant compassion to wrongdoers (Exod. 34:6–7; Num. 14:18; Mic. 7:18)?

It is important to notice the specific nature of transgression in Josh. 24:19–20. At issue is Yahweh's expectation of allegiance and how he deals with the idolatry of his covenant partners. As the only holy God, Yahweh requires exclusive devotion. Service to another god is a rejection of his divine status. A covenant partner, who has experienced his mercy, must treat Yahweh with steadfast loyalty. The abandonment of the exclusive worship of Yahweh is not simply misconduct but all-out rebellion against his name (Exod. 23:21). Defiant idolatry terminates the covenant relationship.

ANSWER KEY

1. *Parse:* (1) תּוּכְל֖וּ (Qal PC 2MP יכל "be able"). (2) תַעַזְב֖וּ (Qal PC 2MP עזב "leave"). (3) וַעֲבַדְתֶּ֖ם (Qal *wəqātal* 2MP עבד "serve"). (4) וְשָׁ֖ב (Qal *wəqātal* 3MS שׁוב "turn back"). (5) וְהֵרַ֥ע (Hiphil *wəqātal* 3MS רעע "bring misfortune"). (6) וְכִלָּ֖ה (Piel *wəqātal* 3MS כלה "destroy"). (7) הֵיטִ֥יב (Hiphil SC 3MS יטב "bring fortune").

2. *Identify:* (A) The first כִּ֥י (v. 19) indicates the basis or grounds for true and proper worship of Yahweh. The כִּ֥י in verse 20 initiates the exclusive terms and conditions for reverence of Yahweh. (B) The subject of לֹא־יִשָּׂא is Yahweh, and each element of the compound object is designated with *lamed* (לְפִשְׁעֲכֶם וּלְחַטֹּאותֵיכֶם). The verb נשא can use the preposition for its object (e.g., Exod. 23:21; 1 Sam. 25:28), but not always (e.g., Gen. 50:17; Exod. 34:7; Num. 14:18; Job 7:21; Ps. 32:5; Mic. 7:18).

3. *Translate:* "Joshua warned the people: 'You will not be able to serve Yahweh on account of the fact that he is a holy and jealous God, not forgiving your waywardness and affronts if you abandon Yahweh to serve foreign gods. As a consequence, he will turn away from you, bring harm, and destroy you even after he dealt so kindly with you.'"

DAY 36: JOSHUA 24:21–22

STEP ONE: Read aloud the text at least five times.

וַיֹּ֨אמֶר²² : וַיֹּ֤אמֶר הָעָם֙ אֶל־יְהוֹשֻׁ֔עַ לֹ֕א כִּ֥י אֶת־יְהוָ֖ה נַעֲבֹֽד

יְהוֹשֻׁ֜עַ אֶל־הָעָ֗ם עֵדִ֤ים אַתֶּם֙ בָּכֶ֔ם כִּֽי־אַתֶּ֞ם בְּחַרְתֶּ֥ם לָכֶ֛ם

אֶת־יְהוָ֖ה לַעֲבֹ֣ד אוֹת֑וֹ וַיֹּאמְר֖וּ עֵדִֽים :

STEP TWO: Parse the following verbs.

	Stem	Conj.	Pers.	Gend.	Numb.	Root	Trans.
(1) נַעֲבֹד							
(2) בְּחַרְתֶּם							

STEP THREE: Identify the following.

A. What is the negative (לֹא) answering? _____

B. How does כִּי function in verse 21? _____

C. Why do the people respond with only one word (עֵדִים)? _____

STEP FOUR: Translate the text into understandable English.

_____

_____

> **VOCABULARY**
>
> עֵד   witness
>
> בחר   Qal: choose; examine

STEP FIVE: Notice significant exegetical insights.

- בָּכֶם: The prepositional phrase functions to designate the one against whom a testimony is proclaimed. It is unusual to see witnesses testify against themselves. More commonly, one individual or group testifies for or against someone else indicated with בְּ (e.g., Exod. 20:16; Num. 5:13; 1 Sam. 12:5), or someone or something serves as the certification of an agreement between two other people or groups with בֵּין (Gen. 31:44, 48, 50; Josh. 22:27–28, 34). In this case, the people—and their own words (כִּי אֶת־יְהוָה נַעֲבֹד)—serve as the witness and evidence.

- אַתֶּם בְּחַרְתֶּם לָכֶם: The repetition of the second-person plural pronouns puts additional emphasis on the responsibility of those directly addressed. The agent of choosing (אַתֶּם) and the benefactor of choosing (לָכֶם) are the people. Neither of these elements is required by the verb, but both place the burden squarely on the people to choose to be faithful to the covenant.

FOR THE JOURNEY

A witness (עֵד) functions as a kind of evidence, verification, or proof. Inanimate witnesses can memorialize a shared relationship between parties. For example, the two and a half trans-Jordanian tribes built an altar on the west bank of the Jordan as a monument demonstrating their allegiance to Israel and Yahweh (Josh. 22:9–29, esp. 27–28, 34). The location of Galeed (גַּלְעֵד "cairn of witness") served to commemorate Laban and Jacob's oath (Gen. 31:43–54), with God as the ultimate arbiter (vv. 49–50). Such objects and places witnessed a covenant inasmuch as they served as memorials for ritualized liturgy and/or pedagogy for future encounters (Josh. 4:6).

The prescribed transcription and recitation of the Song of Moses (Deut. 32) functions in a similar fashion (see Deut. 31:12, 19). The people's singing of its words evinces the covenant. And the affirmation of later generations, as in these verses of Josh. 24 (cf. Deut. 5:3), renews the relationship with Yahweh in each new generation.

ANSWER KEY

1. *Parse:* (1) נַעֲבֹד (Qal PC 1CP עבד "serve"). (2) בְּחַרְתֶּם (Qal SC 2MP בחר "choose").

2. *Identify:* (A) The negative (לֹא) reverses the condition in verse 20: "We will *not* abandon Yahweh and serve foreign gods." (B) The conjunction כִּי functions as an asseverative—that is, an earnest assertion or positive vow. (C) Unlike a negative response to a statement with לֹא, an affirmation involves echoing the central part of the claim. The statement "You are witnesses" expects the positive rejoinder expressed simply as עֵדִים ("[We are] witnesses").

3. *Translate:* "The people responded to Joshua: 'Certainly not, we shall serve only Yahweh!' Joshua said to the people: 'You are witnesses against yourselves because you yourselves have chosen to serve Yahweh.' They replied: 'We are witnesses!'"

JOURNEY 2 · CONTINUING

DAY 37: JOSHUA 24:23–24

STEP ONE: Read aloud the text at least five times.

וְעַתָּ֗ה הָסִ֙ירוּ֙ אֶת־אֱלֹהֵ֤י הַנֵּכָר֙ אֲשֶׁ֣ר בְּקִרְבְּכֶ֔ם וְהַטּוּ֙
אֶת־לְבַבְכֶ֔ם אֶל־יְהוָ֖ה אֱלֹהֵ֥י יִשְׂרָאֵֽל׃ ²⁴וַיֹּאמְר֥וּ הָעָ֖ם
אֶל־יְהוֹשֻׁ֑עַ אֶת־יְהוָ֤ה אֱלֹהֵ֙ינוּ֙ נַעֲבֹ֔ד וּבְקוֹל֖וֹ נִשְׁמָֽע׃

STEP TWO: Parse the following verbs.

	Stem	Conj.	Pers.	Gend.	Numb.	Root	Trans.
(1) הָסִ֙ירוּ							
(2) וְהַטּוּ							
(3) נִשְׁמָע							

STEP THREE: Identify the following.

A. What is the function of וְעַתָּה?

B. What is notable about the word order of the final two clauses?

STEP FOUR: Translate the text into understandable English.

> VOCABULARY
>
> נֵכָר foreignness; foreigner

STEP FIVE: Notice significant exegetical insights.

• The initial discourse frame is missing but implied in verse 23. One would expect the change of speaker to start with the narrative notation וַיֹּאמֶר יְהוֹשֻׁעַ אֶל־הָעָם "Joshua said to the people" as at the beginning of verses 2, 19, and 22.

- **בְּקִרְבְּכֶם**: The foreign gods are described as the ones located in the midst of the people. This command to remove the native idols connects with the instruction not to make a covenant with the people in the land (Exod. 34:15; cf. Josh. 9:7–27) and not to be enticed to worship the Canaanite gods (Deut. 31:16; Josh. 24:16–17).

- **וּבְקוֹלוֹ נִשְׁמָע**: Alongside the final assertion that they will serve Yahweh, the people make explicit their devotion to his word. The verb שׁמע ("to hear, pay attention to") is used with the sense of "obey" or "submit to," particularly when the preposition בְּ follows with the object קוֹל ("voice," i.e., what has been said).

FOR THE JOURNEY

Joshua commands the people to turn from the temptation of idolatry. The metaphor involves the idea of bending or bowing one's heart in submission to Yahweh (נטה את־לבב). The idiom is also used to describe inducing others to support one's military or political cause (2 Sam. 19:15; Judg. 9:3). When Yahweh is in view, it involves full obedience to his word along with walking in his ways and keeping his commandments (1 Kings 8:58; also see Ps. 119:112; Prov. 2:2).

The same expression can be used negatively. Four times it describes Solomon's abandonment of Yahweh for foreign gods (1 Kings 11:2, 3, 4, 9). The prophet Jeremiah narrates Israel's covenant unfaithfulness and insolence using similar language of disobedience (Jer. 7:24) as not inclining their ear and walking according to the stubbornness of their evil heart (Jer. 11:8).

The verbal object involves a body part: לב(ב) "heart/mind" or אֹזֶן "ear." The singular form is regularly used for a group. While it is true that each person possesses their own heart, the singular and shared commitment is embodied with a shared intent. The people are called to obey as one, Israel proclaims their unified commitment to being God's covenant people, and together they either succeed or fail to uphold their promise to Yahweh.

ANSWER KEY

1. *Parse:* (1) הָסִירוּ (Hiphil IMV MP סור "remove"). (2) וְהַטּוּ (Hiphil *wəqātal* 3MP נטה "incline"). (3) נִשְׁמָע (Qal PC 1CP שמע "hear").

2. *Identify:* (A) The conjunction וְעַתָּה "and now" functions as a major transition or inferential statement in a discourse (see day 26, 2 Sam. 7:8). (B) The final two clauses invert the typical word order by placing the verbal complement (object) before the verb. In both instances, the order serves to highlight the object of the people's obedience as Yahweh and his voice.

3. *Translate:* "'Therefore, remove the foreign gods from among you, and incline your heart to Yahweh the God of Israel.' The people replied to Joshua: 'We will serve Yahweh our God, and we will obey his voice.'"

DAY 38: JOSHUA 24:25

STEP ONE: **Read** aloud the text at least five times.

וַיִּכְרֹת יְהוֹשֻׁעַ בְּרִית לָעָם בַּיּוֹם הַהוּא וַיָּשֶׂם לוֹ חֹק וּמִשְׁפָּט
בִּשְׁכֶם:

STEP TWO: **Parse** the following verbs.

	Stem	Conj.	Pers.	Gend.	Numb.	Root	Trans.
(1) וַיָּשֶׂם							

STEP THREE: **Identify** the following.

A. What is the object of וַיִּכְרֹת? _____

B. What is the object of וַיָּשֶׂם? _____

C. How is the initial preposition functioning with בִּשְׁכֶם? _____

STEP FOUR: **Translate** the text into understandable English.

_____

_____

VOCABULARY

חֹק ordinance, regulation, rule

שְׁכֶם Shechem

STEP FIVE: **Notice** significant exegetical insights.

- וַיִּכְרֹת . . . בְּרִית: The most common verb to describe covenant making is כרת ("cut"). The notion of cutting is widely understood as part of the ceremonial initiation of the agreement. (Notice the use of the verb בתר "cut in two" at Gen. 15:10.) Other covenant-formulating verbs are used less commonly than כרת, including הקים "raise up" (e.g., Gen. 6:18) and נתן "give" (e.g., Gen. 17:2).

- לוֹ: The pronominal suffix replaces the noun in the corresponding preposition phrase from the first clause, לְעָם "for the people." The noun עַם can be referenced by a singular or plural pronoun. The prepositional phrase precedes the indefinite verbal object because it is a known (or previously identified) entity. The experiencers of both verbs are the people.

FOR THE JOURNEY

The settlement of Shechem (שְׁכֶם) and its environs has special significance in the history of the people of God. It is the first place that is mentioned in Abram's migration from Haran (Gen. 12:6). His grandson Jacob camped there after coming back into the land, he purchased a nearby field, and he built an altar there (33:18–20). Shechem is an important city in the allotment of the tribe of Ephraim. It is both a city of refuge (Josh. 20:7) and a Levitical city (21:21). Later Joseph's bones are buried in this location (24:32; Acts 7:15–16). Both Abimelech son of Jerubbaal and Rehoboam are anointed as king there (Judg. 9:6; 1 Kings 12:1).

In Josh. 24, Shechem is the place where the people assemble for the last time under Joshua's leadership, who was Ephraim's favored son. It is closely associated with the nearby mountains of Ebal and Gerizim as the site of the covenant renewal (Deut. 11:29–30). Along with Josh. 8:30–35, the covenant renewal in this passage connects the promise of Yahweh to his redeemed people in this place.

ANSWER KEY

1. *Parse:* (1) וַיָּשֶׂם (Qal *wayyiqtol* 3ms שׂים "put").
2. *Identify:* (A) The object of וַיִּכְרֹת is the indefinite word בְּרִית "a covenant." (B) The object of וַיָּשֶׂם is the compound phrase חֹק וּמִשְׁפָּט "statute and judgment." (C) The initial preposition with בִּשְׁכֶם functions as a location marker, similar to English "at" or "in."
3. *Translate:* "Joshua cut a covenant for the people on that day. He established a statute and judgment for them at Shechem."

DAY 39: JOSHUA 24:26

STEP ONE: **Read** aloud the text at least five times.

וַיִּכְתֹּב יְהוֹשֻׁעַ אֶת־הַדְּבָרִים הָאֵלֶּה בְּסֵפֶר תּוֹרַת אֱלֹהִים וַיִּקַּח
אֶבֶן גְּדוֹלָה וַיְקִימֶהָ שָּׁם תַּחַת הָאַלָּה אֲשֶׁר בְּמִקְדַּשׁ יְהוָה:

STEP TWO: **Parse** the following verb.

	Stem	Conj.	Pers.	Gend.	Numb.	Root	Trans.
(1) וַיְקִימֶהָ							

STEP THREE: **Identify** the following.

A. What is the referent of the 3FS suffix (וַיְקִימֶהָ)?

_____

STEP FOUR: **Translate** the text into understandable English.

_____

_____

VOCABULARY

סֵפֶר   document; letter; scroll

אַלָּה   tree (≈ אֵלָה "oak")

מִקְדָּשׁ   sanctuary

STEP FIVE: **Notice** significant exegetical insights.

- סֵפֶר תּוֹרַת אֱלֹהִים: The construct phrase has three members. The final noun does not include the article but can be considered definite because it refers uniquely to God.

- הָאַלָּה: The mention of "the tree" connects this ceremony with other important events occurring in the precinct of this oak known from the narratives of both Jacob (Gen. 35:4) and Abram (12:6).

FOR THE JOURNEY

The Shechem ceremony ends with Joshua producing a written record and setting up a commemorative site. Similar situations are found with other covenant accounts (e.g., Exod. 24:4; Deut. 27:3; Josh. 8:32–34).

The content and location of the record deserve reflection. First, the content is described as "these words" (הַדְּבָרִים הָאֵלֶּה). This description is a common way to allude to past events (Josh. 24:29) or spoken discourse (Deut. 32:45). Here in Josh. 24:26, it might best be understood as the material involved in the covenant rite at Shechem witnessing to the people's commitment to Yahweh (i.e., vv. 2–24; see also, Deut. 11:26–32).

Second, Joshua's record is said to be in "the scroll of the Torah of God" (סֵפֶר תּוֹרַת אֱלֹהִים). This description is rare and found elsewhere only in the book of Ezra-Nehemiah (Neh. 8:18; 10:29–30). More common are the labels the "scroll of the/this Torah" (Deut. 28:61; 29:21; 30:10; 31:26; Josh. 1:8; 8:34) and "the scroll of the Torah of Moses" (Josh. 8:31; 23:6). These archival writings appear to be separate from "the covenant scroll" (סֵפֶר הַבְּרִית, Exod. 24:7), "the tablets of the testimony" (שְׁנֵי לֻחֹת הָעֵדֻת, 31:18), and "the ten words" (עֲשֶׂרֶת הַדְּבָרִים, 34:28; Deut. 4:13).

The written account of the Shechem covenant serves to ratify the people's commitment to Yahweh at the end of Joshua's life. It represents the final act in Yahweh's faithful deliverance of his people and is meant to motivate the reader to be devoted to serve Yahweh alone.

ANSWER KEY

1. *Parse:* (1) וַיְקִימֶהָ (Hiphil *wayyiqtol* 3MS קוּם "erect" + 3FS SF).
2. *Identify:* (A) The 3FS suffix (וַיְקִימֶהָ) refers to the large stone (אֶבֶן גְּדוֹלָה).
3. *Translate:* "Joshua wrote these words on the scroll of the Torah of God. Then he took a large stone and erected it there under the oak at Yahweh's sanctuary."

DAY 40: JOSHUA 24:27–28

STEP ONE: **Read** aloud the text at least five times.

וַיֹּאמֶר יְהוֹשֻׁעַ אֶל־כָּל־הָעָם הִנֵּה הָאֶבֶן הַזֹּאת תִּהְיֶה־בָּנוּ
לְעֵדָה כִּי־הִיא שָׁמְעָה אֵת כָּל־אִמְרֵי יְהוָה אֲשֶׁר דִּבֶּר עִמָּנוּ
וְהָיְתָה בָכֶם לְעֵדָה פֶּן־תְּכַחֲשׁוּן בֵּאלֹהֵיכֶם: ²⁸וַיְשַׁלַּח יְהוֹשֻׁעַ
אֶת־הָעָם אִישׁ לְנַחֲלָתוֹ:

STEP TWO: **Parse** the following verbs.

	Stem	Conj.	Pers.	Gend.	Numb.	Root	Trans.
(1) תִּהְיֶה							
(2) שָׁמְעָה							
(3) וְהָיְתָה							
(4) תְּכַחֲשׁוּן							
(5) וַיְשַׁלַּח							

STEP THREE: **Identify** the following.

A. How is the construction היה ל- being used in the expressions
תִּהְיֶה־בָּנוּ לְעֵדָה and וְהָיְתָה בָכֶם לְעֵדָה?

STEP FOUR: **Translate** the text into understandable English.

_____

_____

_____

> **VOCABULARY**
>
> עֵדָה   witness
> אֹמֶר   speech; word (PL CSTR אִמְרֵי)
> פֶּן   lest
> כחש   Piel: betray, be deceitful

123

STEP FIVE: **Notice** significant exegetical insights.

- כִּי־הִיא שָׁמְעָה ... דִּבֶּר: The כִּי marks the basis on which the stone acts as a witness against Israel. The verbs shift from a prefix conjugation (תִּהְיֶה) to suffix forms that reference anterior (past and completed) events.

- פֶּן־תְּכַחֲשׁוּן בֵּאלֹהֵיכֶם: The verb כחשׁ ("be deceitful") can designate its complement with the preposition בְּ (see Lev. 5:21; 19:11; Isa. 59:13; Jer. 5:12). The action describes taking advantage of one's neighbor through fraud and intentional disregard of God's word.

- אִישׁ לְנַחֲלָתוֹ: The individualizing formula (אִישׁ לְ) serves to depict how Joshua sent the people away from Shechem. The reference to "inheritance" reminds the reader of the fulfillment of Yahweh's promises (Num. 26:52–56; Deut. 4:38; 12:9; Josh. 11:23), the end of the conquest (Num. 32:18), and the ongoing commission to individual tribes to inhabit the land (Josh. 13:1–6). It also serves as a link to the book of Judges (2:6).

FOR THE JOURNEY

The people are witnesses (עֵדִים) to their own promise to serve and obey Yahweh (Josh. 24:22), and the erected stone serves into the future as a memorial witness (עֵדָה) to the covenant (v. 26–27). The monument marks the final remembrance of Yahweh's faithfulness in the book of Joshua. This concluding episode connects with the stone memorial commemorating God's mighty act of bringing his people into the land at the beginning of the book (Josh. 4:6–7, 20–21).

Outside of the book of Joshua, stone monuments serve to mark important treaties and places of divine rescue. Laban and Jacob establish a cairn (גַּל) and standing stone (מַצֵּבָה) to mark a pact (Gen. 31:45–52). Other standing stones designate theophanies (Exod. 24:4) and sanctuaries where humans commune with God (Gen. 28:18–22; 31:13).

In this way, the stones hear and speak to the people about their obligations. They cry out in witness to Yahweh's promises, even if all other voices are silent (Hab. 2:10–11; Luke 19:40).

1. *Parse:* (1) תִּהְיֶה (Qal PC 3FS היה "be"). (2) שָׁמְעָה (Qal SC 3FS שמע "hear").
   (3) וְהָיְתָה (Qal *wəqātal* 3FS היה "be"). (4) תְּכַחֵשׁוּן (Piel PC 2MP כחשׁ "betray";
   the final *nun* is described as paragogic, a vestige of an older form of תְּכַחֵשׁוּ).
   (5) וַיְשַׁלַּח (Piel *wayyiqtol* 3MS שׁלח "send [out]").

2. *Identify:* (A) In both instances, the construction ל- היה designates a change of
   state (*x becomes y*) where the subject is recast as the prepositional object.

3. *Translate:* "Joshua said to all the people: 'Take notice! This stone has become a
   witness against us because it heard all the words of Yahweh that he has spoken
   with us. It is a witness against you in case you should betray your God.' Then
   Joshua sent the people out, each to his own allotment."

ROUTE 7

Isaiah 6:1–13

STEP ONE: **Read** aloud the text at least five times.

בִּשְׁנַת־מוֹת הַמֶּלֶךְ עֻזִּיָּהוּ וָאֶרְאֶה אֶת־אֲדֹנָי יֹשֵׁב עַל־כִּסֵּא רָם
וְנִשָּׂא וְשׁוּלָיו מְלֵאִים אֶת־הַהֵיכָל:

STEP TWO: **Parse** the following verbs.

	Stem	Conj.	Pers.	Gend.	Numb.	Root	Trans.
(1) וָאֶרְאֶה							
(2) רָם							
(3) נִשָּׂא							
(4) מְלֵאִים							

STEP THREE: **Identify** the following.

A. Who or what do the three singular participles describe
(יֹשֵׁב . . . רָם וְנִשָּׂא)? _____

B. Who or what does the participle מְלֵאִים describe?
_____

126

STEP FOUR: **Translate** the text into understandable English.

> **VOCABULARY**
>
> עֻזִּיָּהוּ   Uzziah
>
> כִּסֵּא   seat; throne
>
> רוּם   Qal: be high; be exalted
>
> שׁוּל   hem of robe (PL + 3MS SF שׁוּלָיו)
>
> הֵיכָל   palace; temple

STEP FIVE: **Notice** significant exegetical insights.

- בִּשְׁנַת־מוֹת הַמֶּלֶךְ עֻזִּיָּהוּ: The initial noun phrase has a temporal function. It describes the time frame of the theophany. The main clause begins with the following *wayyiqtol* form (וָאֶרְאֶה). Elsewhere, the initial frame וַיְהִי may be used to introduce such chronological markers.

- וְשׁוּלָיו מְלֵאִים אֶת־הַהֵיכָל: The verb מלא ("to fill") can be intransitive or transitive. In this clause, the subject denotes the thing that fills the object. For more on this metaphor, see "For the Journey" below.

FOR THE JOURNEY

The vision of the divine throne room stands in contrast with the death of the great Judean king.

Uzziah, also known as Azariah, had a long fifty-two-year reign (2 Kings 15:2; 2 Chron. 26:3). Even though he was a remarkably effective leader, his final years were marked by arrogance, unfaithfulness, and controversy (2 Chron. 26:16–23).

Despite the failures of this long-lived king, God still rules over his creation. Isaiah envisions Yahweh as enthroned on a lofty seat within the temple (1 Kings 22:19). God's vestments expand and permeate the entire space. His habitation is unrestricted and not vulnerable to the whims of overconfident earthly kings and powers. The divine presence is visible and awe-inspiring. His glory is promised to those who approach appropriately (Lev. 9:5–6).

In special moments of Israel's history, God inhabits the created realm to reveal his power and purposes. Even so, the divine manifestation is veiled. Clouds cover the tabernacle (Exod. 40:34–35), fill the inner court (Ezek. 10:3), and inhabit the entire structure (1 Kings 8:10). Yahweh's glory is shrouded in tempestuous coverings (Exod. 16:10; 24:16–17; 1 Kings 8:11–12). In Isaiah's encounter, the Holy One of Israel is likewise distant and obscured, and contact is mediated through other divine beings.

ANSWER KEY

1. *Parse:* (1) וָאֶרְאֶה (Qal *wayyiqtol* 1cs ראה "see"). (2) רָם (Qal ACT PTCL MS רום "be high"). (3) נִשָּׂא (Niphal PTCL MS נשא "be lifted"). (4) מְלֵאִים (Qal ACT PTCL MP מלא "fill").

2. *Identify:* (A) The first participle (יֹשֵׁב) describes who Isaiah saw, אֲדֹנָי ("the Lord"). The following two participles (רָם וְנִשָּׂא) likely depict כִּסֵּא as the place where God sits in the temple. (B) The participle מְלֵאִים explains the extent of the Lord's vestments.

3. *Translate:* "In the year of King Uzziah's death, I saw the Lord sitting on a lofty and raised throne, with the hems of his robe filling the temple."

DAY 42: ISAIAH 6:2–3

STEP ONE: **Read** aloud the text at least five times.

שְׂרָפִ֨ים עֹמְדִ֣ים | מִמַּ֣עַל ל֗וֹ שֵׁ֣שׁ כְּנָפַ֖יִם שֵׁ֣שׁ כְּנָפַ֣יִם לְאֶחָ֑ד
בִּשְׁתַּ֣יִם | יְכַסֶּ֣ה פָנָ֗יו וּבִשְׁתַּ֛יִם יְכַסֶּ֥ה רַגְלָ֖יו וּבִשְׁתַּ֥יִם יְעוֹפֵֽף:
³וְקָרָ֨א זֶ֤ה אֶל־זֶה֙ וְאָמַ֔ר קָד֧וֹשׁ | קָד֛וֹשׁ קָד֖וֹשׁ יְהוָ֣ה צְבָא֑וֹת
מְלֹ֥א כָל־הָאָ֖רֶץ כְּבוֹדֽוֹ:

STEP TWO: **Parse** the following verbs.

	Stem	Conj.	Pers.	Gend.	Numb.	Root	Trans.
(1) עֹמְדִים							
(2) יְכַסֶּה							
(3) יְעוֹפֵף							
(4) וְקָרָא							

STEP THREE: **Identify** the following.

A. What spatial position does the compound preposition מִמַּ֣עַל ל֗וֹ indicate? _____

B. How is the sequence זֶ֤ה אֶל־זֶה functioning? _____

STEP FOUR: **Translate** the text into understandable English.

_____

_____

VOCABULARY

שָׂרָף	type of serpent
כָּנָף	wing; extremity, edge (DU כְּנָפַיִם)
כסה	Piel: cover
עוף	Polel: fly around

קָדוֹשׁ	sacred, holy
מְלֹא	fullness
כָּבוֹד	glorious; glory; honor

STEP FIVE: **Notice** significant exegetical insights.

- שְׂרָפִים: The divine beings are described in curious terms: they take the form of venomous snakes (Isa. 30:6). Similarly named beasts responded with a lethal incursion against the rebellion of the people in the wilderness wanderings (Num. 21:4–7). Only the ensign of a bronze *saraph* heralded the hope for an antidote (Num. 21:8–9; John 3:14–15), even though it became an idol in the time of Uzziah and later (2 Kings 18:4). The dual capacity of these creatures as agents of both death and deliverance suggests that this vision is anything but safe to the observer!

- שֵׁשׁ כְּנָפַיִם שֵׁשׁ כְּנָפַיִם לְאֶחָד: The repetition of the number of *saraph* wings ("six wings, six wings for each one") specifies a distributive. That is to say, each being had six appendages. Winged creatures recall those in the most holy place (1 Kings 6:23–28). The depiction in Chronicles is even more vivid. In 2 Chron. 5:7–8, the ark is brought into the holy place and placed under the cherubs' wings, forming a cover.

- קָדוֹשׁ קָדוֹשׁ קָדוֹשׁ: The adjective קָדוֹשׁ ("holy") forms a common title for Yahweh in the book of Isaiah, קְדוֹשׁ יִשְׂרָאֵל ("The Holy One of Israel"; e.g., 1:4; 10:20; 17:7; 30:15; 31:1; 41:16; 45:11; 55:5). It sometimes is accompanied by additional descriptors: גֹּאֵל "Redeemer" (43:14; 48:17; 49:7), בּוֹרֵא "Creator" (43:15), and/or מוֹשִׁיעֶךָ "your Savior" (43:3). The threefold repetition expresses a superlative as compared with the twofold expression קֹדֶשׁ קָדָשִׁים used to describe consecrated individuals (Exod. 30:29; 1 Chron. 23:13), places (Exod. 29:37; 40:10; Ezek. 43:12; 45:3; 48:12), or gifts (Exod. 30:36; Lev. 2:3; 6:18; 7:1; 10:12; 14:13; 24:9; Num. 18:9).

FOR THE JOURNEY

Perhaps the most shocking part of the message of the heralds is their declaration of divine omnipresence. Yahweh is not merely a spiritual being filling heavenly or sacred space (Isa. 6:1). The Creator inhabits the entire earthly realm. The astounding claim is "The fullness of all the earth is his glory" (v. 3). The creation, and not just the temple, is inhabited by divine glory. The entire earthly domain manifests his holiness, and God is acting in the world bringing about restoration and redemption (Isa. 35:2; 40:5; 58:8; 60:1).

The glory of God is immanent and infiltrates the world with his purposes. Like water covering the sea, the knowledge of his glory saturates the heavens and the earth (Hab. 2:14; 3:3). The metaphor of "filling the earth" is part of the creature mandate reverberating from creation (Gen. 1:22, 28; 9:1; 48:19; Exod. 1:7). Divine glory ensures Yahweh's enduring work (Num. 14:21). It is an outworking of his power to act (Ps. 72:19). And no place escapes his view (Jer. 23:24).

ANSWER KEY

1. *Parse:* (1) עֹמְדִים (Qal ACT PTCL MP עמד "stand"). (2) יְכַסֶּה (Piel PC 3MS כסה "cover"). (3) יְעוֹפֵף (Polel PC 3MS עוף "fly around"). (4) וְקָרָא (Qal *wəqātal* 3MS קרא "call").

2. *Identify:* (A) The compound preposition מִמַּעַל לֹ֫ו combines the spatial idea of "above" and the goal notion ("to") with the same object, the Lord, to indicate the orientation and location where the attendants stood in the throne room. (B) The sequence זֶה אֶל־זֶה functions adverbially to describe an antiphonal exchange between the serpents (*this serpent would call to that one*).

3. *Translate:* "The fiery serpents were standing above him. Each had six wings apiece. With two it would cover its face, and with two it would cover its feet, and with two it would flutter about. One would call to another and say: 'Yahweh of Hosts is Most Holy. His glory fills the whole earth.'"

DAY 43: ISAIAH 6:4–5

STEP ONE: **Read** aloud the text at least five times.

וַיָּנֻעוּ֙ אַמּ֣וֹת הַסִּפִּ֔ים מִקּ֖וֹל הַקּוֹרֵ֑א וְהַבַּ֖יִת יִמָּלֵ֥א עָשָֽׁן: ⁵וָאֹמַ֞ר
אֽוֹי־לִ֣י כִֽי־נִדְמֵ֗יתִי כִּ֣י אִ֣ישׁ טְמֵֽא־שְׂפָתַ֜יִם אָנֹ֗כִי וּבְתוֹךְ֙
עַם־טְמֵ֤א שְׂפָתַ֨יִם֙ אָנֹכִ֣י יוֹשֵׁ֔ב כִּ֗י אֶת־הַמֶּ֛לֶךְ יְהוָ֥ה צְבָא֖וֹת
רָא֥וּ עֵינָֽי:

STEP TWO: **Parse** the following verbs.

	Stem	Conj.	Pers.	Gend.	Numb.	Root	Trans.
(1) וַיָּנֻעוּ							
(2) יִמָּלֵא							
(3) וָאֹמַר							
(4) נִדְמֵיתִי							

STEP THREE: **Identify** the following.

A. What is the subject of וַיָּנֻעוּ? _____

B. Identify the relationship between קוֹל and הַקּוֹרֵא? _____

_____

STEP FOUR: **Translate** the text into understandable English.

_____

_____

VOCABULARY

נוע Qal: totter; tremble, quiver

אַמָּה doorpost (PL אַמּוֹת)

סַף threshold (PL סִפִּים)

עָשָׁן smoke

אוֹי alas! woe!

דמה Niphal: be destroyed

טְמֵא unclean

שָׂפָה lip; language; edge (DU שְׂפָתַיִם)

STEP FIVE: **Notice** significant exegetical insights.

- וָאֹמַר . . . וַיָּנֻעוּ: The last narrative form initiated the vision (וָאֶרְאֶה "I saw," v. 1). The first three verses serve as a unit describing what Isaiah saw. Verse 4 explains the consequence of the theophany on the temple complex ("then the foundations of the thresholds shook"). And verse 5 continues Isaiah's reaction as a first-person report ("next I said").

- וְהַבַּיִת יִמָּלֵא עָשָׁן: Corresponding to the doorways quaking, the building was filled with a cloud (see also Ezek. 10:4). Smoke (עָשָׁן) is commonly associated with the divine presence (Exod. 19:18). We can identify the enveloping smoke with God's vestments (שׁוּלָיו, Isa. 6:1), and the resulting earthquake signals his physical manifestation (וַיֶּחֱרַד כָּל־הָהָר מְאֹד) "the entire mountain shook intensely" Exod. 19:18).

- אוֹי־לִי: The exclamation is a common outcry responding to divine appearance and judgment (1 Sam. 4:7–8; Isa. 24:16; Jer. 4:13; etc.). Three reasons follow that describe the basis of the prophet's panic. Each is identified with the discourse element כִּי.

- אִישׁ טְמֵא־שְׂפָתַיִם . . . עַם־טְמֵא שְׂפָתַיִם: Notice the parallel structures. Both sequences of three words are construct phrases. Isaiah identifies himself as "a man of impurity of [two] lips" living among "a people of impurity of [two] lips." The contrast comes with the statement identifying the king (אֶת־הַמֶּלֶךְ יְהוָה צְבָאוֹת רָאוּ עֵינָי) as the one who is seen with his very own two eyes! The difference between Yahweh's holy dwelling and entourage (יֹשֵׁב עַל־כִּסֵּא, v. 1) and the prophet's contemptible situation among an impure people (v. 5) is striking and suggests the source of his fear.

FOR THE JOURNEY

Isaiah's characterization as having unclean lips is unprecedented and illuminates the internal and external aspects of religious purity.

The status of impurity ordinarily results when a human physically engages with something external and acquires uncleanness from that entity (טמא, e.g., Hag. 2:13). Unclean objects include, among other things, certain animals (Lev. 11:1–47; 22:5, 8), polluted foods (11:34), dead bodies, infected skin, or bodily fluids (22:4). Such encounters contaminate the body and require separation from the community for a time (Num. 19). Ritual cleansing marks the transition back to a state of purity (Lev. 22:6–7). In acknowledging his and his people's unclean lips, the prophet demonstrates emphatically that he should not be in the presence of God. Unclean persons cannot travel in the way of holiness (Isa. 35:8) and are prohibited from entering Yahweh's holy place (52:1, 11).

But there is more to this claim. Isaiah recognizes that the purity system has an internal, moral component. It applies to the fullness of the temple and the whole earth. Unclean lips signal iniquity and alienation. Sin contaminates, motivates God's anger, and prevents salvation (Isa. 64:4–7). The unclean will perish (66:17). On the other hand, virtuous living is analogous to the purity of one's hands and heart (Ps. 24:4), heart and lips (Prov. 22:11), and eyes (Hab. 1:13). Uncleanness is not only a characteristic of things without but also applies to what is within a person (see Mark 7:15–23; Matt. 15:11–20).

ANSWER KEY

1. *Parse:* (1) וַיָּנֻעוּ (Qal *wayyiqtol* 3ms נוע "tremble"). (2) יִמָּלֵא (Niphal PC 3ms מלא "be filled"). (3) וָאֹמַר (Qal *wayyiqtol* 1cs אמר "say"). (4) נִדְמֵיתִי (Niphal SC 1cs דמה "be destroyed").

2. *Identify:* (A) The subject of וַיָּנֻעוּ is likely "the doorway foundations" (אַמּוֹת הַסִּפִּים) even though it appears to be mismatched in grammatical gender. Alternatively, they could be the object, but the Hiphil verb form וַיָּנִעוּ may be expected in that case. (B) The sequence קוֹל הַקּוֹרֵא appears to be a construct phrase: "the sound of the speaking." The participle could instead be understood as an agent noun (*the speaker*); however, since the sound is produced by multiple heavenly creatures, it may be better to understand הַקּוֹרֵא as their collective vocal reverberation.

3. *Translate:* "Then the entryway foundations shook at the sound of the pronouncement as the building filled with smoke. And I responded: 'Oy me—I'm doomed! I have unclean lips and live among people with unclean lips! My eyes have seen the king, Yahweh of Hosts!'"

DAY 44: ISAIAH 6:6–7

STEP ONE: **Read** aloud the text at least five times.

וַיָּעָף אֵלַי אֶחָד מִן־הַשְּׂרָפִים וּבְיָדוֹ רִצְפָּה בְּמֶלְקַחַיִם לָקַח
מֵעַל הַמִּזְבֵּחַ: ⁷וַיַּגַּע עַל־פִּי וַיֹּאמֶר הִנֵּה נָגַע זֶה עַל־שְׂפָתֶיךָ
וְסָר עֲוֺנֶךָ וְחַטָּאתְךָ תְּכֻפָּר:

STEP TWO: **Parse** the following verbs.

	Stem	Conj.	Pers.	Gend.	Numb.	Root	Trans.
(1) וַיָּעָף							
(2) וַיַּגַּע							
(3) וְסָר							
(4) תְּכֻפָּר							

STEP THREE: **Identify** the following.

A. How is אֶחָד מִן־הַשְּׂרָפִים functioning in the clause?

B. What is the form of פִּי?

C. What is the referent of זֶה?

STEP FOUR: **Translate** the text into understandable English.

VOCABULARY

עוּף Qal: fly
שָׂרָף type of serpent
רִצְפָּה smoldering coal
מֶלְקָחַיִם tongs, snuffer

נגע Qal: touch; strike; reach
שָׂפָה lip; language; edge
כפר Pual: be atoned (for)

STEP FIVE: **Notice** significant exegetical insights.

- **בְּמֶלְקַחַיִם לָקַח מֵעַל הַמִּזְבֵּחַ**: This clause functions like a relative clause even though it does not begin with **אֲשֶׁר**. It describes the place ("the altar") from which the indefinite noun **רִצְפָּה** ("coal") was removed and the way ("with tongs") it was removed.

- **נָגַע זֶה עַל־שְׂפָתֶיךָ**: The touching of the prophet's *lips* corresponds to the confession in verse 5: **אִישׁ טְמֵא־שְׂפָתַיִם אָנֹכִי וּבְתוֹךְ עַם־ טְמֵא שְׂפָתַיִם אָנֹכִי יוֹשֵׁב** ("I have unclean lips and live among people with unclean lips"). The actions of the divine being serve as a response to Isaiah's distress.

- **וְסָר עֲוֹנֶךָ וְחַטָּאתְךָ תְּכֻפָּר**: The word pair for Isaiah's transgression ("your iniquity" and "your sin") corresponds to a word pair describing its remedy ("is removed" and "is atoned for"). This chiastic parallelism structure (AB–B′A′) enacts magnanimous forgiveness and sanctions clemency for the prophet who has just acknowledged his unworthiness to appear in God's presence.

FOR THE JOURNEY

The language of sacrifice is profuse in Isaiah's temple vision, even though any description of a particular sacrifice is conspicuously lacking.

The winged serpents attend the Holy One in his holy habitation. They are the heavenly priests. They herald Yahweh and his superlative character. As emissaries, they serve as intermediaries between the supplicant and God. The altar is aflame with a blazing fire. Tongs are used to extract a burning ember. The rite of expiation involves touching the coal to the prophet's mouth. But no slaughter or offering is depicted.

Apart from his confession of guilt and a contrite heart, Isaiah makes no overt sacrifice (Ps. 51:2–6). Yet, Isaiah experiences Yahweh's unmerited forgiveness. His response of ruin is replaced by a revelation of rescue. He is pardoned. And he participates in the activities of the holy place.

The question remains: What about the people with whom Isaiah lives? Will they call out for mercy? Will they also receive clemency?

1. *Parse:* (1) וַיָּ֫עָף (Qal *wayyiqtol* 3MS עוף "fly"). (2) וַיַּגַּע (Hiphil *wayyiqtol* 3MS נגע "touch"). (3) וְסָר (Qal *wəqātal* 3MS סור "remove"). (4) תְּכֻפָּר (Pual PC 2MS כפר "be atoned for").

2. *Identify:* (A) The partitive phrase אֶחָד מִן־הַשְּׂרָפִים "one from among the serpents" is the subject of the main verb (וַיָּ֫עָף). (B) For the noun פֶּה ("mouth"), the first-person pronominal suffix form and the construct form look alike (פִּי); in this verse, it is functioning as the first-person pronominal suffix form. (C) The MS referent of זֶה is not altogether clear: it most likely designates רִצְפָּה "coal" even though the grammatical gender appears to be mismatched (cf. the plural is רְצָפִים at 1 Kings 19:6). Alternatively, the demonstrative could relate to יָד ("hand"), which is construed as masculine in some cases.

3. *Translate:* "One of the serpents flew toward me. In its hand was a fiery cinder that it had taken with tongs off the altar. Then (the serpent) touched my lips and said, 'Since this has touched your lips, your iniquity has departed, and your sin is expiated.'"

STEP ONE: **Read** aloud the text at least five times.

וָאֶשְׁמַע אֶת־קוֹל אֲדֹנָי אֹמֵר אֶת־מִי אֶשְׁלַח וּמִי יֵלֶךְ־לָנוּ
וָאֹמַר הִנְנִי שְׁלָחֵנִי:

STEP TWO: **Parse** the following verbs.

	Stem	Conj.	Pers.	Gend.	Numb.	Root	Trans.
(1) וָאֶשְׁמַע							
(2) אֹמֵר							
(3) יֵלֶךְ							
(4) וָאֹמַר							
(5) שְׁלָחֵנִי							

STEP THREE: **Identify** the following.

  A. What is the difference between אֶת־מִי and מִי?

  B. What is the form of לָנוּ, and how is it functioning?

STEP FOUR: **Translate** the text into understandable English.

STEP FIVE: **Notice** significant exegetical insights.

- קוֹל אֲדֹנָי אֹמֵר: In verses 3–4, the divine beings spoke about the Lord and the sound shook the foundations of the temple. Verse 8 details "the voice of the Lord" as a construct phrase and further specifies God's question and his subsequent commission (v. 9). The participle (אֹמֵר) depicts the words expressed by the voice, but they are not directed toward a particular individual. Yet, of all the heavenly attendants, Isaiah responds.

- אֶת־מִי אֶשְׁלַח וּמִי יֵלֶךְ־לָנוּ: The speaker has shifted from the prophet narrating the vision (וָאֶשְׁמַע) to the Lord asking two questions. The verb אֶשְׁלַח of the first question is first-person singular, and the suffix on the preposition לָנוּ ("for us") is first-person plural. Both are divine and self-referential. The latter "us" could refer to the heavenly hosts and/or God (day 3, Gen. 1:26). Then Isaiah's first-person narration resumes with the subsequent *wayyiqtol* form (וָאֹמַר).

- הִנְנִי: The particle הִנֵּה punctuates various types of discourse with unexpected and even surprising news. The pronoun identifies Isaiah as the speaker exclaiming "Look at me!" We could even think of the expression as a presentative, like a student replying "I'm here!" to a teacher checking attendance.

FOR THE JOURNEY

The Lord's two queries anticipate that the same individual is the answer to both. But the order of the questions and the response appear to be reversed. It demonstrates that the Lord's call is not merely about who will go but about who is chosen as the divine representative.

The first question asks for someone to be sent from the divine realm. In the heavenly throne room, multiple parties could be issued such orders. The one commissioned receives a special status and task.

The second question anticipates that the one sent would convey a dispatch as an emissary of the divine king. (Only in the following verses are the message and purpose specified.) The mission is not just about movement. The divine king propels a herald to proclaim with royal authority. At issue is the dissemination of the regal message.

The prophet's response repeats the same order. He does not say "I will go, send me." Isaiah directly and candidly volunteers to be chosen. Like an exuberant child vying for a spot on a schoolyard team, he shouts "Pick me!" Among all the created beings suited for the task, he brazenly advises the King of kings "I'm your man. Send me."

Isaiah, in his vision, acknowledges that the divine calling is primary. God's messenger must first and foremost be willing to be commissioned to the divine task before knowing the mission, the message, or even the outcome.

ANSWER KEY

1. *Parse:* (1) וָאֶשְׁמַע (Qal *wayyiqtol* 1cs שמע "hear"). (2) אֹמֵר (Qal ACT PTCL MS אמר "say"). (3) יֵלֶךְ (Qal PC 3MS הלך "go"). (4) וָאֹמַר (Qal *wayyiqtol* 1cs אמר "say"). (5) שְׁלָחֵנִי (Qal IMV MS שלח "send" + 1cs SF).

2. *Identify:* (A) The sequence with the object marker אֶת־מִי indicates that the answer to the question is the object of the verb ("whom?"), whereas the answer to the interrogative pronoun without the object marker is the subject ("who?"). (B) The form of לָנוּ is the preposition with the 1CP pronominal suffix. It designates the one benefiting from the main action ("for us").

3. *Translate:* "Then I heard the Lord's voice, speaking: 'Whom will I send? Who will go for us?' I answered, 'Me, me! Send me!'"

DAY 46: ISAIAH 6:9–10

STEP ONE: **Read** aloud the text at least five times.

וַיֹּאמֶר לֵךְ וְאָמַרְתָּ לָעָם הַזֶּה שִׁמְעוּ שָׁמוֹעַ וְאַל־תָּבִינוּ
וּרְאוּ רָאוֹ וְאַל־תֵּדָעוּ: ¹⁰הַשְׁמֵן לֵב־הָעָם הַזֶּה וְאָזְנָיו הַכְבֵּד
וְעֵינָיו הָשַׁע פֶּן־יִרְאֶה בְעֵינָיו וּבְאָזְנָיו יִשְׁמָע וּלְבָבוֹ יָבִין
וָשָׁב וְרָפָא לוֹ:

STEP TWO: **Parse** the following verbs.

	Stem	Conj.	Pers.	Gend.	Numb.	Root	Trans.
(1) לֵךְ							
(2) וְאָמַרְתָּ							
(3) תָּבִינוּ							
(4) תֵּדָעוּ							
(5) הַשְׁמֵן							
(6) וָשָׁב							

STEP THREE: **Identify** the following.

A. What is the construction שִׁמְעוּ שָׁמוֹעַ and where else is the same construction used in this passage? _____

B. What is the subject of the verbs following פֶּן? _____

STEP FOUR: **Translate** the text into understandable English.

_____

_____

בין   Qal: understand; discern

שמן   Hiphil: make fat; cause to grow fat

אֹזֶן   ear (PL + 3MS SF אָזְנָיו)

כבד   Hiphil: make heavy, cause to be heavy

שעע   Hiphil: make blind, cause to be blind

פֶּן   lest; perhaps

רפא   Qal: heal

STEP FIVE: **Notice** significant exegetical insights.

- וְאַל־תָּבִינוּ . . . וְאַל־תֵּדָעוּ: Listening and seeing produce a negative outcome. The consequence is this people will *not* comprehend God's message. The ordinary response is subverted.

- לֵב־הָעָם . . . וְאָזְנָיו . . . וְעֵינָיו: An extended metaphor of hearing, seeing, and knowing is developed using the corresponding anatomic terms ears, eyes, and heart. The expected function of each collective body part is subverted through various somatic impairments. Isaiah's message apparently will have a deleterious result: the people's heart becomes fattened (i.e., indolent and apathetic; cf. 4Q424 3.3–6), their ears are heavy (i.e., deaf; cf. Isa. 59:1), and their eyes are besmeared (i.e., blind; cf. Isa. 32:3).

- וְשָׁב וְרָפָא: Three prefix conjugations (יְרָאֶה . . . יִשְׁמָע . . . יָבִין "... see ... hear ... understand") resolve with two *wǝqātal* verbs. The final two verbs וְשָׁב וְרָפָא signal a consequential relationship ("so that [the people] would repent, and then [God] would heal [the people]").

FOR THE JOURNEY

The prophet's personal confession incriminates his countrymen (v. 5). They, like him, are characterized as having unclean lips. Following his confession, Isaiah receives atonement (v. 6). Divine reconciliation appears to be no less possible for his audience. A humble response would yield forgiveness (2 Kings 22:15–20).

But the people would not respond in contrition. God tasks the prophet to announce judgment. Such a proclamation would appear to bear an opportunity to turn from their wickedness and impending disaster (Jer. 18:8). Yet, God ominously declares that the opposite will occur. Their mouths will not confess, and they will not receive healing. Their reaction motivates further disbelief and represses understanding. The people hear and see the message, but like Pharaoh, they harden their hearts. And their lack of repentance results in the privation of healing.

ANSWER KEY

1. *Parse:* (1) לֵךְ (Qal IMV MS הלך "go"). (2) וְאָמַרְתָּ (Qal *wəqāṭal* 2MS אמר "say"). (3) תָּבִינוּ (Qal PC 2MP בין "understand"). (4) תֵּדְעוּ (Qal PC 2MP ידע "know"). (5) הַשְׁמֵן (Hiphil IMV MS שמן "make fat"). (6) וְשָׁב (Qal *wəqāṭal* 3MS שוב "turn").

2. *Identify:* (A) The construction שִׁמְעוּ שָׁמוֹעַ ("listen carefully") includes an imperative with a cognate infinitive absolute and conveys a form of verbal prominence. The same sequence occurs later in the verse (וּרְאוּ רָאוֹ "look intently"). (B) The subject of the 3MS verbs following פֶּן is the same group (הָעָם הַזֶּה) being addressed and indicated by the preceding 3MS pronominal suffixes (i.e., וְאָזְנָיו . . . וְעֵינָיו).

3. *Translate:* "[The Lord] said, 'Go, say to this people: "Listen carefully, but do not understand; look intently, but do not distinguish." Engorge this people's heart, weigh down their ears, and besmear their eyes, lest they see with their eyes, hear with their ears, and understand in their heart, such that they repent, and he heal them.'"

DAY 47: ISAIAH 6:11–12

STEP ONE: **Read** aloud the text at least five times.

וַיֹּ֨אמֶר עַד־מָתַ֣י אֲדֹנָ֔י וַיֹּ֗אמֶר עַ֣ד אֲשֶׁר֩ אִם־שָׁא֨וּ עָרִ֜ים מֵאֵ֣ין
יוֹשֵׁ֗ב וּבָתִּים֙ מֵאֵ֣ין אָדָ֔ם וְהָאֲדָמָ֖ה תִּשָּׁאֶ֥ה שְׁמָמָֽה׃ ¹²וְרִחַ֥ק
יְהוָ֖ה אֶת־הָאָדָ֑ם וְרַבָּ֥ה הָעֲזוּבָ֖ה בְּקֶ֥רֶב הָאָֽרֶץ׃

STEP TWO: **Parse** the following verbs.

	Stem	Conj.	Pers.	Gend.	Numb.	Root	Trans.
(1) וַיֹּ֨אמֶר							
(2) שָׁא֨וּ							
(3) תִּשָּׁאֶ֥ה							
(4) וְרִחַ֥ק							
(5) וְרַבָּ֥ה							
(6) הָעֲזוּבָ֖ה							

STEP THREE: **Identify** the following.

A. How is אֲדֹנָי functioning? _____

B. What are the singular forms of the irregular plurals עָרִים and
בָּתִּים? _____

STEP FOUR: **Translate** the text into understandable English.

_____

_____

STEP FIVE: **Notice** significant exegetical insights.

- וְהָאֲדָמָה תִּשָּׁאֶה שְׁמָמָה: The definite element ("the ground/earth") is the subject of the passive verb. This devastation recalls the Edenic judgment (Gen. 3:17–19) and other covenant curses (Lev. 26:32–33). The final indefinite clause element (שְׁמָמָה) functions as an adverb describing the extent of the desolation: "as a wasteland."

- הָעֲזוּבָה: The nearest referent is in the previous verse. The feminine entity abandoned is the ground (הָאֲדָמָה). The collapse will extend not just to the inhabited and populous places but to the very earth. Widespread and utter obliteration is in view; as a result, the land will be uninhabitable.

FOR THE JOURNEY

"How long?" may be understood in two primary ways.

The question could be asking the length of time the prophet should anticipate being the divine emissary. In this way, it explains the command: לֵךְ וְאָמַרְתָּ לָעָם הַזֶּה "Go, say to this people" (v. 9). The response would establish how long Isaiah should expect to continue preaching the message.

Alternatively, the query could be requesting the timeline for Israel's continued disobedience and devastation. When will the people turn to Yahweh in repentance? How long before the land and people receive their healing?

The response favors the latter interpretation. God's opening words mirror the question: עַד אֲשֶׁר אִם "until that time when." Rather than describing the temporal extent of the prophet's ministry, the circumstances specify the extent of the destruction of the dwellings and ground. The land will experience devastation on account of the people's unwillingness to return to Yahweh (Isa. 1:7–15). Repentance will not, however, be forthcoming in his generation. The people are to experience the entirety of the covenant curses (see Lev. 26:14–20). There is no escape. Destruction is their end (see Ps. 74:1–11). The only remaining question is how long the judgment will last before Yahweh intervenes (Ps. 74:9–10).

1. *Parse:* (1) וָאֹמַר (Qal *wayyiqtol* 1cs אמר "say"). (2) שָׁאוּ (Qal sc 3cp שאה "be desolate"). (3) תִּשָּׁאֶה (Niphal pc 3fs שאה "be devastated"). (4) וְרִחַק (Piel *wǝqātal* 3ms רחק "remove"). (5) וְרַבָּה (Qal *wǝqātal* 3fs רבב "be large"). (6) הָעֲזוּבָה (def art + Qal pass ptcl fs עזב "abandon").

2. *Identify:* (A) The title אֲדֹנָי "Lord" is a vocative of address. (B) The singular form of עָרִים is עִיר "city," and the singular of בָּתִּים is בַּיִת "house."

3. *Translate:* "I asked: 'How long, Lord?' He responded: 'Until the cities are desolate without inhabitant, houses without humans, and the ground is devastated as a wasteland. Then Yahweh will remove the humans, and the desertion will be abundant in the land.'"

DAY 48: ISAIAH 6:13

STEP ONE: **Read** aloud the text at least five times.

וְעוֹד בָּהּ עֲשִׂרִיָּה וְשָׁבָה וְהָיְתָה לְבָעֵר כָּאֵלָה וְכָאַלּוֹן אֲשֶׁר
בְּשַׁלֶּכֶת מַצֶּבֶת בָּם זֶרַע קֹדֶשׁ מַצַּבְתָּהּ׃

STEP TWO: **Parse** the following verbs.

	Stem	Conj.	Pers.	Gend.	Numb.	Root	Trans.
(1) וְשָׁבָה							
(2) וְהָיְתָה							
(3) לְבָעֵר							

STEP THREE: **Identify** the following.

A. How is וְעוֹד being used? _____

B. What is the feminine referent of בָּהּ? _____

C. What is the plural referent of בָּם? _____

STEP FOUR: **Translate** the text into understandable English.

_____

_____

VOCABULARY

עֲשִׂירִי tenth (part)

בער Piel: kindle; consume, devour

אֵלָה terebinth tree

אַלּוֹן tree; oak (?)

שַׁלֶּכֶת felling (of a tree)

מַצֶּבֶת stump; pillar (cf. מַצֵּבָה)

STEP FIVE: **Notice** significant exegetical insights.

- וְשָׁבָה וְהָיְתָה לְבָעֵר: The initial accent on the verb שָׁבָה differentiates it from the active participle (שָׁבָה). It functions as an auxiliary verb denoting repetition with the following periphrastic formulation, וְהָיְתָה לְבָעֵר "it [the land] will again be devoured."

- אֲשֶׁר בְּשַׁלֶּכֶת מַצֶּבֶת בָּם: Textual variants along with semantic and grammatical issues present difficulties for understanding this relative clause. The Great Isaiah Scroll from Qumran reads the second word as a passive participle and the final word perhaps as a noun—אשר משלכת מצבת במה ("which is being discarded from the pillar of the high place")—which is not entirely transparent either. The term מַצֶּבֶת is used twice, perhaps referring to the different parts of a cut tree (i.e., its trunk and its stump). Commentators debate the best explanation. That said, the MT version may refer to the flammability of a felled tree. Even if one escapes the devastation described in verses 11–12, little hope remains not to be consumed by the final conflagration.

FOR THE JOURNEY

Isaiah employs several dendrological metaphors to describe the people. Trees can stand for kings and monarchical lineages (see Judg. 9:8–15). Seeds and vegetative growth represent the rise of kingdoms and empires over which God exercises ultimate power (Isa. 40:24). A severed tree can represent a fallen political power or ruler, and a barren tree an unfruitful people (Jer. 8:13; Mark 11:14). Notably, Jesse's stump is said to resprout by the Spirit and establish justice and righteousness in the land (Isa. 11).

Isaiah 6 relates the tree to the holy seed. The prophet reveals that Israel is fallen and aflame! There is no optimism of regrowth; even the remnant is devastated and consumed. Hope has gone up in smoke. The promise to Abraham is in jeopardy and subject to ruin. Yet, the holy seed is reborn in the second part of the book—namely, Isa. 40–66. Yahweh sustains Israel, even though they may be distant from the land (41:8–10). They will multiply and live in God's presence (48:19). His spirit will enliven them (59:21). The holy seed will be blessed again and bless the nations (61:9). Yahweh is loyal to his promises. Even the unfaithfulness of his people will not deter his ultimate purposes.

ANSWER KEY

1. *Parse:* (1) וְשָׁבָה (Qal *wəqātal* 3FS שׁוּב "turn," here "again"). (2) וְהָיְתָה (Qal *wəqātal* 3FS היה "be"). (3) לְבָעֵר (PREP + Piel INF CSTR בער "consume").

2. *Identify:* (A) The adverb עוֹד is being used to modify the nominal clause as a restrictive, like "still" or "yet." (B) The feminine referent of בָּהּ (also מַצֶּבְתָּה as well as the head of the adjective עֲשִׂרִיָּה and verbs וְשָׁבָה וְהָיְתָה) is הָאָרֶץ ("the land") from the end of the previous clause. Metaphorically, עֲשִׂרִיָּה could be further denoting the inhabitants of the land. (C) The plural suffix with בָּם appears to refer to the two trees (כָּאֵלָה וְכָאַלּוֹן).

3. *Translate:* "Even though a tenth part is still in the land, it will again burn like a terebinth or oak whose trunk is felled—its stump is the holy seed."

ROUTE 8

Exodus 2:1–25

STEP ONE: **Read** aloud the text at least five times.

וַיֵּלֶךְ אִישׁ מִבֵּית לֵוִי וַיִּקַּח אֶת־בַּת־לֵוִי: ²וַתַּהַר הָאִשָּׁה וַתֵּלֶד
בֵּן וַתֵּרֶא אֹתוֹ כִּי־טוֹב הוּא וַתִּצְפְּנֵהוּ שְׁלֹשָׁה יְרָחִים:

STEP TWO: **Parse** the following verbs.

	Stem	Conj.	Pers.	Gend.	Numb.	Root	Trans.
(1) וַיֵּלֶךְ							
(2) וַתַּהַר							
(3) וַתֵּלֶד							
(4) וַתֵּרֶא							
(5) וַתִּצְפְּנֵהוּ							

STEP THREE: **Identify** the following.

A. What is the sense of the idiom הלך מִן ("go from")?

B. How is כִּי functioning in verse 2?

STEP FOUR: **Translate** the text into understandable English.

> VOCABULARY
>
> הרה Qal: conceive, become pregnant
>
> צפן Qal: hide; save
>
> יֶרַח month (PL יְרָחִים)

STEP FIVE: **Notice** significant exegetical insights.

- **בַּת־לֵוִי . . . בֵּית לֵוִי**: The unnamed man is identified only as coming from the house of Levi. His wife is described as "a daughter of Levi." In Exod. 6:18–20, the man is designated as Levi's grandson, Amram (also 1 Chron. 6:3). He is married to Jochebed, the sister of his father Kohath. They had two other children: Aaron and Miriam (Num. 26:59).

- **וַתֵּרֶא אֹתוֹ כִּי־טוֹב הוּא**: This sequence is reminiscent of several important descriptions. In the creation account of Gen. 1, God sees various created elements as good: the light (v. 4), dry land (v. 10), vegetation (v. 12), heavenly bodies (v. 18), fish and birds (v. 21), and animals (v. 25). In the early narratives, the woman observes that the forbidden tree is good for food (3:6), and the sons of God see that the daughters of humankind are good (6:2). The inverse is also informative: God observes that the earth is filled with wickedness (6:5) and corruption (6:12).

FOR THE JOURNEY

It is tempting to read the particulars of these verses as inconsequential. The seemingly unimportant details, however, relate to the previous narrative and anticipate the coming exodus from Egypt.

First, the genealogical notice connects the husband and wife to Leah's third son (Gen. 29:34; 35:23; Exod. 1:2) and relates this family of Levites to the forthcoming priestly leadership in the cultic activities in Israel (Deut. 18:1–8).

Second, the anxious birth of a son recounts the events of the previous chapter. Jacob's family also lived as a displaced community in a time of concern about foreign incursion and internal insurgency (Exod. 1:10). Fearing the non-native population, the Egyptian king decreed the killing of all male children to encourage societal assimilation (v. 16). Against this climate of death and ethnic cleansing, the family and persistent community (v. 17) again must trust in Yahweh's deliverance.

Third, Moses's life is saved through the faith of a lone mother in a foreign land. The child's goodly appearance motivates his mother to act to save him. She risks contravening the immoral statute because she sees that he is a special child, blessed by God and purposed to save his people (Acts 7:20).

Fourth, the family concealed the baby for three months. In the NT, the author of Hebrews commends Moses's parents, Amram and Jochebed, for their defiance of Pharaoh's evil edict and their stubborn faith in God (Heb. 11:23).

ANSWER KEY

1. *Parse:* (1) וַיֵּלֶךְ (Qal *wayyiqtol* 3MS הלך "go"). (2) וַתַּהַר (Qal *wayyiqtol* 3FS הרה "conceive"). (3) וַתֵּלֶד (Qal *wayyiqtol* 3FS ילד "bear"). (4) וַתֵּרֶא (Qal *wayyiqtol* 3FS ראה "see"). (5) וַתִּצְפְּנֵהוּ (Qal *wayyiqtol* 3FS צפן "hide" + 3MS SF).

2. *Identify:* (A) The movement idiom הלך מִן indicates heredity, like the English phrase "he comes from the family of X." (B) In verse 2, the clause beginning with כִּי provides an adnominal description of the verbal object (see day 2, Gen. 1:4).

3. *Translate:* "A man came from the family of Levi, and he wedded a daughter of Levi. His wife conceived and gave birth to a son. She saw that he was goodly and hid the baby for three months."

DAY 50: EXODUS 2:3

STEP ONE: **Read** aloud the text at least five times.

וְלֹא־יָכְלָה עוֹד֙ הַצְּפִינוֹ֒ וַתִּקַּֽח־לוֹ֙ תֵּבַת גֹּ֔מֶא וַתַּחְמְרָ֥ה בַחֵמָ֖ר
וּבַזָּ֑פֶת וַתָּ֤שֶׂם בָּהּ֙ אֶת־הַיֶּ֔לֶד וַתָּ֥שֶׂם בַּסּ֖וּף עַל־שְׂפַ֥ת הַיְאֹֽר׃

STEP TWO: **Parse** the following verbs.

	Stem	Conj.	Pers.	Gend.	Numb.	Root	Trans.
(1) יָכְלָה							
(2) הַצְּפִינוֹ							
(3) וַתִּקַּח							
(4) וַתַּחְמְרָה							
(5) וַתָּשֶׂם							

STEP THREE: **Identify** the following.

A. What is the preposition doing with בְחֵמָר וּבַזָּפֶת?

B. What is the referent of the suffix with בָּהּ?

STEP FOUR: **Translate** the text into understandable English.

VOCABULARY

יכל	Qal: be able	זֶפֶת	pitch, tar
צפן	Hiphil: hide	יֶלֶד	child; boy
תֵּבָה	ark	סוּף	reed(s)
גֹּמֶא	reed; papyrus	שָׂפָה	lip; edge
חמר	Qal: apply a substance	יְאֹר	stream; the Nile
חֵמָר	bitumen, asphalt		

153

STEP FIVE: **Notice** significant exegetical insights.

- וְלֹא־יָכְלָה עוֹד הַצְּפִינוֹ: The sequence of *wayyiqtol* forms in the first two verses is interrupted with the first clause of verse 3. It pauses the narrative and builds suspense around the three-month effort to conceal the boy and explains his mother's fated decision. The clause expresses her incapacity to continue the situation of the first three months of his life, so Moses's mother demonstrates her care by constructing an impermeable and floatable craft. She is not simply abandoning her son but strategically positioning the vessel (and her daughter?) to lead to its discovery. In all this, she is deliberately subverting the evil command of the Egyptian Pharaoh (Exod. 1:22).

- תֵּבַת גֹּמֶא: The initial term, traditionally translated "ark," does not describe a standard nautical craft. More common terms would be אֳנִיָּה "ship," שְׂכִיָּה "boat," or רִיחַ "coracle" (a round vessel). The description rather denotes something like a container, perhaps even a rectangular chest. The word elsewhere only describes Noah's vessel (e.g., Gen. 6:14–16). Its material is described as "reed" (גֹּמֶא), a type of water-plant or perhaps grass (Isa. 35:7). Isaiah 18:2 describes "reed vessels" (כְּלֵי גֹמֶא) used by a Cushite envoy.

FOR THE JOURNEY

The three-month time frame of verse 2 forestalls the family's limited ability to safeguard their lineage. Like the midwives (Exod. 1:15–20), the unnamed mother defies the king's order and protects her vulnerable child. Yet even great faith requires God's intervention. The birth could not be hidden forever. Yahweh would have to bring deliverance to this favored infant boy and his beset family.

Analogously, Yahweh's involvement was needed to rescue his own son, Israel. Jacob and his twelve sons entered Egypt with favored status, but political turmoil and non-native population growth elicited oppression and fear (1:7) that led to enslavement (1:9–10). Four hundred years was the time frame of Israel's sojourn in Egypt, according to Yahweh's disclosure to Abram (Gen. 15:13–16). God promised restoration of the people in the fourth generation and judgment on the enslaving nation. This child was the fourth ancestor from Jacob

(Levi>Kohath>Amram>Moses; Num. 26:57–59). As their circumstances deteriorated and subjugation increased, the hope for deliverance became more palpable, but the people were not able to save themselves from the oppressive regime of Egypt. The fourth generation had arrived expectantly but also with ruptured expectations and infanticide (Matt. 2:16–18). Yahweh needed to send a rescuer.

ANSWER KEY

1. *Parse:* (1) יָכְלָה (Qal SC 3FS יכל "be able"). (2) הַצְּפִינוֹ (Hiphil INF CSTR צפן "hide" + 3MS SF). (3) וַתִּקַּח (Qal *wayyiqtol* 3FS לקח "take"). (4) Read as וַתַּחְמְרָה (Qal *wayyiqtol* 3FS חמר "cover" + 3FS SF). (5) וַתָּשֶׂם (Qal *wayyiqtol* 3FS שׂים "put, place").

2. *Identify:* (A) The prepositions with בַחֵמָר וּבַזָּפֶת indicate the material applied to the ark. (B) The referent of the suffix בָּהּ is תֵּבַת גֹּמֶא "reed ark."

3. *Translate:* "When she was no longer able to hide him, she took a reed box and covered it with bitumen and tar. She put the child in it and positioned it among the reeds by the shore of the Nile."

DAY 51: EXODUS 2:4–6A

STEP ONE: **Read** aloud the text at least five times.

וַתֵּתַצַּב אֲחֹתוֹ מֵרָחֹק לְדֵעָה מַה־יֵּעָשֶׂה לוֹ: ⁵וַתֵּרֶד בַּת־פַּרְעֹה
לִרְחֹץ עַל־הַיְאֹר וְנַעֲרֹתֶיהָ הֹלְכֹת עַל־יַד הַיְאֹר וַתֵּרֶא
אֶת־הַתֵּבָה בְּתוֹךְ הַסּוּף וַתִּשְׁלַח אֶת־אֲמָתָהּ וַתִּקָּחֶהָ:
⁶וַתִּפְתַּח וַתִּרְאֵהוּ אֶת־הַיֶּלֶד וְהִנֵּה־נַעַר בֹּכֶה

STEP TWO: **Parse** the following verbs.

	Stem	Conj.	Pers.	Gend.	Numb.	Root	Trans.
(1) וַתֵּתַצַּב							
(2) לְדֵעָה							
(3) יֵּעָשֶׂה							
(4) וַתֵּרֶד							
(5) הֹלְכֹת							
(6) וַתִּקָּחֶהָ							
(7) וַתִּרְאֵהוּ							

STEP THREE: **Identify** the following.

A. What is the function of מַה? _____

B. How is the motion specified by הֹלְכֹת עַל־יַד הַיְאֹר?
_____

STEP FOUR: **Translate** the text into understandable English.

_____

_____

VOCABULARY

יצב   Hitpael: take a stand; station oneself

אָחוֹת   sister (FS + 3MS SF אֲחֹתוֹ)

רָחוֹק   distance (מֵרָחֹק "at a distance")

רחץ   Qal: wash, bathe

יְאֹר   stream; the Nile

נַעֲרָה   young girl; maidservant (PL + 3FS SF נַעֲרֹתֶיהָ)

תֵּבָה   ark

סוּף   reed(s)

אָמָה   female slave (+ 3FS SF אֲמָתָהּ)

פתח   Qal: open

יֶלֶד   child; boy

בכה   Qal: weep

STEP FIVE: **Notice** significant exegetical insights.

- אֲחֹתוֹ . . . בַּת־פַּרְעֹה . . . וְנַעֲרֹתֶיהָ: Three new characters or groups are introduced in succession: the child's sister, the daughter of Pharaoh, and her entourage. No names are given for any of these women—similar to the child's parents. These nameless actors are contrasted with the identification of the child in verse 10 and the previous acknowledgment of Shiphrah and Puah, the faithful Hebrew midwives (Exod. 1:15). Later, of course, Miriam is named and recognized as a prophet (15:20).

- וְהִנֵּה־נַעַר בֹּכֶה: The murderous edict of the Egyptian king is sharply contrasted with the magnanimous empathy of his daughter. Beyond the surprise of finding a child abandoned in a box beside the river, the boy is weeping! It is possible that his cries are the very reason he could no longer be hidden. Yet his crying also leads to his discovery and compassionate adoption into his persecutor's family.

FOR THE JOURNEY

Several satiric elements in the story subvert human authority and demonstrate God's ultimate control.

In chapter 1, the Egyptian king directs the midwives to eradicate the Hebrew sons but allows the daughters to live (v. 16). Pharaoh's orders, however, go unheeded. With the failure of that scheme, Pharaoh turns to his own people to carry out ethnic cleansing by male infanticide. They are instructed to throw (שׁלך) every son into the Nile (v. 22). No one—besides the child's mother—is said to abide by the latter edict. In both cases, the actions of women subvert these abhorrent commands.

In chapter 2, deliverance is not inevitable but is facilitated by the empathy and shrewd disobedience of multiple Hebrew and Egyptian daughters, perhaps pointing back to Pharaoh's provision of female clemency. The infant's rescue involves a daughter of Levi (2:1), her daughter (2:4), and Pharaoh's own daughter with her attendants (2:5). Under duress, the boy's mother is forced to abandon him. Yet she takes care to give him a chance to survive. She prepares a watertight chest, places it at the edge of the river, and even stations his sister as a lookout and scout. In heroic defiance, Egyptian women from within Pharaoh's own household intervene to save the child. The least powerful characters usher in divine deliverance and upset the king's capricious, homicidal directives.

Yahweh's deliverance of his son, Israel, harnesses the faith of a mother, the empathy of a foreign princess, and her interaction with a young Hebrew woman to bring about the rescuer's rescue.

ANSWER KEY

1. *Parse:* (1) וַתֵּתַצַּב (Hitpael *wayyiqtol* 3FS יצב "stand"). (2) לְדֵעָה (PREP + Qal INF CSTR ידע "know"). (3) יֵעָשֶׂה (Niphal PC 3MS עשׂה "be done"). (4) וַתֵּרֶד (Qal *wayyiqtol* 3FS ירד "go down"). (5) הֹלְכֹת (Qal ACT PTCL FP הלך "go"). (6) וַתִּקָּחֶהָ (Qal *wayyiqtol* 3FS לקח "take" + 3FS SF [i.e., הַתֵּבָה]). (7) וַתִּרְאֵהוּ (Qal *wayyiqtol* 3FS ראה "see" + 3MS SF, with 3MS SF in apposition to אֶת־הַיֶּלֶד).

2. *Identify:* (A) The element מַה functions to embed a content clause to specify the object of ידע. (B) The motion הלך is further delimited by the locative preposition עַל and noun phrase יַד הַיְאֹר, "by the hand of [i.e., beside] the Nile."

3. *Translate:* "His sister stood at a distance to know what would happen to him. Pharaoh's daughter went down to bathe beside the Nile, while her domestics were walking along by the banks of the Nile. She saw the box among the reeds and sent her handmaiden. She took and opened it, and she saw the child—there was a boy crying!"

DAY 52: EXODUS 2:6B–8A

STEP ONE: **Read** aloud the text at least five times.

וַתַּחְמֹל עָלָיו וַתֹּאמֶר מִיַּלְדֵי הָעִבְרִים זֶה: ⁷וַתֹּאמֶר אֲחֹתוֹ
אֶל־בַּת־פַּרְעֹה הַאֵלֵךְ וְקָרָאתִי לָךְ אִשָּׁה מֵינֶקֶת מִן הָעִבְרִיֹּת
וְתֵינִק לָךְ אֶת־הַיָּלֶד: ⁸וַתֹּאמֶר־לָהּ בַּת־פַּרְעֹה לֵכִי

STEP TWO: **Parse** the following verbs.

	Stem	Conj.	Pers.	Gend.	Numb.	Root	Trans.
(1) וַתַּחְמֹל							
(2) הַאֵלֵךְ							
(3) וְקָרָאתִי							
(4) מֵינֶקֶת							
(5) וְתֵינִק							
(6) לֵכִי							

STEP THREE: **Identify** the following.

A. What is the first element of הַאֵלֵךְ? _____

B. What is the function of the preposition מִן with מִיַּלְדֵי הָעִבְרִים? _____

STEP FOUR: **Translate** the text into understandable English.

_____

_____

VOCABULARY

חמל Qal: spare, have compassion
יֶלֶד child; boy; youth
עִבְרִי Hebrew
אָחוֹת sister
ינק Hiphil: nurse

STEP FIVE: **Notice** significant exegetical insights.

- הָעִבְרִית . . . הָעִבְרִים: The gentilic identifier "Hebrew" originates with Abram (Gen. 14:13), perhaps connected to his eponymous ancestor, Eber (11:16). It serves as an ethnic marker connected to Joseph's origins (40:15) and his lineage (39:14) coupled with his enslaved status (39:14, 17; 41:12). It is used in the first two books of the Bible by Egyptians as a basis of derision (Exod. 1:19) and discrimination (Gen. 43:32).

- הַאֵלֵךְ וְקָרָאתִי . . . וְתֵינִק: The linking of a pc, *wəqātal*, and *waw* + prefix conjugation indicates a marked sequence of volitive semantics. The first verb initiates the volitive sequence ("Should I go?"). The response of Pharaoh's daughter affirms the entire string by simply echoing the initial verb: לְכִי "go." The second verb is dependent on the first, forming an ordered series ("and then call"). The final verb in the sequence indicates the purpose or result ("so that she may nurse").

FOR THE JOURNEY

The detailed description of the child's hiding place and his slow reveal builds the reader's anticipation for the response of Pharaoh's daughter. What will be her reaction? Will she comply with or contravene the homicidal edict of her father? How will God save Israel's rescuer?

Upon finding the crying boy, even though he is incriminated as an ill-fated foreigner ("This is a Hebrew child," v. 6b), the Egyptian king's daughter has compassion on him. She knows that she is expected to cast him into the river (1:22), but she refuses to kill the Hebrew boy. When she encounters the condemned infant face-to-face, this Egyptian woman responds with bold compassion and resolute action.

In full view of her attendants, she disregards Pharaoh's evil directive and affirms the Hebrew daughter's intrepid request. The dialogue with the child's sister reverses the last Egyptian-Hebrew interaction (1:15–19). Pharaoh's disloyal daughter does not ignore the boy's cries but provides for his care. Together with her attendants, she intervenes on behalf of the defenseless, immigrant child and saves his life. These women, like the midwives before them (1:17, 21), fear God more than man.

JOURNEY 2 · CONTINUING

1. *Parse:* (1) וַתַּחְמֹל (Qal *wayyiqtol* 3FS חמל "empathize"). (2) הַאֵלֵךְ (INT + Qal PC 1CS הלך "go"). (3) וְקָרָאתִי (Qal *wəqātal* 1CS קרא "call"). (4) מֵינֶקֶת (Hiphil PTCL FS ינק "nurse"). (5) וְתֵינִק (CJ + Hiphil PC FS ינק "nurse"). (6) לְכִי (Qal IMV FS הלך "go").

2. *Identify:* (A) The first element of הַאֵלֵךְ is the interrogative הַ that marks a yes-no question. (B) The preposition מִן with מִיַּלְדֵי הָעִבְרִים indicates the partitive (i.e., "*one from among* the children of the Hebrews"), and it functions similarly as מִן הָעִבְרִיֹּת ("from the Hebrew women") in verse 7.

3. *Translate:* "[Pharaoh's daughter] had compassion on him and said, 'This must be a Hebrew child!' His sister responded to Pharaoh's daughter, 'Should I go and summon a nursing Hebrew woman for you so she might nurse the child for you?' Pharaoh's daughter replied to her, 'Go!'"

DAY 53: EXODUS 2:8B–9

STEP ONE: **Read** aloud the text at least five times.

וַתֵּלֶךְ הָעַלְמָה וַתִּקְרָא אֶת־אֵם הַיָּלֶד: ⁹וַתֹּאמֶר לָהּ בַּת־פַּרְעֹה
הֵילִיכִי אֶת־הַיֶּלֶד הַזֶּה וְהֵינִקִהוּ לִי וַאֲנִי אֶתֵּן אֶת־שְׂכָרֵךְ
וַתִּקַּח הָאִשָּׁה הַיֶּלֶד וַתְּנִיקֵהוּ:

STEP TWO: **Parse** the following verbs.

	Stem	Conj.	Pers.	Gend.	Numb.	Root	Trans.
(1) וַתֵּלֶךְ							
(2) הֵילִיכִי							
(3) וְהֵינִקִהוּ							
(4) אֶתֵּן							
(5) וַתִּקַּח							
(6) וַתְּנִיקֵהוּ							

STEP THREE: **Identify** the following.

A. Who is הָעַלְמָה?

STEP FOUR: **Translate** the text into understandable English.

___

VOCABULARY

עַלְמָה young woman
יֶלֶד child; boy
ינק Hiphil: nurse
שָׂכָר payment (+ 2FS SF שְׂכָרֵךְ)

STEP FIVE: **Notice** significant exegetical insights.

- הָעַלְמָה: This description indicates the age and social standing of the young woman. She is living within her parent's household and old enough to be relied on to fetch someone to take care of the child. On the other hand, the shift in language from "his sister" (v. 7) downplays her relationship to the child and even *her* mother (אֵם הַיֶּלֶד). Perhaps the narrator uses this generic expression as a way to highlight her clandestine familial connection. There is no indication that Pharaoh's daughter knows that the child is related to the girl or the Hebrew nurse.

- הֵילִיכִי אֶת־הַיֶּלֶד הַזֶּה: Speaking to the Hebrew nurse, Pharaoh's daughter echoes her earlier order to the sister (v. 8). The Hiphil of הלך indicates that she is given the task to take care, guide, and provide for the child (cf. Josh. 24:3; 2 Kings 6:19; Isa. 42:16).

- וְהֵינִקֵהוּ לִי: Pharoah's daughter reiterates the request of the child's sister for someone to nurse the boy (v. 7). It is clear that she takes on the responsibility for the child's welfare, repeating the beneficial element לִי "for me" (cf. לָךְ in v. 7). The Egyptian princess willingly takes on the fostering of the orphaned refugee.

FOR THE JOURNEY

The Israelites experienced genocidal policies and oppressive treatment as foreigners in Egypt. Their servitude and economic mistreatment (Exod. 1:11–13) compelled Yahweh's intervention (2:23; 3:7, 9).

God's redemptive plan and provision play out in the life of this Hebrew family. Even though they are enslaved, this Egyptian woman of privilege rescues the child and promises to pay a wage for taking care of her adopted son (Exod. 2:9; see 3:21; 12:36).[1] Included in the instructions of Pharaoh's daughter is a subtle acknowledgment of both the value and the costs of raising a child. Contrasted with the oppressive actions of her father, she treats the family justly rather than exploiting their vulnerable status. Political and economic persecution do not prevail over her intent to save the life of the boy.

---

1. Similar expressions describe the compensation given to laborers (Gen. 30:28), soldiers (Ezek. 29:19), and sailors (Jon. 1:3).

In the exodus, Yahweh rescues his people from subjugation and calls them to a countercultural socio-economic ideal. The intercession of Moses's adopted mother mirrors in small measure his own later ministry to his people. The rescued rescuer would bring about justice for the oppressed Hebrews and legislate their proper conduct one to another. Torah mandates just treatment of the refugee, fatherless, and widow in reference to their subjugation in Egypt (Exod. 22:21–23). The need for fair dealings becomes an outcome of sabbath theology (Deut. 5:15). And the lack of timely payment brings guilt on the oppressor (24:15).

ANSWER KEY

1. *Parse:* (1) וַתֵּלֶךְ (Qal *wayyiqtol* 3FS הלך "go"). (2) הֵילִיכִי (Hiphil IMV FS הלך "go"). (3) וְהֵינִקֵהוּ (CJ + Hiphil IMV FS ינק "nurse" + 3MS SF). (4) אֶתֵּן (Qal PC 1CS נתן "give"). (5) וַתִּקַּח (Qal *wayyiqtol* 3FS לקח "take"). (6) וַתְּנִיקֵהוּ (Hiphil *wayyiqtol* 3FS ינק "nurse" + 3MS SF).

2. *Identify:* (A) The child's sister (אֲחֹתוֹ vv. 4, 7) is identified as הָעַלְמָה "the young woman" in verse 8.

3. *Translate:* "The young woman went and called the child's mother. Pharaoh's daughter said to her, 'Take this child and nurse him for me. I will compensate you.' The woman took the child, and she nursed him."

DAY 54: EXODUS 2:10

STEP ONE: **Read** aloud the text at least five times.

וַיִּגְדַּל הַיֶּלֶד וַתְּבִאֵהוּ לְבַת־פַּרְעֹה וַיְהִי־לָהּ לְבֵן וַתִּקְרָא שְׁמוֹ מֹשֶׁה וַתֹּאמֶר כִּי מִן־הַמַּיִם מְשִׁיתִהוּ׃

STEP TWO: **Parse** the following verbs.

	Stem	Conj.	Pers.	Gend.	Numb.	Root	Trans.
(1) וַיִּגְדַּל							
(2) וַתְּבִאֵהוּ							
(3) מְשִׁיתִהוּ							

STEP THREE: **Identify** the following.

A. Who is the subject of the verb וַתְּבִאֵהוּ?

STEP FOUR: **Translate** the text into understandable English.

VOCABULARY

גדל   Qal: grow up

יֶלֶד   child; boy

משה   Qal: draw, pull (out)

STEP FIVE: **Notice** significant exegetical insights.

• וַיְהִי־לָהּ לְבֵן: This construction indicates a possessive predicate, like "she *had* a son" in English. The negative formulation is similar: לֹא־הָיָה לוֹ בֵן "he did not have a son" (2 Kings 1:17). Other related constructions express covenant relationships (Exod. 6:7), including adoption (Esther 2:15) and marriage (Gen. 24:67). As part of this sequence, it indicates the child's transformed status from enslaved child to royal son.

- וַתִּקְרָא שְׁמוֹ מֹשֶׁה: The nearest feminine referent for the subject of the verb is Pharaoh's daughter rather than his birth mother. This conclusion is supported by the following description since she is the one who pulls him out of the water (כִּי מִן־הַמַּיִם מְשִׁיתִהוּ).

FOR THE JOURNEY

The Hebrew boy's name was given by his adoptive Egyptian mother. As a child of two ethnic worlds, Moses's name finds different and special significances in both.

Several Pharaohs had Egyptian names with a similar *m-s* component meaning "child" or "offspring." Ra-meses and Thut-mose are well-known examples. Their names mean something akin to "born of Ra" and "child of Thoth," respectively. They claimed to be the offspring of these divinities. Even though Moses's name lacks an explicit theophoric component, it signaled his status as a chosen *son* to his adoptive family. He was a child not naturally born but granted favored status in the Egyptian king's household, in a sense *Pharaoh's son*.

According to the Exodus account, his Hebrew name relates to his extraordinary rescue from the Nile. Pharaoh's daughter "pulled him out" (מְשִׁיתִהוּ). The narrative etymology even specifies the place of his deliverance: "from the waters" (מִן־הַמַּיִם). For the favored child, the means of judgment (Exod. 1:22) became the site of his deliverance (2:5). What's more, the grammatical form מֹשֶׁה acknowledges the one who rescued him. It is not the feminine form, מֹשָׁה ("she is pulling out"). The name perhaps unexpectedly is the *masculine* singular active participle form (like the divine descriptions נֹצֵר and נֹשֵׂא at Exod. 34:7). God—rather than Pharaoh's daughter—was the one pulling him out from a watery grave and giving him a redeemed life.

Moses's rescue and his name were reminders of the broader setting, which was ripe for the hope of God's promised redemption for his favored son, Israel.

ANSWER KEY

1. *Parse:* (1) וַיִּגְדַּל (Qal *wayyiqtol* 3MS גדל "grow up"). (2) וַתְּבִאֵהוּ (Hiphil *wayyiq-tol* 3FS בוא "bring in" + 3MS SF). (3) מְשִׁיתִהוּ (Qal SC 1CS משה "pull out" + 3MS SF).

2. *Identify:* (A) The subject of the verb וַתְּבִאֵהוּ is הָאִשָּׁה from verse 9 (i.e., Moses's biological mother).

3. *Translate:* "The child grew up. She brought him to Pharaoh's daughter, and he became her son. She named him Moses. 'For I pulled him out of the water,' she said."

DAY 55: EXODUS 2:11–12

STEP ONE: **Read** aloud the text at least five times.

וַיְהִ֣י ׀ בַּיָּמִ֣ים הָהֵ֗ם וַיִּגְדַּ֤ל מֹשֶׁה֙ וַיֵּצֵ֣א אֶל־אֶחָ֔יו וַיַּ֖רְא בְּסִבְלֹתָ֑ם
וַיַּ֗רְא אִ֤ישׁ מִצְרִי֙ מַכֶּ֣ה אִישׁ־עִבְרִ֔י מֵאֶחָֽיו׃ ¹²וַיִּ֤פֶן כֹּה֙ וָכֹ֔ה
וַיַּ֖רְא כִּ֣י אֵ֣ין אִ֑ישׁ וַיַּךְ֙ אֶת־הַמִּצְרִ֔י וַֽיִּטְמְנֵ֖הוּ בַּחֽוֹל׃

STEP TWO: **Parse** the following verbs.

	Stem	Conj.	Pers.	Gend.	Numb.	Root	Trans.
(1) מַכֶּ֣ה							
(2) וַיַּךְ							
(3) וַיִּטְמְנֵהוּ							

STEP THREE: **Identify** the following.

A. Who is referred to as אֶחָיו?

B. What is the meaning of כֹּה וָכֹה (see Num. 11:31; 23:15)?

STEP FOUR: **Translate** the text into understandable English.

> **VOCABULARY**
>
> גדל   Qal: grow up; become strong; become great
>
> סְבָלוֹת   laborious burdens (+ 3MS SF סִבְלֹתָם)
>
> מִצְרִי   Egyptian
>
> עִבְרִי   Hebrew
>
> פנה   Qal: turn
>
> טמן   Qal: hide, conceal
>
> חוֹל   sand

STEP FIVE: **Notice** significant exegetical insights.

- וַיְהִי בַּיָּמִים הָהֵם: Narrative time can be indicated by the construction וַיְהִי בְּ functioning much like a temporal *when*-clause in English. In this case, "those days" is a reference to the passage of years or an extended length of time rather than just a few days. Moses has grown (גדל) into a man—that is, to maturity (Judg. 11:2; Ruth 1:13)—and is no longer a mere child. The expectation is that his ministry would soon start (1 Sam. 3:19).

- וַיֵּצֵא אֶל־אֶחָיו: The verb יצא indicates exiting a circumscribed location or group. It is the inverse of בוא ("enter"). In this instance, it indicates that Moses was raised away from his biological family. After he was weaned, Pharaoh's daughter had brought him into Pharaoh's house (וַתְּבִאֵהוּ לְבַת־פַּרְעֹה, v. 10). He had to leave the confines of his privileged setting to observe the plight of his relatives.

FOR THE JOURNEY

Repetition in a narrative plays a key role in communicating an essential notion or description. The recurring action "he saw" (וַיַּרְא) occurs three times in these two verses. The outcome of Moses's visit with his Israelite relatives was to observe their onerous situation. Their toil was unrelenting. What previously he perhaps had known about only through word of mouth, he now understood firsthand. Moses observed the ruthless cruelty and enslavement of his brothers (1:13–14). He saw (וַיַּרְא) an Egyptian beating a Hebrew. The narrator uses repetition to build suspense and empathy. The Hebrew man is described as "from among his relatives" (מֵאֶחָיו). But what could one person—even one of such privileged status—do to relieve their burdens?

Taking a clear side, Pharaoh's adopted grandson metes out individual retribution and covers his trail. The euphemistic language for manslaughter is unmistakable. Moses took it upon himself to be this Egyptian's judge and executor. He may not have been able to deliver every Hebrew from mistreatment, but this brother was saved. His covert action, however principled and altruistic, was carefully orchestrated so as not to be seen.

God was not unaware of his people's difficulties. In fact, he had predicted it (Gen. 15:13–14). At the end of Exod. 2, the narrator details that God heard the Israelites' cries for relief and deliverance (Exod. 2:24). God has seen (וַיַּרְא) and knows their plight (2:25). His retribution will be clear and decisive. Unlike Moses's limited response, Yahweh will act to deliver the entire nation for all to see (3:7–10).

ANSWER KEY

1. *Parse:* (1) מַכֶּה (Hiphil PTCL MS נכה "strike"). (2) וַיַּךְ (Hiphil *wayyiqtol* 3MS נכה "strike"). (3) וַיִּטְמְנֵהוּ (Qal *wayyiqtol* 3MS טמן "hide" + 3MS SF).

2. *Identify:* (A) "His brothers" (אֶחָיו) are Moses's Hebrew relatives. (B) The idiom כֹּה וָכֹה refers to two different options or specifically locations, like English "this and that" or "here and there" (Num. 11:31; 23:15).

3. *Translate:* "After some time, Moses matured, went out to his relatives, and saw their toil. He saw an Egyptian man striking a Hebrew man from among his relatives. He turned this way and that. He saw no one. He struck down the Egyptian and hid him in the sand."

DAY 56: EXODUS 2:13–15A

STEP ONE: **Read** aloud the text at least five times.

וַיֵּצֵא בַּיּוֹם הַשֵּׁנִי וְהִנֵּה שְׁנֵי־אֲנָשִׁים עִבְרִים נִצִּים וַיֹּאמֶר
לָרָשָׁע לָמָּה תַכֶּה רֵעֶךָ: ¹⁴וַיֹּאמֶר מִי שָׂמְךָ לְאִישׁ שַׂר וְשֹׁפֵט
עָלֵינוּ הַלְהָרְגֵנִי אַתָּה אֹמֵר כַּאֲשֶׁר הָרַגְתָּ אֶת־הַמִּצְרִי וַיִּירָא
מֹשֶׁה וַיֹּאמַר אָכֵן נוֹדַע הַדָּבָר: ¹⁵וַיִּשְׁמַע פַּרְעֹה אֶת־הַדָּבָר
הַזֶּה וַיְבַקֵּשׁ לַהֲרֹג אֶת־מֹשֶׁה

STEP TWO: **Parse** the following verbs.

	Stem	Conj.	Pers.	Gend.	Numb.	Root	Trans.
(1) נִצִּים							
(2) תַכֶּה							
(3) שָׂמְךָ							
(4) הַלְהָרְגֵנִי							
(5) נוֹדַע							
(6) וַיְבַקֵּשׁ							

STEP THREE: **Identify** the following.

A. Who or what does לָרָשָׁע refer to? _____

STEP FOUR: **Translate** the text into understandable English.

_____

_____

VOCABULARY

שֵׁנִי	second	הרג	Qal: kill; slay
עִבְרִי	Hebrew	מִצְרִי	Egyptian
נצה	Niphal: fight	אָכֵן	surely
רֵעַ	companion, neighbor, friend (רֵעֲךָ + 2MS SF)		

STEP FIVE: **Notice** significant exegetical insights.

- וַיֵּצֵא בַּיּוֹם הַשֵּׁנִי: The time frame is specified as "on the second day." The day of the assault is considered day 1. The second day is the next one (cf. Gen. 1:8; Josh. 6:14). The verb יצא is repeated from Exod. 2:11. It is unclear whether his previous departure was intended to be a permanent exodus from the palace or a temporary departure. The reader can only guess where Moses went after he buried the Egyptian taskmaster in the sand. But again on the next day, he found himself encountering Hebrews.

- אַתָּה אֹמֵר: The antagonist's accusation ("Are you saying?") suggests that Moses's interruption comes with an implicit claim. The illocution could be understood as "Why should I relent? Are you threatening to stop me?!"

- וַיֹּאמֶר אָכֵן נוֹדַע הַדָּבָר: Discourse is commonly used in narrative as a tool to state explicitly the thoughts and opinions of a character about a situation or event. In this case, Moses's fear is expressed as direct speech. Even though he had considered the matter a secret (v. 12), he discovers that his intervention is known.

FOR THE JOURNEY

The aggressive antagonist unsuspectingly spews a prophetic pronounce-ment. *Who made you to be a prince and judge over us?* The knowledge-able reader answers "God did!" God would call this man to be Israel's prince and judge (שַׂר וְשֹׁפֵט). Paradoxically the derisive indictment anticipates Moses's vocation (Exod. 3:10). Moses would not only be Israel's leader and mediator, but he would also appoint others to do the same. As commander-in-chief and chief justice, Moses would assign capable men as leaders (Exod. 18:21, 25; Deut. 1:15) and judges over the people (Exod. 18:26; Deut. 1:16).

Yet before these appointments are given to Moses, he experiences some unexpected digressions. His story staggers between a life of great privilege and promise and one of alienation and abandonment. It is punctuated by his childhood deliverance, this unsuccessful rebellion, a fearful exile, and reticence in his mission. The first chapters of Exodus demonstrate that God alone accomplishes the liberation of his people.

It is guaranteed, but it takes place according to his plan and in his time. Even the divinely called person must wait for God's preparation and schedule to accomplish his will.

ANSWER KEY

1. *Parse:* (1) נִצִּים (Niphal PTCL MP נצה "fight"). (2) תַּכֶּה (Hiphil PC 2MS נכה "strike"). (3) שָׂמְךָ (Qal SC 3MS שׂים "place" + 2MS). (4) הַלְהָרְגֵנִי (INT + PREP + Qal INF CSTR הרג "kill" + 1CS). (5) נוֹדַע (Niphal SC 3MS ידע "be known"). (6) וַיְבַקֵּשׁ (Piel *wayyiqtol* 3MS בקשׁ "seek").

2. *Identify:* (A) Moses directed his question "to the evil one" (לְרָשָׁע), referring to the man at fault in the struggle with his neighbor (רֵעֶךָ).

3. *Translate:* "Moses went out on the next day. There were two Hebrew men fighting. He said to the antagonist: 'Why would you strike your neighbor?' He responded: 'Who made you to be a prince and judge over us? Are you threatening to kill me as you killed the Egyptian?' Moses was afraid and said: 'The matter is definitely known.' Pharaoh heard of this matter and sought to kill Moses."

DAY 57: EXODUS 2:15B–17

STEP ONE: **Read** aloud the text at least five times.

וַיִּבְרַ֨ח מֹשֶׁה֙ מִפְּנֵ֣י פַרְעֹ֔ה וַיֵּ֥שֶׁב בְּאֶֽרֶץ־מִדְיָ֖ן וַיֵּ֥שֶׁב עַֽל־הַבְּאֵֽר׃
16וּלְכֹהֵ֥ן מִדְיָ֖ן שֶׁ֣בַע בָּנ֑וֹת וַתָּבֹ֣אנָה וַתִּדְלֶ֗נָה וַתְּמַלֶּ֙אנָה֙
אֶת־הָ֣רְהָטִ֔ים לְהַשְׁק֖וֹת צֹ֥אן אֲבִיהֶֽן׃ 17וַיָּבֹ֥אוּ הָרֹעִ֖ים וַיְגָרְשׁ֑וּם
וַיָּ֤קָם מֹשֶׁה֙ וַיּ֣וֹשִׁעָ֔ן וַיַּ֖שְׁקְ אֶת־צֹאנָֽם׃

STEP TWO: **Parse** the following verbs.

	Stem	Conj.	Pers.	Gend.	Numb.	Root	Trans.
(1) וַתָּבֹ֣אנָה							
(2) וַתִּדְלֶ֗נָה							
(3) וַתְּמַלֶּ֙אנָה֙							
(4) לְהַשְׁק֖וֹת							
(5) וַיְגָרְשׁ֑וּם							
(6) וַיּ֣וֹשִׁעָ֔ן							
(7) וַיַּ֖שְׁקְ							

STEP THREE: **Identify** the following.

A. What are the two meanings conveyed by וַיֵּ֥שֶׁב in verse 15?

_____

B. Does צֹ֥אן אֲבִיהֶֽן refer to a lone animal or a group?

_____

STEP FOUR: **Translate** the text into understandable English.

_____

_____

VOCABULARY

ברח	Qal: flee; go through
מִדְיָן	Midian
בְּאֵר	well, pit
דלה	Qal: draw (water)
רַהַט	trough
שׁקה	Hiphil: give a drink
רעה	Qal: shepherd, graze; pasture; feed
גרשׁ	Piel: drive out
ישׁע	Hiphil: deliver, save; assist

STEP FIVE: **Notice** significant exegetical insights.

- וּלְכֹהֵן מִדְיָן שֶׁבַע בָּנוֹת: The nonverbal clause functions to introduce several new characters into the narrative—the priest of the region of Midian (Reuel, see v. 18; Num. 10:29; elsewhere called Jethro) and, more immediately salient, his seven daughters. Jethro appears at important moments throughout Moses's Midian wanderings up to Exod. 4, and then again upon his return in Exod. 18.

- וַיְגָרְשׁוּם: The subject and the object are both designated as third-person masculine plural entities. The participle הָרֹעִים ("shepherds") acts like an agentive noun and continues the subject from the previous clause (וַיָּבֹאוּ). The masculine plural object is more uncertain. Possible referents could be the daughters (שֶׁבַע בָּנוֹת), who were the subject of the three finite verbs in verse 16, or their father's flock (צֹאן אֲבִיהֶן). The former does not agree in grammatical gender with the pronominal suffix, and the latter is a mismatch in morphological number but could agree in sense, referring to the multiple sheep rather than a flock. The best solution is either to see it as a reference to the mixed group (i.e., the daughters and their flock) or simply the animals.

- וַיּוֹשִׁעָן: Moses arises (קוּם) and rescues (ישׁע) the seven daughters of the Midianite priest from the rogue shepherds. Elsewhere this verb is used most commonly to refer to what Yahweh does for his people (e.g., Exod. 14:30; Num. 10:9; Deut. 20:4). The resolution includes the provision of water as well for their physical needs (וַיַּשְׁקְ אֶת־צֹאנָם).

FOR THE JOURNEY

As a child, Moses requires saving, but after he grows up, he finds himself in a position to save others. He first rescues a Hebrew laborer from a brutal Egyptian taskmaster and then intervenes between another Hebrew victim and a belligerent countryman. After his life is threatened and he flees Egypt, Moses intercedes again, this time on behalf of a group of Midianite women and their sheep. His status as a type of proto-savior for individual Hebrews, non-Hebrews, and even animals anticipates his future part in the redemption of God's people.

Moses's actions also emulate his later roles in Israel's deliverance from Egypt. He serves as a leader for the fledgling people and as an arbiter of internal disputes (Exod. 18). He stands up against the aggression of outside groups (17:8–13) and leads the Israelites through the desert while seeking out water for them (15:22–27; 17:1–7). Eventually, Moses will return to this same territory with the Israelites and worship Yahweh in the wilderness (3:1, 12).

The salvation Moses experiences and his attempts at saving others in his youth hint at what is to come. God works through his chosen human agent to bring about redemption, build his people, establish his kingdom, and accomplish his miraculous acts.

ANSWER KEY

1. *Parse:* (1) וַתָּבֹאנָה (Qal *wayyiqtol* 3FP בוא "enter"). (2) וַתִּדְלֶנָה (Qal *wayyiqtol* 3FP דלה "draw water"). (3) וַתְּמַלֶּאנָה (Piel *wayyiqtol* 3FP מלא "fill"). (4) לְהַשְׁקוֹת (PREP + Hiphil INF CSTR שקה "give drink"). (5) וַיְגָרְשׁוּם (Piel *wayyiqtol* 3MP גרש "drive out" + 3MP SF). (6) וַיּוֹשִׁעָן (Hiphil *wayyiqtol* 3MS ישע "rescue" + 3FP SF). (7) וַיַּשְׁקְ (Hiphil *wayyiqtol* 3MS שקה "give water").

2. *Identify:* (A) The successive clauses with וַיֵּשֶׁב in verse 15 locate Moses's sojourn in the land of Midian ("to dwell") and position him beside a known water source ("to sit"). (B) The construct phrase צֹאן אֲבִיהֶן refers to a group of small herd animals.

3. *Translate:* "Moses fled from Pharaoh's authority. He dwelt in the land of Midian and sat down by its well. As it turned out, there was a Midianite priest who had seven daughters. They came, drew water, and filled the watering troughs to give water to their father's sheep. The shepherds came and drove them away, but Moses stood up, rescued them, and gave water to their sheep."

DAY 58: EXODUS 2:18–20

STEP ONE: **Read** aloud the text at least five times.

וַתָּבֹ֙אנָה֙ אֶל־רְעוּאֵ֣ל אֲבִיהֶ֔ן וַיֹּ֕אמֶר מַדּ֛וּעַ מִהַרְתֶּ֥ן בֹּ֖א הַיּֽוֹם׃
¹⁹וַתֹּאמַ֕רְןָ אִ֣ישׁ מִצְרִ֔י הִצִּילָ֖נוּ מִיַּ֣ד הָרֹעִ֑ים וְגַם־דָּלֹ֤ה דָלָה֙ לָ֔נוּ
וַיַּ֖שְׁקְ אֶת־הַצֹּֽאן׃ ²⁰וַיֹּ֥אמֶר אֶל־בְּנֹתָ֖יו וְאַיּ֑וֹ לָ֤מָּה זֶּה֙ עֲזַבְתֶּ֣ן
אֶת־הָאִ֔ישׁ קִרְאֶ֥ן ל֖וֹ וְיֹ֥אכַל לָֽחֶם׃

STEP TWO: **Parse** the following verbs.

	Stem	Conj.	Pers.	Gend.	Numb.	Root	Trans.
(1) וַתָּבֹ֙אנָה֙							
(2) מִהַרְתֶּ֥ן							
(3) וַתֹּאמַ֕רְןָ							
(4) הִצִּילָ֖נוּ							
(5) דָּלֹ֤ה							
(6) וַיַּ֖שְׁקְ							
(7) עֲזַבְתֶּ֣ן							
(8) קִרְאֶ֥ן							
(9) וְיֹ֥אכַל							

STEP THREE: **Identify** the following.

A. Who or what is the subject of the FP verbs (e.g., וַתָּבֹ֙אנָה֙)?

B. What does the metaphor יַד הָרֹעִים mean?

C. Who is the referent of the 3MS suffix (וְאַיּ֑וֹ)?

STEP FOUR: **Translate** the text into understandable English.

VOCABULARY

רְעוּאֵל   Reuel

מַדּוּעַ   why?

מהר   Piel: hurry, (come) quickly

מִצְרִי   Egyptian

רעה   Qal: shepherd, graze; pasture; feed

דלה   Qal: draw (water)

אֵי   where? (+ 3MS SF, אַיּוֹ)

STEP FIVE: **Notice** significant exegetical insights.

- **מְהַרְתֶּן בֹּא**: The sequence of מהר and an infinitive construct is a fairly common construction (e.g., Gen. 18:7; 27:20; 41:32; Exod. 10:16; 12:33). It indicates expediency and urgency in undertaking the second verbal action.

- **אִישׁ מִצְרִי**: Many have speculated about the identification of Moses as an Egyptian. His appearance, clothing, or language could have given him away. Perhaps, more importantly, the detail is relevant here because he is a foreigner and unknown to this Midianite family. What's more, the identification marks a literary connection and reminder about the Egyptian man whom Moses killed (Exod. 2:11–14).

- **קִרְאֶן לוֹ וְיֹאכַל לָחֶם**: An imperative followed by a (*waw* +) prefix conjugation provides both a command and a resulting purpose statement. They are to extend a request to join the family to eat.

FOR THE JOURNEY

The interaction between Reuel and his daughters illuminates the impact of Moses's actions. His deeds were no ordinary involvement or expected intervention. The daughters were so surprised by his altruistic intervention, effective liberation, and compassionate response of drawing water that they immediately rushed back to their father.

Reuel is also stunned by their hasty return and astounding abandonment of their rescuer. The back-and-forth dialogue and brief replies summarize the basic events. A foreigner delivered them from danger and provided for the herd. His questions give a sense that deserting this foreigner was impolite and undignified. Proper decorum—even apart from his role as their deliverer—assumed the care for the stranger. How much more should they have extended hospitality to the one that acted to save them?

ANSWER KEY

1. *Parse:* (1) וַתָּבֹאנָה (Qal *wayyiqtol* 3FP בוא "enter"). (2) מִהַרְתֶּן (Piel SC 2FP מהר "act hastily"). (3) וַתֹּאמַרְןָ (Qal *wayyiqtol* 3FP אמר "say"). (4) הִצִּילָנוּ (Hiphil SC 3MS נצל "save" + 1CP SF). (5) דָּלֹה (Qal INF ABS דלה "draw water"). (6) וַיַּשְׁקְ (Hiphil *wayyiqtol* 3MS שקה "give water"). (7) עֲזַבְתֶּן (Qal SC 2FP עזב "abandon"). (8) קְרֶאןָ (Qal IMV FP קרא "call"). (9) וְיֹאכַל (Qal *wayyiqtol* 3MS אכל "eat").

2. *Identify:* (A) The subject of the FP verbs (וַתָּבֹאנָה) is the "seven daughters" (שֶׁבַע בָּנוֹת) of the Midianite priest (v. 16). (B) The metaphor יַד הָרֹעִים describes the shepherds' dominance and the powerlessness of the daughters to counter their influence. (C) The referent of the 3MS suffix (וְאַיּוֹ) is אִישׁ מִצְרִי (i.e., Moses).

3. *Translate:* "[The daughters] went to their father Reuel. He said, 'How come you rushed back already?' They said, 'An Egyptian man delivered us from the hand of the shepherds. He even drew up water for us and gave water to the sheep.' He said to his daughters, 'So where is he? Why have you abandoned this man? Invite him to dinner!'"

DAY 59: EXODUS 2:21–22

STEP ONE: **Read** aloud the text at least five times.

וַיּ֣וֹאֶל מֹשֶׁ֔ה לָשֶׁ֖בֶת אֶת־הָאִ֑ישׁ וַיִּתֵּ֛ן אֶת־צִפֹּרָ֥ה בִתּ֖וֹ
לְמֹשֶֽׁה: ²²וַתֵּ֣לֶד בֵּ֔ן וַיִּקְרָ֥א אֶת־שְׁמ֖וֹ גֵּרְשֹׁ֑ם כִּ֣י אָמַ֔ר גֵּ֣ר
הָיִ֔יתִי בְּאֶ֖רֶץ נָכְרִיָּֽה:

STEP TWO: **Parse** the following verbs.

	Stem	Conj.	Pers.	Gend.	Numb.	Root	Trans.
(1) וַיּ֣וֹאֶל							
(2) לָשֶׁ֖בֶת							
(3) וַתֵּ֣לֶד							
(4) הָיִ֔יתִי							

STEP THREE: **Identify** the following.

A. What is the function of the initial element of אֶת־הָאִ֑ישׁ?

B. Who is הָאִ֑ישׁ?

STEP FOUR: **Translate** the text into understandable English.

VOCABULARY

יאל Hiphil: be willing; decide
צִפֹּרָה Zipporah
גֵּרְשֹׁם Gershom
גֵּר sojourner
נָכְרִי foreign

STEP FIVE: **Notice** significant exegetical insights.

- וַיּוֹאֶל מֹשֶׁה לָשֶׁבֶת אֶת־הָאִישׁ: Moses determines to stay with the Midianite priest and his daughters. He is integrated into the household through marriage and occupation (3:1). Eventually, he will ask for his father-in-law's blessing to return to his people (4:18–20).

- וַיִּתֵּן אֶת־צִפֹּרָה בִתּוֹ לְמֹשֶׁה: The idiom of "giving a daughter" is enshrined in the traditional English ceremony of matrimony, with the officiant asking: "Who giveth this woman to be married to this man?" Similar Hebrew expressions for marriage are found in Gen. 29:26; Judg. 21:1; 1 Chron. 2:35; Dan. 11:17.

- בְּאֶרֶץ נָכְרִיָּה: The foreign land refers to Midian (v. 15). The land of Moses's birth is Egypt. He spends decades away as a sojourner before answering the call of God to deliver his people from Egypt to their own land (Exod. 3:8). Eventually, he will return with the Israelites to this land and the mountain of God (3:12)

FOR THE JOURNEY

Even while it may seem that the main story of divine redemption is on hold or faltering, God is rescuing and drawing others into his story in unexpected ways.

Like his ancestors Abraham, Jacob, and Joseph, Moses travels into a distant land and is separated for a prolonged period from his extended relatives. In what appears to be a redemptive hiatus, Yahweh acts through his human agent to rescue other people along the way. Part of this recurring story includes God's chosen agent receiving hospitality from curious sources as well forming a family in a foreign place.

Moses's story follows this familiar pattern. Moses prospers in Midian. Reuel provides him safe harbor. He marries Zipporah and has two sons (Exod. 18:3–4). Yet he still longs for his home and his people. Gershom's name signifies Moses's yearning to be in a familiar land with the people he loves. Amid Moses's eventual return to Egypt, Zipporah intervenes to save his life (4:24–26). As he is away, his wife and children find refuge with their Midianite family (18:2–6). His father-in-law celebrates Israel's redemption upon hearing of Yahweh's miraculous salvation (18:7–10) and offers Yahweh exclusive worship (18:11–12). He advises Moses wisely (18:13–26) but does not join the Israelites in their trek to the promised land (Num. 10:29–32).

All told, Yahweh acts providentially to prepare and provide for Moses in Midian. He acts to save the vulnerable in a foreign land and to multiply his people. Non-Israelites become a vital part of God's redemption, and they respond with worship.

ANSWER KEY

1. *Parse:* (1) וַיּוֹאֶל (Hiphil *wayyiqtol* 3ms יאל "decide"). (2) לָשֶׁבֶת (PREP + Qal INF CSTR ישׁב "dwell"). (3) וַתֵּלֶד (Qal *wayyiqtol* 3FS ילד "give birth"). (4) הָיִיתִי (Qal SC 1CS היה "be").

2. *Identify:* (A) The initial element of the phrase אֶת־הָאִישׁ is the preposition ("with"). Without suffixes, the preposition is identical in form to the definite direct-object marker (e.g. אֶת־צִפֹּרָה). (B) הָאִישׁ refers to Reuel (Exod. 2:18).

3. *Translate:* "Moses determined to stay with the man. He gave Zipporah his daughter to Moses, and she had a son. He called his name Gershom because he said, 'I am a refugee in a foreign land.'"

DAY 60: EXODUS 2:23–25

STEP ONE: **Read** aloud the text at least five times.

וַיְהִי֩ בַיָּמִ֨ים הָרַבִּ֜ים הָהֵ֗ם וַיָּ֙מָת֙ מֶ֣לֶךְ מִצְרַ֔יִם וַיֵּאָנְח֧וּ
בְנֵֽי־יִשְׂרָאֵ֛ל מִן־הָעֲבֹדָ֖ה וַיִּזְעָ֑קוּ וַתַּ֧עַל שַׁוְעָתָ֛ם אֶל־הָאֱלֹהִ֖ים
מִן־הָעֲבֹדָֽה׃ ²⁴וַיִּשְׁמַ֥ע אֱלֹהִ֖ים אֶת־נַאֲקָתָ֑ם וַיִּזְכֹּ֤ר אֱלֹהִים֙
אֶת־בְּרִית֔וֹ אֶת־אַבְרָהָ֖ם אֶת־יִצְחָ֥ק וְאֶֽת־יַעֲקֹֽב׃ ²⁵וַיַּ֥רְא
אֱלֹהִ֖ים אֶת־בְּנֵ֣י יִשְׂרָאֵ֑ל וַיֵּ֖דַע אֱלֹהִֽים׃

STEP TWO: **Parse** the following verbs.

	Stem	Conj.	Pers.	Gend.	Numb.	Root	Trans.
(1) וַיֵּאָנְחוּ							
(2) וַתַּ֫עַל							

STEP THREE: **Identify** the following.

A. What is the sense of the prepositional phrase מִן־הָעֲבֹדָה?

_____

STEP FOUR: **Translate** the text into understandable English.

_____

_____

VOCABULARY

אנח   Niphal: groan, sigh

עֲבֹדָה   work

זעק   Qal: cry (out), call (for help)

שַׁוְעָה   cry (+ 3MP SF שַׁוְעָתָם)

נְאָקָה   groan (+ 3MP SF נַאֲקָתָם)

STEP FIVE: **Notice** significant exegetical insights.

- וַיְהִי בַיָּמִים הָרַבִּים הָהֵם: The initial construction of וַיְהִי with the temporal phrase marks a chronological time stamp connecting the previous account with the following sequence of events. "In those many days" (בַיָּמִים הָרַבִּים הָהֵם) designates both the extended period when Moses was in Midian and the simultaneous events occurring in Egypt described in these verses.

- הָעֲבֹדָה: The labor of the Israelites is framed in the context of a new king (cf. 1:8) who is just as unjust. While God blessed Israel, Egypt oppressed them (1:12–14). Israel's helpless cry brings God's involvement into their powerlessness. God will intervene to end their slavery and rescue them! Throughout the Scriptures, Yahweh declares that he is on the side of the weak and disadvantaged. And he promises to come to the aid of those who depend on him (Isa. 30:19).

- וַיִּשְׁמַע . . . וַיִּזְכֹּר . . . וַיַּרְא . . . וַיֵּדַע: This series of divine actions both acknowledges Yahweh's awareness of Israel's bondage and gives the basis on which he will act on behalf of his people. God (אֱלֹהִים) is the expressed subject of each verb. The end of chapter 2 marks a turning point in the oppression of God's people. Their wait is over. Redemption is near. In Exod. 6, God reassures Moses of his plans by repeating these same notions: "I have heard Israel's groan" (v. 5), "I have remembered my covenant" (v. 5), "you will see what I will do to Pharaoh" (v. 1), and "you will know that I am Yahweh your God, who is bringing you out from Egyptian toil" (v. 7).

FOR THE JOURNEY

Yahweh's covenant is an unalterable guarantee. But from the human perspective, the promises can appear, at times, to be anything but certain. During their Egypt enslavement, Israel's identity had been challenged, their sons killed, and their dignity wiped out. Cries for mercy were ignored. No sympathy occurred, and no rescue materialized. Their toil and pain amounted to tacit sacrifice to a God who must be either absent or impotent.

As months lengthened to years, years to decades, and decades to centuries, all hope must have been lost. Yahweh had not heard their cries. He had forgotten them. Even those who tried to intervene to bring redemption—like a young Moses—were driven into exile in fear of Pharaoh.

But the older folks recalled a distant prophecy and passed along a whispered account of a frightful promise. Egypt's supremacy was not unlimited. Israel would be delivered. A land of promise would be theirs. Judgment and reward would come in the fourth generation (Gen. 15:13). Yet, as four centuries had passed, hope seemed distant.

Had Yahweh even noticed their pain? How much longer would Yahweh delay? Were his promises still sure?

ANSWER KEY

1. *Parse:* (1) וַיֵּאָנְחוּ (Niphal *wayyiqtol* 3MP אנח "groan"). (2) וַתַּעַל (Qal *wayyiqtol* 3FS עלה "go up").

2. *Identify:* (A) The prepositional phrase מִן־הָעֲבֹדָה ("from the work") identifies the basis, or grounds, of the people's beleaguered cries.

3. *Translate:* "In the ensuing days, the Egyptian king died. The Israelites groaned because of their bondage and cried out, and their call came up to God because of their bondage. God heard their distraught plea and remembered his covenant with Abraham, Isaac, and Jacob. God saw the Israelites, and God knew."

Journey 3

EXPANDING

ROUTE 9

Ruth 1:1–2:1

STEP ONE: **Read** aloud the text at least five times.

וַיְהִ֗י בִּימֵי֙ שְׁפֹ֣ט הַשֹּׁפְטִ֔ים וַיְהִ֥י רָעָ֖ב בָּאָ֑רֶץ וַיֵּ֨לֶךְ אִ֜ישׁ מִבֵּ֧ית
לֶ֣חֶם יְהוּדָ֗ה לָגוּר֙ בִּשְׂדֵ֣י מוֹאָ֔ב ה֥וּא וְאִשְׁתּ֖וֹ וּשְׁנֵ֥י בָנָֽיו׃

STEP TWO: **Parse** the following verbs.

	Stem	Conj.	Pers.	Gend.	Numb.	Root	Trans.
(1) הַשֹּׁפְטִים							
(2) וַיֵּלֶךְ							

STEP THREE: **Translate** the text into understandable English.

> ### VOCABULARY
>
> רָעָב   hunger; famine
> בֵּית לֶחֶם   Bethlehem
> גּוּר   Qal: live as a foreigner or displaced person
> מוֹאָב   Moab

STEP FOUR: **Notice** significant exegetical insights.

- וַיְהִי: The clause-initial construction וַיְהִי serves several functions in narrative. With a temporal phrase (בִּימֵי שְׁפֹט הַשֹּׁפְטִים), it marks the setting for the following sequence of events. With a simple subject-predicate clause (רָעָב בָּאָרֶץ), it specifies a situation that frames the reader's conception of the forthcoming account.

- וַיֵּלֶךְ . . . לָגוּר: Fleeing political upheaval and food scarcity as a refugee is an all-too-familiar pattern. Similar references to escaping famine occur in Genesis (12:10; 26:1; 43:1; 47:4) and 2 Kings 8:1–2. The book of Judges mentions several individuals who leave their homeland and resettle elsewhere. Notably, two of these are connected with Bethlehem: a Levite in Judg. 17 fled from Bethlehem of Judah (Judg. 17:8–9), and a woman affiliated with another displaced Levite was from Bethlehem (Judg. 19:1).

- הוּא וְאִשְׁתּוֹ וּשְׁנֵי בָנָיו: While the 3MS subject of וַיֵּלֶךְ focuses the topic on the yet-to-be-named man, the following noun phrase clarifies that he is not alone in fleeing the famine in his homeland. The members of his household—particularly his wife—are, in fact, more noteworthy in the unfolding of the story. She takes a significant role in the ensuing narrative and the book's concluding lineage (Ruth 4:17).

FOR THE JOURNEY

The setting of the book of Ruth is anything but inconsequential. The circumstances and locations elicit important ideas and concepts from Scripture. Great significance is found in considering the many connections both without and within the story.

The time of the judges is characterized by widespread unfaithfulness to Yahweh. His people repeatedly abandon the covenant. Their leaders do not fear God or encourage Israel to follow God's path. Because of their disloyalty, God hands them over to their enemies (Judg. 2:14–15), and each tribe finds itself under the tyranny of Canaanite oppressors. One could reasonably ask: Were there any who were faithful to Yahweh during these days? The book of Judges contains few candidates. The story of Ruth, however, is an account of the faithful actions of not only

Israelites but also non-Israelites (i.e., Moabites, Gen. 19:30–37), who together constitute the family of promise.

Famine in the land flowing with milk and honey draws particular attention to the covenant curses. Bethlehem—the "House of Bread"— lacks bread. Moses had warned of the reversal of God's favor should the people be disobedient (Deut. 28:15–68), and the alienation and hardship experienced due to the unfaithfulness of the Judges genera- tion seem to bear this out (v. 48). The people had rejected Yahweh and his covenant. Yet hope remained because God was faithful. Bethlehem of Judah would ultimately be known not as a place of curse or death (Gen. 35:19–20) but as a place of restoration and hope (Ruth 4:12; Mic. 5:1; Matt. 2:6).

ANSWER KEY

1. *Parse:* (1) הַשֹּׁפְטִים (DEF ART + Qal ACT PTCL MP שפט "judge"). (2) וַיֵּלֶךְ (Qal *wayyiqtol* 3MS הלך "go").

2. *Translate:* "In the time when the judges judged and a famine was in the land, a man left Bethlehem of Judah with his wife and two sons to reside temporarily in the fields of Moab."

DAY 62: RUTH 1:2–3

STEP ONE: **Read** aloud the text at least five times.

וְשֵׁם הָאִישׁ אֱלִימֶלֶךְ וְשֵׁם אִשְׁתּוֹ נָעֳמִי וְשֵׁם שְׁנֵי־בָנָיו ׀ מַחְלוֹן
וְכִלְיוֹן אֶפְרָתִים מִבֵּית לֶחֶם יְהוּדָה וַיָּבֹאוּ שְׂדֵי־מוֹאָב
וַיִּהְיוּ־שָׁם: ³וַיָּמָת אֱלִימֶלֶךְ אִישׁ נָעֳמִי וַתִּשָּׁאֵר הִיא וּשְׁנֵי בָנֶיהָ:

STEP TWO: **Parse** the following verbs.

	Stem	Conj.	Pers.	Gend.	Numb.	Root	Trans.
(1) וַיָּבֹאוּ							
(2) וַתִּשָּׁאֵר							

STEP THREE: **Translate** the text into understandable English.

_____

_____

> ### VOCABULARY
>
> אֱלִימֶלֶךְ   Elimelech
> נָעֳמִי   Naomi
> מַחְלוֹן   Mahlon
> כִּלְיוֹן   Chilion
> אֶפְרָתִי   Ephrathite
> בֵּית לֶחֶם   Bethlehem
> מוֹאָב   Moab
> שׁאר   Niphal: be left over

STEP FOUR: **Notice** significant exegetical insights.

- וְשֵׁם: Prior to continuing the narrative, the family members' names are listed. They follow the order presented in the previous noun phrase (הוּא וְאִשְׁתּוֹ וּשְׁנֵי בָנָיו) "he, his wife, and his two sons"). Each presages an important element of the forthcoming story (see "For the Journey" below).

- אֶפְרָתִים מִבֵּית לֶחֶם יְהוּדָה: The family is identified by an eponym. The origin of the name Ephrath is uncertain but could refer to a place (Gen. 35:19; 48:7; Ruth 4:11), a matriarch (1 Chron. 2:19, 50; 4:4), or a clan (1 Sam. 17:12). The village at some point became known by two names: Ephrathah and Bethlehem (Mic. 5:1). The latter name, Bethlehem, describes two locations—one in the tribal allotment of Judah (south of Jerusalem, the birthplace of Jesus; Matt. 2:1; Luke 2:4) and another one in Zebulun (Josh. 19:15).

- אֱלִימֶלֶךְ אִישׁ נָעֳמִי . . . הִיא וּשְׁנֵי בָנֶיהָ: While the book begins with Naomi described as the man's wife (אִשְׁתּוֹ) and their children as his sons (שְׁנֵי בָנָיו), verse 3 portrays Elimelech as "Naomi's husband" and their children as "her two sons." This change highlights Naomi's central role in the subsequent story. She is now the leader of the family.

FOR THE JOURNEY

The names of this Ephrathite family anticipate important details in the story. Generally, names serve as unique identifiers of persons. Hebrew names are readily evocative, like the English names Joy, Hope, Grace, Faith, Rose, Olive, May, Scarlet, Willow, Brook, River, Archer, Royal, Dean, Sunny, and Christian. Unlike most proper nouns in English, nearly all names of Hebrew characters have transparent meaning.

Mahlon and *Chilion* may refer to the physical fragility of the two sons as "Weak" and "Sickly." Alternatively, their names could signify the difficulties leading to the family's need to flee their homeland. They had experienced "Affliction" (חלה, Deut. 29:21) and "Catastrophe" (כִּלָּיוֹן, Deut. 28:65), but their troubles were not restricted to the land of Israel. In exile, every male family member dies, leaving a precarious future for the women left behind.

Bethlehem ("House of Bread") anticipates provision, yet the family experiences food scarcity. Attempting to escape insecurity, their situation worsens in the region of Moab. Upon arriving back in the land, grain and food production is the backdrop for the restoration of their household (e.g., Ruth 1:6, 22; 2:2–3, 17–18, 23; 3:3). The House of Bread would be restored.

Naomi was known as "Pleasant" prior to leaving Bethlehem. When she returns without her husband or sons, she identifies herself instead as "Bitter" (מָרָא, Ruth 1:20–21), but her story takes yet another turn and ends with blessing and the reinstatement of her original name (4:14, 17).

Finally, *Elimelech* points to the religious and political turmoil in the time of the judges. "My God is King" stands in opposition to the ominous concluding refrain, "there was no king in Israel" (Judg. 17:6; 18:1; 19:1; 21:25). Perhaps his parents hoped for a time when Yahweh would be established as Israel's king and reign righteously over Israel. The fulfillment of that desire would be a part of his story (Ruth 4:17).

ANSWER KEY

1. *Parse:* (1) וַיָּבֹאוּ (Qal *wayyiqtol* 3MP בוא "enter"). (2) וַתִּשָּׁאֵר (Niphal *wayyiqtol* 3FS שאר "remain").

2. *Translate:* "The man's name was Elimelech, and his wife's name was Naomi. The names of his two sons were Mahlon and Chilion. They were Ephrathites from Bethlehem of Judah. They entered the fields of Moab and stayed there. Then Naomi's husband, Elimelech, died. She remained [in Moab] with her two sons."

DAY 63: RUTH 1:4–5

STEP ONE: **Read** aloud the text at least five times.

וַיִּשְׂאוּ לָהֶם נָשִׁים מֹאֲבִיּוֹת שֵׁם הָאַחַת עָרְפָּה וְשֵׁם הַשֵּׁנִית
רוּת וַיֵּשְׁבוּ שָׁם כְּעֶשֶׂר שָׁנִים: ⁵וַיָּמוּתוּ גַם־שְׁנֵיהֶם מַחְלוֹן
וְכִלְיוֹן וַתִּשָּׁאֵר הָאִשָּׁה מִשְּׁנֵי יְלָדֶיהָ וּמֵאִישָׁהּ:

STEP TWO: **Parse** the following verb.

	Stem	Conj.	Pers.	Gend.	Numb.	Root	Trans.
(1) וַתִּשָּׁאֵר							

STEP THREE: **Translate** the text into understandable English.

_____

_____

VOCABULARY

מֹאֲבִי   Moabite

עָרְפָּה   Orpah

שֵׁנִי   second

רוּת   Ruth

מַחְלוֹן   Mahlon

כִּלְיוֹן   Chilion

שׁאר   Niphal: be left over

יֶלֶד   child; boy; youth

STEP FOUR: **Notice** significant exegetical insights.

• שֵׁם הָאַחַת עָרְפָּה וְשֵׁם הַשֵּׁנִית רוּת: The wives' names are not presented in accordance with the birth order of Naomi's sons (Ruth 1:2, 5, but compare 4:9). Orpah was Chilion's wife, even though she is listed first. And Mahlon is Ruth's husband (Ruth 4:10). Perhaps first and second here refers to their marriage order.

- כְּעֶשֶׂר שָׁנִים: The time frame of "about ten years" means the famine lasted a long time. Even so, Naomi had not given up hope of returning to Bethlehem (Ruth 1:6). In that decade, neither of the sons' marriages produced children. The family lineage stopped with Elimelech's sons at their deaths. Both Moabite women remained under the care of their mother-in-law, who as a widow herself was in a precarious position without a living male counterpart or heir.

- וַתִּשָּׁאֵר הָאִשָּׁה: The verb denotes more than the fact that Naomi stayed in Moab. In several contexts, שׁאר is used to indicate that someone is left alone (Deut. 3:11) or is the only remaining relative in a family (Gen. 42:38; 2 Chron. 21:17).

- מִשְּׁנֵי יְלָדֶיהָ וּמֵאִישָׁהּ: The מִן prepositions designate a privative meaning, that is, she remained "without" her two children or her husband.

FOR THE JOURNEY

A curious shift describes Naomi's sons. According to verse 3, Naomi stayed in Moab with "her two *sons*" (שְׁנֵי בָנֶיהָ). Two verses later, similar language describes their tragic death and notes that Naomi remained alone in Moab. The relational terminology, however, designates them as "her two *boys*" (שְׁנֵי יְלָדֶיהָ, v. 5). One could assume that the difference between "son" and "boy" is merely stylistic, but the rest of verse 5 is nearly identical to verse 3. This subtle variation may point to the intriguing conclusion of the story.

In Ruth 4, Naomi resurfaces and takes a central role. Yahweh intervenes and grants the formerly barren Ruth a boy with Boaz (4:13). Before the child is named, however, the Bethlehem women bless Naomi (4:14–17; cf. 1:19)! Even through exile and the hopelessness in the death of her family, Yahweh had not abandoned Naomi or withheld a promised redeemer. Her Moabite daughter-in-law Ruth saved her through covenant devotion, and Boaz would be her adopted son, providing for her in her old age.

Naomi becomes the caretaker of "the boy" (הַיֶּלֶד, 4:16). Reversing the terminology from chapter 1, the women of Bethlehem considered him to be Naomi's "son" (יֻלַּד־בֵּן לְנָעֳמִי "A son has been born to Naomi," 4:17). And the women name him Obed ("servant"). We know him as the father of Jesse, the father of King David (4:22; 1 Chron. 2:12; Matt. 1:5–6; Luke 3:32).

ANSWER KEY

1. *Parse:* (1) וַתִּשָּׁאֵר (Niphal *wayyiqtol* 3FS שאר "remain").
2. *Translate:* "They married Moabite women, one named Orpah and the other Ruth. They resided there for about ten years, and then both Mahlon and Chilion also died. The woman remained [in Moab] without her two children and her husband."

STEP ONE: Read aloud the text at least five times.

וַתָּקָם הִיא וְכַלֹּתֶיהָ וַתָּשָׁב מִשְּׂדֵי מוֹאָב כִּי שָׁמְעָה בִּשְׂדֵה
מוֹאָב כִּי־פָקַד יְהוָה אֶת־עַמּוֹ לָתֵת לָהֶם לָחֶם: ⁷וַתֵּצֵא
מִן־הַמָּקוֹם אֲשֶׁר הָיְתָה־שָׁמָּה וּשְׁתֵּי כַלֹּתֶיהָ עִמָּהּ וַתֵּלַכְנָה
בַדֶּרֶךְ לָשׁוּב אֶל־אֶרֶץ יְהוּדָה:

STEP TWO: Parse the following verbs.

	Stem	Conj.	Pers.	Gend.	Numb.	Root	Trans.
(1) וַתָּקָם							
(2) וַתָּשָׁב							
(3) שָׁמְעָה							
(4) וַתֵּצֵא							
(5) הָיְתָה							
(6) וַתֵּלַכְנָה							

STEP THREE: Translate the text into understandable English.

_____

_____

VOCABULARY

כַּלָּה   bride; daughter-in-law (PL + 3FS SF כַּלֹּתֶיהָ)

STEP FOUR: Notice significant exegetical insights.

- וַתָּקָם הִיא וְכַלֹּתֶיהָ וַתָּשָׁב . . . וַתֵּצֵא . . . וַתֵּלַכְנָה: Naomi continues to be the main actor until the last clause of verse 7 when the mainline narrative verb changes to the feminine plural form. Up to that point, her daughters-in-law accompany her but are repeatedly given secondary agency. The question becomes: How devoted are Naomi's daughters-in-law? Are they going to leave their homeland

and family? Once they are on the way together, all three women are given equal agency for their travels. This motivates Naomi's prolonged and sorrowful goodbye (vv. 8–14).

- לָתֵת לָהֶם לָחֶם: These three words create assonance at the end of this important statement. These sound pairings hearken back to the Hebrew name of Bethlehem (בֵּית לֶחֶם), reminding the listener of the village's previous lack of bread (לֶחֶם). After ten years, Yahweh's return visit signals a relief to punishment and the provision of sustenance in the land of Israel (Deut. 28:5, 8).

FOR THE JOURNEY

The verb פקד takes a staggering assortment of translation values in English. A partial list includes "to visit, to remember, to investigate, to muster, to miss, to punish, to number." We should not try to read all these meanings into each occurrence; context must determine which sense is in view. In Ruth 1:7, for instance, Yahweh is *not* visiting, investigating, mustering, missing, punishing, and numbering his people by giving them food (פָּקַד יְהוָה אֶת־עַמּוֹ). Rather, the action of providing bread is a move of divine generosity and grace. English translations render the narrator's explanation in various ways to elicit this notion: Yahweh "paid attention to" (CSB), "had visited" (ESV), "had considered" (NRSV), "had come to the aid of" (NIV), "had taken note of" (Tanakh), and "had shown concern for" (NET) his people.

While translations attend to the setting and situation, other nuances of language can be, at times, lost in the choices of the translators. For instance, the alliteration of לָתֵת לָהֶם לָחֶם and בֵּית לֶחֶם is absent in English: "to give to them bread" (see note above). Any reverberation with the earlier famine is restricted to a notional or semantic reversal. And the irony of the House of Bread again having bread is at best relegated to a footnote. The Hebrew text arguably builds on this link with the verb פקד.

Because Yahweh's visiting of this people could convey either a positive or negative outcome, the reader would connect the curse described in the initial verses of the book with Yahweh returning the blessing in this narrative description.

ANSWER KEY

1. *Parse:* (1) וַתָּקָם (Qal *wayyiqtol* 3FS קום "arise"). (2) וַתָּשָׁב (Qal *wayyiqtol* 3FS שוב "return"). (3) שָׁמְעָה (Qal sc 3FS שמע). (4) וַתֵּצֵא (Qal *wayyiqtol* 3FS יצא "leave"). (5) הָיְתָה (Qal sc 3FS היה "be"). (6) וַתֵּלַכְנָה (Qal *wayyiqtol* 3FP הלך "go").

2. *Translate:* "[Naomi] arose with her daughters-in-law to return from the fields of Moab because she had heard that Yahweh arranged to give his people bread. She left the place where she was, her two daughters-in-law were with her, and they traveled along the way to go back to the land of Judah."

DAY 65: RUTH 1:8-10

STEP ONE: **Read** aloud the text at least five times.

וַתֹּאמֶר נָעֳמִי לִשְׁתֵּי כַלֹּתֶיהָ לֵכְנָה שֹּׁבְנָה אִשָּׁה לְבֵית
אִמָּהּ יַעֲשֶׂה יְהוָה עִמָּכֶם חֶסֶד כַּאֲשֶׁר עֲשִׂיתֶם עִם־הַמֵּתִים
וְעִמָּדִי: ⁹יִתֵּן יְהוָה לָכֶם וּמְצֶאןָ מְנוּחָה אִשָּׁה בֵּית אִישָׁהּ
וַתִּשַּׁק לָהֶן וַתִּשֶּׂאנָה קוֹלָן וַתִּבְכֶּינָה: ¹⁰וַתֹּאמַרְנָה־לָּהּ
כִּי־אִתָּךְ נָשׁוּב לְעַמֵּךְ:

STEP TWO: **Parse** the following verbs.

	Stem	Conj.	Pers.	Gend.	Numb.	Root	Trans.
(1) וַתֹּאמֶר							
(2) לֵכְנָה							
(3) שֹּׁבְנָה							
(4) יַעֲשֶׂה							
(5) עֲשִׂיתֶם							
(6) הַמֵּתִים							
(7) יִתֵּן							
(8) וּמְצֶאןָ							
(9) וַתִּשַּׁק							
(10) וַתִּשֶּׂאנָה							
(11) וַתִּבְכֶּינָה							
(12) וַתֹּאמַרְנָה							
(13) נָשׁוּב							

STEP THREE: **Translate** the text into understandable English.

_____

_____

VOCABULARY

נָעֳמִי   Naomi

כַּלָּה   daughter-in-law

עִמָּדִי   with (עִם + 1cs sf)

מְנוּחָה   rest; resting place

STEP FOUR: **Notice** significant exegetical insights.

- יַעֲשֶׂה יְהוָה עִמָּכֶם חֶסֶד: The Tiberian Masoretic text preserves a reading of the verb that is different from its spelling. The reading underlying the consonants is יַעֲשֶׂה "he will do" (Ruth 1:17), but the Tiberian tradition reads the form as a third-person jussive: יַעַשׂ "may he do." The subtle distinction affects the strength of the assertion regarding how (or if) Yahweh will respond. The latter reading could have arisen to preserve divine agency in Naomi's assertion, since the jussive would be understood as less obligatory than the imperfective.

- אִשָּׁה לְבֵית אִמָּהּ . . . אִשָּׁה בֵּית אִישָׁהּ: Naomi urges her daughters-in-law to return each to her mother's household. This statement continues the matriarchal theme of the book of Ruth. It may also acknowledge the wider connection of food scarcity and endemic mortality. Could it be that both daughters-in-law had experienced the loss of their husbands *and* their fathers? The hope is that Yahweh will look kindly on them and that they will each find rest in their (future) husband's household. The inference is that each widow would marry a Moabite husband. Naomi releases them from any duty they might feel toward their Hebrew husbands or mother-in-law.

- וַתִּשַּׁק לָהֶן: A kiss contains several culturally significant connotations. It can be used as a gesture of fond appreciation in a greeting (Gen. 33:4; Exod. 4:27), worship (1 Kings 19:18; Hosea 13:2), and when parting ways (1 Sam. 10:1; 20:41). Naomi's final farewell includes this affectionate goodbye. The response of all three women is to weep over the regretful prospect of never seeing one another again (cf. Gen. 21:16).

FOR THE JOURNEY

Orpah and Ruth remain devoted to their widowed mother-in-law for more than a decade. Their mutual commitment continues beyond the untimely deaths of their husbands. They are not quick to abandon Naomi. They choose to journey with her to her home, to her people, even though it will mean entering a foreign country with an uncertain future far from the familiarity of their own home.

While the famine may have lifted in Bethlehem, Naomi does not imagine that the curse on her family would likewise be assuaged. She is returning only to die and be buried with her people. Her daughters-in-law would experience the same fate. She has nothing to offer them. The loyalty of Orpah and Ruth would only return more sorrow in Judah. Naomi considers the covenant incorporation of these Moabite women as a death wish. Their only hope remains in staying and marrying into a Moabite family.

Because of these realities, Naomi blesses Orpah and Ruth, acknowledges their loyalty, and releases them from any covenant responsibility they still have to her and her family. She prays that as they have done with her, so Yahweh will deal faithfully with them (Exod. 20:6; Zech. 7:9–10). Echoing the request of her relative, Boaz's mother Rahab (Josh. 2:12), Naomi entreats the favor of Yahweh on behalf of an outsider showing loyalty to the people of God. Surely he will honor such fidelity once more!

ANSWER KEY

1. *Parse:* (1) וַתֹּאמֶר (Qal *wayyiqtol* 3FS אמר "say"). (2) לֵכְנָה (Qal IMV FP הלך "go"). (3) שֹׁבְנָה (Qal IMV FP שוב "return"). (4) יַעֲשֶׂה (*Qere*: Qal JUSS 3MS עשה "do"; see step 4 above for a discussion of PC יַעֲשֶׂה). (5) עֲשִׂיתֶם (Qal SC 2FP עשה "do"). (6) הַמֵּתִים (DEF ART + Qal ACT PTCL MP מות "die"). (7) יִתֵּן (Qal JUSS 3MS נתן "give"). (8) וּמְצֶאןָ (CJ + Qal IMV FP מצא "find"). (9) וַתִּשַּׁק (Qal *wayyiqtol* 3FS נשק "kiss"). (10) וַתִּשֶּׂאנָה (Qal *wayyiqtol* 3FP נשא "lift"). (11) וַתִּבְכֶּינָה (Qal *wayyiqtol* 3FP בכה "weep"). (12) וַתֹּאמַרְנָה (Qal *wayyiqtol* 3FP אמר "say"). (13) נָשׁוּב (Qal PC 1CP שוב "return").

2. *Translate:* "Naomi said to her two daughters-in-law, 'Go back each of you to her own mother's house. May Yahweh treat you faithfully as you have treated the dead and me. May Yahweh allow each of you to find rest in the house of a husband.' She kissed them, and they cried aloud and wept. They said to her, 'Absolutely not! Allow us to return with you to your people.'"

DAY 66: RUTH 1:11–13

STEP ONE: **Read** aloud the text at least five times.

וַתֹּאמֶר נָעֳמִי שֹׁבְנָה בְנֹתַי לָמָּה תֵלַכְנָה עִמִּי הַעוֹד־לִי בָנִים
בְּמֵעַי וְהָיוּ לָכֶם לַאֲנָשִׁים: 12שֹׁבְנָה בְנֹתַי לֵכְןָ כִּי זָקַנְתִּי מִהְיוֹת
לְאִישׁ כִּי אָמַרְתִּי יֶשׁ־לִי תִקְוָה גַּם הָיִיתִי הַלַּיְלָה לְאִישׁ וְגַם
יָלַדְתִּי בָנִים: 13הֲלָהֵן| תְּשַׂבֵּרְנָה עַד אֲשֶׁר יִגְדָּלוּ הֲלָהֵן תֵּעָגֵנָה
לְבִלְתִּי הֱיוֹת לְאִישׁ אַל בְּנֹתַי כִּי־מַר־לִי מְאֹד מִכֶּם כִּי־יָצְאָה
בִי יַד־יְהוָה:

STEP TWO: **Parse** the following verbs.

	Stem	Conj.	Pers.	Gend.	Numb.	Root	Trans.
(1) וַתֹּאמֶר							
(2) שֹׁבְנָה							
(3) תֵלַכְנָה							
(4) וְהָיוּ							
(5) לֵכְןָ							
(6) תְּשַׂבֵּרְנָה							
(7) תֵּעָגֵנָה							
(8) יָצְאָה							

STEP THREE: **Translate** the text into understandable English.

_____

_____

VOCABULARY

מֵעֶה   internal parts, entrails (PL + 1CS SF מֵעַי)

לָכֶם   to you (i.e., the daughters-in-law, despite 2MP SF)

זקן   Qal: be old; grow old

יֵשׁ   there is

תִּקְוָה   hope

לָהֵן   therefore; on account of this

שׂבר   Piel: hope; wait

גדל   Qal: grow up; become strong; become great

עגן   Niphal: shut oneself off

בִּלְתִּי   no, not (+ INF)

מרר   Qal: be bitter

STEP FOUR: **Notice** significant exegetical insights.

- שֹׁבְנָה בְנֹתַי: Twice Naomi responds to the request of Orpah and Ruth to follow her (v. 10). Each time she refers to "her daughters-in-law" (כַּלֹּתֶיהָ, v. 6) with the familial address "my daughters" (בְנֹתַי, vv. 11, 12). Her pain is heightened even more on account of their covenant relationship—these women are her daughters.

- אַל בְּנֹתַי: With each directive, Naomi presents a more and more dire situation. First, her two rhetorical questions demonstrate that they have no prospect of remarrying within the family (Deut. 25:5). Second, she expounds a romantic fantasy in which she is still a young woman, yet even then they would have to wait decades before they could marry (Gen. 38:11). Naomi finally answers her own musings. "No, my daughters!" (אַל בְּנֹתַי). The categorical negative answer to her own questions and imaginings is expressed in the final address to her daughters-in-law. They must return. They must not go with her. She sees no solution (not even a miraculous one) to their predicament.

- כִּי־מַר־לִי מְאֹד מִכֶּם: Some translations render this clause as contrasting Naomi's grief with that of her daughters-in-law. This understanding is based on reading the מִן as a comparison: "It is more bitter for me than for you" (NIV). Such a statement may seem callous and overly self-absorbed. All three women have lost a spouse and are destitute! It may be better to understand

Naomi's bitterness as exponentially worse on account of the fact that (causal מִ) she cannot care for her daughters-in-law, and her disfavored condition would result in even more hardship for them ("it grieves me very much for your sakes," NKJV).

- כִּי־יָצְאָה בִי יַד־יְהוָה: The circumstances are much more dismal than they may appear. Naomi is not merely bad luck. She views her acrimonious circumstances as her destiny. It is the result of Yahweh's direct maleficence. She wants what remains of her loyal family not to continue sharing her calamitous life.

FOR THE JOURNEY

Naomi's perspective—with good reason based on her past experiences—is anything but hopeful. She does not have a husband. If she did, old age would prevent her from having sons. Even if she did miraculously have children to fulfill the duty of the brother-in-law (Gen. 38:8), Orpah and Ruth would need to wait until they were grown to establish families. As she has experienced only divine acrimony, she finds it unthinkable that God would intervene on their behalf now. Her faithful, beloved daughters-in-law are being swept away in the downpour of her disastrous life. Despite her hopelessness, Yahweh would intervene and save (cf. Isa. 59:1). And God's surprising reclamation would outpace even Naomi's most outrageous imagining.

In the final account of the book, those witnessing Boaz's request acknowledge supernatural involvement. As the kinsman-redeemer, Boaz acquires both the economic and familial responsibilities of Naomi's household (Ruth 4:9–10). Unlike his tribe's namesake Judah and his sons, however, he does not fear reprisals assigned to becoming a widow's husband (cf. Tamar, Gen. 38:6–11, 26). The people summon their collective memory to bless the women who will build the house (Ruth 4:11–12). Their poignant reminder of the lineage of Perez, his mother Tamar, and Judah (4:12; 1 Chron. 5:2) connects this story of widowhood to the promises of God and the future king of Israel (Ruth 4:18–22; Matt. 1:3–6; Luke 3:30–33).

ANSWER KEY

1. *Parse:* (1) וַתֹּאמֶר (Qal *wayyiqtol* 3FS אמר "say"). (2) שֹׁבְנָה (Qal IMV FP שוב "return"). (3) תֵּלַכְנָה (Qal PC 2FP הלך "go"). (4) וְהָיוּ (Qal *waqātal* 3CP היה "be"). (5) לֵכְןָ (Qal IMV FP הלך "go"). (6) תְּשַׂבֵּרְנָה (Piel PC 2FP שבר "wait"). (7) תֵּעָגֵנָה (Niphal PC 2FP עגן "shut off"). (8) יָצְאָה (Qal SC 3FS יצא "go out").

2. *Translate:* "Naomi said, 'Return, my daughters! Why go with me? Will I ever again have sons in my womb who could be your husbands? Return, my daughters! Go! I am too old to have a husband. Even if I said I had hope that tonight I will both have a husband and bear sons, would you want to wait until they were grown and constrain yourselves from not having a husband? No, my daughters! My bitterness is exceedingly worse on account of your [situation], for Yahweh's hand has gone out against me.'"

DAY 67: RUTH 1:14–15

STEP ONE: **Read** aloud the text at least five times.

וַתִּשֶּׂנָה קוֹלָן וַתִּבְכֶּינָה עוֹד וַתִּשַּׁק עָרְפָּה לַחֲמוֹתָהּ וְרוּת
דָּבְקָה בָּהּ: ¹⁵וַתֹּאמֶר הִנֵּה שָׁבָה יְבִמְתֵּךְ אֶל־עַמָּהּ
וְאֶל־אֱלֹהֶיהָ שׁוּבִי אַחֲרֵי יְבִמְתֵּךְ:

STEP TWO: **Parse** the following verbs.

	Stem	Conj.	Pers.	Gend.	Numb.	Root	Trans.
(1) וַתִּשֶּׂנָה							
(2) וַתִּבְכֶּינָה							
(3) וַתִּשַּׁק							
(4) דָּבְקָה							
(5) וַתֹּאמֶר							
(6) שָׁבָה							
(7) שׁוּבִי							

STEP THREE: **Translate** the text into understandable English.

> ### VOCABULARY
>
> בכה   Qal: weep
>
> נשק   Qal: kiss
>
> עָרְפָּה   Orpah
>
> חָמוֹת   mother-in-law (sg + 3fs sf חֲמוֹתָהּ)
>
> רוּת   Ruth
>
> דבק   Qal: cling, hold
>
> יְבָמָה   brother's widow, sister-in-law (+ 2fs sf יְבִמְתֵּךְ)

STEP FOUR: **Notice** significant exegetical insights.

- וַתִּשַּׁק עָרְפָּה לַחֲמוֹתָהּ וְרוּת דָּבְקָה בָּהּ: The narrative contrasts the responses of Orpah and Ruth. The grammatical alteration highlights the dissimilar reactions of the two daughters-in-law. These are not sequential events (i.e., *wayyiqtol* + *wayyiqtol*). Rather, the discontinuous series, *wayyiqtol* + subject (וַתִּשַּׁק עָרְפָּה) and *waw* + subject + *qātal* (וְרוּת דָּבְקָה), presents their actions as coinciding but with differing outcomes. Orpah's kiss signals her departure (see v. 9; also 1 Sam. 10:1; 20:41). She heeds Naomi's warning. On the other hand, Ruth is undeterred by her mother-in-law's glum outlook. She demonstrates her loyalty, refusing to leave Naomi's side (cf. 2 Sam. 20:2). The verb דבק can even express covenant faithfulness (e.g., Gen. 2:24; Deut. 10:20).

- הִנֵּה שָׁבָה יְבִמְתֵּךְ . . . שׁוּבִי אַחֲרֵי יְבִמְתֵּךְ: The same root (שׁוּב) links Orpah's response and Naomi's instruction. Naomi requests that they stop following her and both return to Moab (vv. 11–12). Starting with verse 15, the interaction is between only Naomi and Ruth. Naomi points to Orpah's earlier departure (שָׁבָה) and tells Ruth to do the same (שׁוּבִי). Ruth needs to identify with Orpah rather than with Naomi. The distance is also reflected in Naomi's switch from "my daughter" (בִּתִּי) to "your sister-in-law" (יְבִמְתֵּךְ).

FOR THE JOURNEY

Naomi describes Orpah's departure as a return to her people and her gods. "Her people" reiterates Naomi's previous command to go back to your mother's household (Ruth 1:8) and the hope that she would find peace in the house of a Moabite husband (v. 9). However, the inclusion of "her god(s)" is introduced here for the first time (v. 15). Moabite religion is not discussed previously, but several important social assumptions underlie this extension.

The commingling of a people and their god(s) was typical in ancient Near Eastern cultures. Identifying as a member of a certain people group included identifying with that people's gods. Moabites worship Chemosh, Edomites Qos, Arameans Hadad, and Babylonians Marduk. Other gods may also be recognized and venerated alongside these principal national deities. In the book of Jonah, for instance, the sailors inquire of various gods regarding the catastrophic storm. Turning to the prophet, the non-Israelites ask about his travel purpose and his regional, national, and ethnic origins: "Where are you from? What is your land? What people are you from?" (Jon. 1:7–8). Jonah's response is telling: "I am a Hebrew, and I worship Yahweh" (v. 9). By identifying his ethnicity and his deity, Jonah answers their fundamental question about who he is.

It is tempting to take the exclusive religious belief that the God of Israel is the only true god (2 Kings 5:15) and combine it with these cultural assumptions to create harmful implications. Since Israelites worship the one true God, one could conclude that all foreigners are irrevocably and inextricably pagan. Such religious exceptionalism and the strict cultural demarcation of insider and outsider, however, are challenged by many stories in the Bible (e.g., Naaman, Rahab, Zipporah, etc.). Faithfulness to Yahweh—regardless of ethnic origin—is the hallmark of a true believer! Yahweh is Israel's God, but he is also the God of anyone who follows him.

Ruth and Orpah may always be known as Moabites and widows. Their social status is unavoidable. But the more central identifier is whom each *chooses* to be her God. Orpah returns to her family's gods. But Ruth refuses consolation in her upbringing, takes the uncertain path into a foreign context, and trusts her future to Yahweh and his covenant community.

ANSWER KEY

1. *Parse:* (1) וַתִּשֶּׂ֫נָה (Qal *wayyiqtol* 3FP נשׂא "lift"). (2) וַתִּבְכֶּ֫ינָה (Qal *wayyiqtol* 3FP בכה "weep"). (3) וַתִּשַּׁק (Qal *wayyiqtol* 3FS נשׁק "kiss"). (4) דָּבְקָה (Qal sc 3FS דבק "cling"). (5) וַתֹּאמֶר (Qal *wayyiqtol* 3FS אמר "say"). (6) שָׁ֫בָה (Qal sc 3FS שׁוב "return"). (7) שׁ֫וּבִי (Qal IMV FS שׁוב "return").

2. *Translate:* "They cried aloud and wept again. Orpah kissed her mother-in-law [farewell], but Ruth stayed close to her. She said, 'Don't you see? Your sister-in-law has returned to her people and her gods. Return after your sister-in-law.'"

DAY 68: RUTH 1:16–17

STEP ONE: **Read** aloud the text at least five times.

וַתֹּאמֶר רוּת֙ אַל־תִּפְגְּעִי־בִ֔י לְעָזְבֵ֖ךְ לָשׁ֣וּב מֵאַחֲרָ֑יִךְ כִּ֠י
אֶל־אֲשֶׁ֨ר תֵּלְכִ֜י אֵלֵ֗ךְ וּבַאֲשֶׁ֤ר תָּלִ֙ינִי֙ אָלִ֔ין עַמֵּ֣ךְ עַמִּ֔י וֵאלֹהַ֖יִךְ
אֱלֹהָֽי: ¹⁷בַּאֲשֶׁ֤ר תָּמ֙וּתִי֙ אָמ֔וּת וְשָׁ֖ם אֶקָּבֵ֑ר כֹּה֩ יַעֲשֶׂ֨ה יְהוָ֥ה לִ֛י
וְכֹ֥ה יֹסִ֖יף כִּ֣י הַמָּ֔וֶת יַפְרִ֖יד בֵּינִ֥י וּבֵינֵֽךְ:

STEP TWO: **Parse** the following verbs.

	Stem	Conj.	Pers.	Gend.	Numb.	Root	Trans.
(1) תִּפְגְּעִי							
(2) לְעָזְבֵךְ							
(3) תֵּלְכִי							
(4) אֵלֵךְ							
(5) תָּלִינִי							
(6) אָלִין							
(7) תָּמוּתִי							
(8) אָמוּת							
(9) אֶקָּבֵר							
(10) יַעֲשֶׂה							
(11) יֹסִיף							
(12) יַפְרִיד							

STEP THREE: **Translate** the text into understandable English.

_____

_____

VOCABULARY

פגע   Qal: meet; request

לין   Qal: stay the night; dwell

קבר   Niphal: be buried

מָוֶת   death

פרד   Hiphil: separate

STEP FOUR: **Notice** significant exegetical insights.

- כִּי אֶל־אֲשֶׁר . . . וּבַאֲשֶׁר . . . בַּאֲשֶׁר . . . וְשָׁם: The reason for Ruth's plea is introduced by six clauses following כִּי (v. 16). Ruth's central declaration ("Your people will be mine, and your God will be mine") is surrounded before and after by clauses focused on a location where she has never been. Each relative indicates the locality of Naomi migration: "to the place . . . at the place . . . in the place . . . there." Ruth focuses her pledge on living and dying with Naomi. Her commitment is undeterred by locality, separation from her family, or death. She refuses to follow Naomi's warning or to be overwhelmed by hopelessness (vv. 11–13).

- כִּי הַמָּוֶת יַפְרִיד בֵּינִי וּבֵינֵךְ: The second כִּי (v. 17) can be understood in several ways. It may indicate a consequence ("so that death will separate us"), a concessive ("although death will separate us"), or an adversative ("yet death will separate us"). Most English versions translate it as a type of conditional (i.e., "unless death separates us"). Regardless of the exact nuance, the overall promise is clear. Ruth ensures her covenant commitment to Naomi by calling down Yahweh's punishment should she not be faithful. Similar language is used for oaths followed by a conditional clause starting with כִּי (1 Sam. 14:44; 20:13; 2 Sam. 3:9; 35; 1 Kings 2:23) or אִם (1 Sam. 3:17; 25:22; 2 Sam. 19:14; 1 Kings 20:10; 2 Kings 6:31).

FOR THE JOURNEY

Even though she has allied her life to this Hebrew family, likely through an arranged marriage to Mahlon, Ruth continues to be associated with her Moabite kin. Naomi offers to release her from any remaining obligation, insists on parting ways, and knows that Ruth would be taken care of in her mother's house (v. 8). Ruth refuses Naomi's instruction to follow after Orpah and return to her people and her gods (v. 15). Using language akin to covenant realignment, Ruth takes the more vulnerable and insecure path. She joins Naomi's people and embraces Israel's God. Her allegiance is unfaltering. She declares irrevocably her loyalties to her mother-in-law, her people, and her God.

Ruth's response is her first and longest speech in the book. The central assertion comes in verse 17: "Your people will be mine, and your God mine" (עַמֵּךְ עַמִּי וֵאלֹהַיִךְ אֱלֹהָי). This four word declaration repositions her life. Ruth adopts a new people and a new God. The identification forms a kind of pledge of allegiance (Gen. 17:7–8; Zech. 8:8).

This decision was her own and drastically reoriented her future. Migrating to a new home in Bethlehem meant conclusively leaving behind all her cultural and familial relations. She was transferring her allegiance once and for all. She would become part of Israel. There was no going back.

ANSWER KEY

1. *Parse:* (1) תִּפְגְּעִי (Qal juss 2fs פגע "request"). (2) לְעָזְבֵךְ (prep + Qal inf cstr עזב "leave" + 2fs sf). (3) תֵּלְכִי (Qal pc 2fs הלך "go"). (4) אֵלֵךְ (Qal pc 1cs הלך "go"). (5) תָּלִינִי (Qal pc 2fs לין "dwell"). (6) אָלִין (Qal pc 1cs לין "dwell"). (7) תְּמוּתִי (Qal pc 2fs מות "die"). (8) אָמוּת (Qal pc 1cs מות "die"). (9) אֶקָּבֵר (Niphal pc 1cs קבר "be buried"). (10) יַעֲשֶׂה (Qal pc 2ms עשה "do"). (11) יֹסִיף (Hiphil pc 3ms יסף "increase"). (12) יַפְרִיד (Hiphil pc 3ms פרד "separate").

2. *Translate:* "Ruth responded, 'Do not ask me to abandon you and turn back from following you. Where you go to, I will go, and wherever you stay at, I will stay. Your people will be mine, and your God mine! Wherever you die, I will die, and there I will be buried. May Yahweh do so to me and even worse, should anything but death separate between you and me.'"

DAY 69: RUTH 1:18–19

STEP ONE: **Read** aloud the text at least five times.

וַתֵּרֶא כִּי־מִתְאַמֶּצֶת הִיא לָלֶכֶת אִתָּהּ וַתֶּחְדַּל לְדַבֵּר אֵלֶיהָ:
¹⁹וַתֵּלַכְנָה שְׁתֵּיהֶם עַד־בֹּאָנָה בֵּית לָחֶם וַיְהִי כְּבֹאָנָה בֵּית
לֶחֶם וַתֵּהֹם כָּל־הָעִיר עֲלֵיהֶן וַתֹּאמַרְנָה הֲזֹאת נָעֳמִי:

STEP TWO: **Parse** the following verbs.

	Stem	Conj.	Pers.	Gend.	Numb.	Root	Trans.
(1) וַתֵּרֶא							
(2) מִתְאַמֶּצֶת							
(3) וַתֶּחְדַּל							
(4) וַתֵּלַכְנָה							
(5) בֹּאָנָה							
(6) וַתֹּאמַרְנָה							

STEP THREE: **Translate** the text into understandable English.

_____

_____

VOCABULARY

אמץ   Hitpael: prove to be strong; be determined
חדל   Qal: cease; refrain from
הום   Niphal: shout; be in a stir

STEP FOUR: **Notice** significant exegetical insights.

- מִתְאַמֶּצֶת הִיא: The participle is used in a progressive sense. Ruth has set her mind on going with Naomi and is unrelenting in her determination to travel with her to the very end of the journey. This choice is not merely a momentary inclination based on her fondness or sympathy for her mother-in-law. She demonstrates a resolute attachment to her faithful decision. For this reason, she becomes known as a woman of noble character (אֵשֶׁת חַיִל, Ruth 3:11).

- וַתֵּלַכְנָה שְׁתֵּיהֶם: The clause connects with the identical verb that appears in verse 7 (וַתֵּלַכְנָה). In contrast to the beginning of the journey, the subject ("both of them," v. 19) specifies that only two of the women—namely, Naomi and Ruth—reached the destination. Orpah left them with a kiss goodbye (v. 14).

FOR THE JOURNEY

Verse 19 ends with a multilayered question: "Can this be Naomi?" (הֲזֹאת נָעֳמִי). The unanswered question is spoken among the towns-folk, particularly the women of Bethlehem.

On the grammatical level, it expresses a straightforward question. The expected response would simply require an affirmative or a negative reply. Since the story narrates Naomi's return home to Bethlehem, the obvious answer would be "Yes, this is Naomi."

But there is more. The connotation expands beyond the simple identification of an unknown traveler. The question identifies both the content of what the women were saying (וַתֹּאמַרְנָה) and why the entire city was in an uproar (וַתֵּהֹם).

The inquiry reaffirms that a long time had passed since Naomi left her hometown. Her appearance presumably had changed. She was older. Some women may not have recognized her. Others may have known her only by name or reputation. She was the one who left with her husband many years ago to escape the famine.

The query further encapsulates the uproar of the whole city. This may be the same woman, but Naomi is different! Her circumstances have drastically changed. Her pleasant condition had become bitter. The fact that her husband has died may not have been known, and the death of her two sons only adds to the tragedy. What's more, the townsfolk would be concerned about the young Moabite woman who accompanies Naomi. None of this is ordinary or expected.

The real question in their minds is *What happened to Naomi?*

ANSWER KEY

1. *Parse:* (1) וַתֵּרֶא (Qal *wayyiqtol* 3FS ראה "see"). (2) מִתְאַמֶּצֶת (Hitpael PTCL FS אמץ "determine"). (3) וַתֶּחְדַּל (Qal *wayyiqtol* 3FS חדל "cease"). (4) וַתֵּלַכְנָה (Qal *wayyiqtol* 3FP הלך "go"). (5) בֹּאָנָה (Qal INF CSTR בוא "come" + 3FP SF). (6) וַתֹּאמַרְנָה (Qal *wayyiqtol* 3FP אמר "say").

2. *Translate:* "[Naomi] saw that she was determined to go with her, and she stopped speaking to her [about the matter]. Both of them traveled until they arrived at Bethlehem. As they entered Bethlehem, the entire city was in an uproar over them, and the women said: 'Can this be Naomi?'"

DAY 70: RUTH 1:20–21

STEP ONE: **Read** aloud the text at least five times.

וַתֹּאמֶר אֲלֵיהֶן אַל־תִּקְרֶאנָה לִי נָעֳמִי קְרֶאןָ לִי מָרָא כִּי־הֵמַר
שַׁדַּי לִי מְאֹד: ²¹ אֲנִי מְלֵאָה הָלַכְתִּי וְרֵיקָם הֱשִׁיבַנִי יְהוָה לָמָּה
תִקְרֶאנָה לִי נָעֳמִי וַיהוָה עָנָה בִי וְשַׁדַּי הֵרַע לִי:

STEP TWO: **Parse** the following verbs.

	Stem	Conj.	Pers.	Gend.	Numb.	Root	Trans.
(1) וַתֹּאמֶר							
(2) תִּקְרֶאנָה							
(3) קְרֶאןָ							
(4) הֵמַר							
(5) הָלַכְתִּי							
(6) הֱשִׁיבַנִי							
(7) הֵרַע							

STEP THREE: **Translate** the text into understandable English.

_____

_____

VOCABULARY

מַר   bitter (cf. מָרָא)

מרר   Hiphil: cause grief; make bitter

שַׁדַּי   Shaddai

מָלֵא   full

רֵיקָם   emptily, vainly

רעע   Hiphil: treat badly; bring suffering

STEP FOUR: **Notice** significant exegetical insights.

- **מָרָא** . . . **נָעֳמִי**: Naomi responds disapprovingly to the women's question about who she is (v. 19). Her name is no longer Naomi (i.e., "Pleasant"). She is not the same person who left many years before. All her attachments are severed. She has no sweetness, no congeniality, and no hope. Her existence can simply be characterized as Mara (i.e., "Bitter").

- **שַׁדַּי**: This name of God (see also Num. 24:4; Job 5:17; 8:3; 22:25; Pss. 68:15; 91:1; Isa. 13:6; etc.) is a shortened version of **אֵל שַׁדַּי** (Gen. 17:1; Exod. 6:3). It may be understood as a title, God the Almighty (see Job 5:17 LXX παντοκράτωρ, also Rev. 1:8; Latin *omnipotens*), or as a pseudo-name, El Shaddai (Ezek. 10:5 LXX θεοῦ Σαδδαι; Syriac; Aramaic targums). The etymology of the Hebrew is widely debated.

- **וַיהוָה עָנָה בִי**: The verb is translated in various ways: "oppose" (CSB), "testified against" (KJV/ESV/Tanakh), "witnessed against" (NASB95), "dealt harshly" (NRSV), "afflicted" (NIV), "caused to suffer" (NLT). Hebrew lexicons list two meanings for עָנָה that are relevant here: (1) to answer, respond, testify or (2) to be afflicted, be troubled, be humiliated. The latter option fits with the following clause ("Shaddai has brought calamity to me"), but the Qal stem of עָנָה is typically intransitive ("be afflicted"). That is to say, the subject is the one "suffering humiliation" (e.g., Pss. 116:10; 119:67; Zech. 10:2) rather than the one causing it. The Piel of this word has the transitive sense (e.g., Deut. 8:2; Isa. 64:11) rendered by some translations (e.g., CSB, NIV). The other choice of meaning is a response to speech or to an action. With the preposition denoting the respondent (i.e., בִּי "against me"; see 1 Sam. 12:3; Job 15:6), the verb takes on the formality of a judgment or verdict. This sense seems to align with the grammar of the clause, even though its connotation requires some unspoken suppositions. This meaning would assume that Naomi asked Yahweh to deliver her, but his response was not relief but more disaster. She may even be claiming that God has reprimanded her and her family for their prior actions. Whatever the nuance, God's reply was not pleasant but bitter.

FOR THE JOURNEY

Naomi expresses her belief that disaster stems from God's actions in the world. Similar notions are expressed elsewhere in the Scriptures, and they contrast with the modern notion that calamity is a result of restricted control or divine inability to act. The biblical account provides another explanation: God's ways are not our ways, and his word never returns empty (Isa. 55:8–11).

Naomi's experiences lead her to formulate a theology around her tragic life. She describes God's function in the world through three activities: (a) he makes her bitter, (b) he empties her life, and (c) he brings calamity.

She echoes the words of Job. Death comes to the prosperous and the bitter (Job 21:22–26). Justice appears to be inverted in the present world (Job 3:20; 27:2). The loss of one's family brings overwhelming anguish (2 Kings 4:27; Zech. 12:10) and emptiness (Job 22:9). God's actions bring about brokenness and heartache (Ps. 22:1–2). Naomi assumes that widowhood and the loss of her sons were a direct result of God working against her (1 Kings 17:20).

Yet, Naomi's story does not end with chapter 1. God is working for her. Even through real difficulty and bitterness, God redeems and rescues his people (Ruth 4:9–12), and he brings retribution on those who do not turn to him (Exod. 5:22–6:1).

ANSWER KEY

1. *Parse:* (1) וַתֹּאמֶר (Qal *wayyiqtol* 3FS אמר "say"). (2) תִּקְרֶאנָה (Qal JUSS 2FP קרא "call"). (3) קְרֶאןָ (Qal IMV FP קרא "call"). (4) הֵמַר (Hiphil SC 3MS מרר "embitter"). (5) הָלַכְתִּי (Qal SC 1CS הלך "go"). (6) הֱשִׁיבַנִי (Hiphil SC 3MS שוב "make return" + 1CS SF). (7) הֵרַע (Hiphil SC 3MS רעע "afflict").

2. *Translate:* "She responded to the women, 'Do not call me "Naomi" [Pleasant]. Call me "Mara" [Bitter] because Shaddai has made me incredibly bitter. I went away full, but Yahweh returned me empty. Why call me Naomi? Yahweh decided against me, and Shaddai has made me suffer.'"

DAY 71: RUTH 1:22–2:1

STEP ONE: **Read** aloud the text at least five times.

וַתָּשָׁב נָעֳמִי וְרוּת הַמּוֹאֲבִיָּה כַלָּתָהּ עִמָּהּ הַשָּׁבָה מִשְּׂדֵי
מוֹאָב וְהֵמָּה בָּאוּ בֵּית לֶחֶם בִּתְחִלַּת קְצִיר שְׂעֹרִים: ²:¹וּלְנָעֳמִי
מוֹדָע לְאִישָׁהּ אִישׁ גִּבּוֹר חַיִל מִמִּשְׁפַּחַת אֱלִימֶלֶךְ וּשְׁמוֹ בֹּעַז:

STEP TWO: **Parse** the following verbs.

	Stem	Conj.	Pers.	Gend.	Numb.	Root	Trans.
(1) וַתָּשָׁב							
(2) הַשָּׁבָה							

STEP THREE: **Translate** the text into understandable English.

_____

_____

VOCABULARY

מוֹאֲבִי   Moabite

כַּלָּה   bride; daughter-in-law

הֵמָּה   they (i.e., the daughters-in-law, despite 3MP)

תְּחִלָּה   beginning

קָצִיר   harvest, harvesting

שְׂעֹרָה   barley

מוֹדָע   kinsman, relative (*Ketiv*: מְיֻדָּע "one who is known")

גִּבּוֹר   strong, mighty; hero

אֱלִימֶלֶךְ   Elimelech

בֹּעַז   Boaz

STEP FOUR: **Notice** significant exegetical insights.

- הַשָּׁבָה מִשְּׂדֵי מוֹאָב: This is understood either as a participle phrase describing Ruth or a separate (relative) clause perhaps summing up Naomi's journey. As the article is typically not used with finite verbs in Biblical Hebrew, the active particle seems like the more plausible reading, even though the expected accent would be word final (i.e., הַשָּׁבָה; exceptions include Ruth 2:6; 4:3). In either case, it may be best understood as an attributive phrase, reiterating Ruth's faithful decision to follow her mother-in-law and leave her homeland of Moab. The other option is that the clause recapitulates the verb and actor of the previous clause (וַתָּשָׁב נָעֳמִי). The point would be to specify (once again) the source location of Naomi's trek.

- בִּתְחִלַּת קְצִיר שְׂעֹרִים: This temporal description may seem out of place but serves several narrative purposes. The barley is an early crop, harvested in early to mid-spring (Exod. 9:31) and followed by the wheat harvest (Ruth 2:23). In contrast with the previous period of famine (1:1), it is a reminder of the productive land where the people were promised not to be in lack of anything (Deut. 8:7–10). The harvest month, Abib, also looks back to Israel's deliverance from Egypt with the Feast of Unleavened Bread (Exod. 13:3–10) and Passover (Deut. 16:1–8) and anticipates Yahweh's protection of the weak and vulnerable. The setting is ripe for God's redemption.

- וּלְנָעֳמִי מוֹדַע לְאִישָׁהּ . . . מִמִּשְׁפַּחַת אֱלִימֶלֶךְ: The second word can be read as the noun "relative" or the passive participle "one known" (see Ruth 3:2). Regardless, a new person is introduced who is connected to Naomi through her husband. Boaz is closely related to Elimelech as part of Elimelech's "clan" (also 2:3). The importance of this connection is amplified in Ruth 2:20. Boaz is described there as a kinsman-redeemer (גֹּאֵל). This kinsman could take on the obligation of caring for a destitute family through purchasing their residence or land allotment (Lev. 25:23–31). In this case, the situation was even more complicated because of the obligation to preserve the family line (Deut. 25:5–10). The redeemer needed to both purchase Naomi's property and wed Ruth (Ruth 4:1–10).

FOR THE JOURNEY

Even before Boaz is named, Elimelech's kinsman is described as אִישׁ
גִּבּוֹר חָיִל. The phrase is understood variously as "a prominent man
of noble character" (CSB), "a worthy man" (ESV), "a mighty man
of wealth" (KJV), "a man of standing" (NIV), "a prominent rich man"
(NRSV), and "a man of substance" (Tanakh). Also, it is interesting
that the Greek translator of 2 Chron. 3:17 renders the name Boaz
as "strength, might" (Ἰσχύς), perhaps etymologizing the element עֹז
("strength").

Akin to Gideon (Judg. 6:12), Jephthah (Judg. 11:1), David (1 Sam.
16:18), and Naaman (2 Kings 5:1), Boaz is described as a mighty man
(גִּבּוֹר) of strength (חָיִל). These terms can denote able-bodied men
(Judg. 3:29), warriors (Judg. 20:44; 2 Sam. 24:9), brave men (1 Sam.
31:12; 2 Sam. 11:16; Jer. 48:14), and capable or skilled men (Gen. 47:6;
1 Kings 1:42; 1 Chron. 26:7–8). Elsewhere, חָיִל can even indicate wealth
(Gen. 34:29; Num. 31:9; Job 15:29). In this way, Boaz could be thought
to be a man of some affluence, not just brawny acumen.

Finally, the phrase can be connected to the notion of virtue and
good character. In Exodus, Moses's father-in-law describes exemplary
leaders as אַנְשֵׁי־חַיִל—that is, those who fear God, are truthful, and
hate extortion (Exod. 18:21).

Boaz uses a corresponding phrase אֵשֶׁת חַיִל ("a woman of
strength") to describe Ruth's noble character as observed by the people
of Bethlehem (Ruth 3:11) and blessed accordingly (4:11). This assessment is based on her display of covenant faithfulness (חֶסֶד, 3:10) and
self-sacrifice (2:11).

ANSWER KEY

1. *Parse:* (1) וַתָּשָׁב (Qal *wayyiqtol* 3FS שׁוּב "return"). (2) הַשָּׁבָה (DEF ART + Qal
   ACT PTCL FS שׁוּב "return") or הַשָּׁבָה (DEF ART + Qal SC 3FS שׁוּב "return").

2. *Translate:* "Naomi returned, and Ruth her Moabite daughter-in-law was with
   her returning from the fields of Moab. They entered Bethlehem at the start of
   the barley harvest. Now Naomi had [*or*, knew about] a family member on her
   husband's side—a virtuous, valiant man—belonging to Elimelech's family. His
   name was Boaz."

ROUTE 10

Proverbs 31:10–31

STEP ONE: **Read** aloud the text at least five times.

¹⁰אֵשֶׁת־חַיִל מִי יִמְצָא   וְרָחֹק מִפְּנִינִים מִכְרָהּ:

¹¹בָּטַח בָּהּ לֵב בַּעְלָהּ   וְשָׁלָל לֹא יֶחְסָר:

¹²גְּמָלַתְהוּ טוֹב וְלֹא־רָע   כֹּל יְמֵי חַיֶּיהָ:

STEP TWO: **Parse** the following verb.

	Stem	Conj.	Pers.	Gend.	Numb.	Root	Trans.
גְּמָלַתְהוּ (1)							

STEP THREE: **Translate** the text into understandable English.

_____

_____

VOCABULARY

מִי   who?

רָחוֹק   distant, far

פְּנִינִים   pearls of coral

מֶכֶר   value (+ 3FS SF מִכְרָהּ)

בטח   Qal: trust

בַּעַל   lord; husband

שָׁלָל   plunder; gain

חסר   Qal: lack; be in need of

גמל   Qal: repay, deal (kindly) with; wean

חַיִּים   life(time) (+ 3FS SF חַיֶּיהָ)

STEP FOUR: **Notice** significant exegetical insights.

- **אֵשֶׁת . . . . בָּטַח . . . . גְּמָלַתְהוּ:** Starting with verse 10, the first letter of the first word in each of the next twenty-two lines (the number of letters in the Hebrew alphabet) is organized in alphabetical order. Several other psalms and biblical compositions use a similar arrangement (Pss. 9–10; 37; 111; Lam. 1, 2, 4). Sometimes each letter is repeated, as in Lam. 3, where three lines occur with the same letter before proceeding to the next letter. Another well-known example is Ps. 119, where each eight-line stanza begins with the same Hebrew letter for a total of 176 verses (22 letters × 8 verses each). This structuring device serves as an aid for memorization and forms a list that represents totality.

- **אֵשֶׁת־חַיִל מִי יִמְצָא . . . בָּטַח בָּהּ לֵב בַּעְלָהּ וְשָׁלָל לֹא יֶחְסָר:** On account of the alphabetic ordering and the poetic arrangement, the clause structure may augment the typical Hebrew word order: verb followed by object. In verse 10, for instance, the object (אֵשֶׁת־חַיִל, see "For the Journey" below) is presented before the interrogative and the verb (מִי יִמְצָא). The poetic arrangement of the line may also result in nonstandard clause structure. Verse 11 has a chiastic organization. The first half of the line is verb initial (בָּטַח), and the second half of the line is verb final (לֹא יֶחְסָר). The latter clause requires the object (שָׁלָל) to precede the verb, resembling the structure of verse 10.

- טוֹב וְלֹא־רָע כֹּל יְמֵי חַיֶּיהָ: The coupling of "good and evil" is reminiscent of the tree of knowledge (Gen. 2:9, 17), the disregard for God's admonition (3:5–6), and the cause of humanity's expulsion from the Edenic garden (3:22–24). This woman, however, is trustworthy. She dispatches good and remits evil. In contrast to the mother of all living (i.e., "Eve" חַוָּה, Gen. 3:20), her life embodies godly wisdom and results in human flourishing.

FOR THE JOURNEY

The opening words, "a valiant wife" (אֵשֶׁת־חַיִל), serve as the subject matter for the entire twenty-two-verse composition. Every clause is about this woman, her husband, or her household. Outside of Proverbs, the formulation is used only to depict the character of Ruth (Ruth 3:11).

Within Proverbs, אֵשֶׁת־חַיִל describes a woman who is "her husband's crown" (עֲטֶרֶת בַּעְלָהּ) and is contrasted with a shameful wife who is like old rotting bones (12:4). The metaphor of a crown is used to symbolize the reward for a wise life (4:9; 14:24). These crowns adorn those with a valiant wife (12:4), those boasting in the gift of grandchildren (17:6), and those embodying the righteousness that comes with gray hair (16:31).

It is not surprising, then, that the wise counsel of Prov. 31:10–22 is appended to a mother's kingly advice to her son. In verses 8 and 9, King Lemuel's mother encourages her son to speak for the weak, defend the disadvantaged, and judge justly. To avoid the pitfalls of power, she warns him about spending his time indulging certain passions to the exclusion of virtue. The first of these lusts involves giving his strength (חַיִל) to women (31:3). The ideal sought-after spouse, by contrast, is characterized as a woman of her own strength (חַיִל in v. 10; עֹז in vv. 17, 25). She provides for the weak and the needy (v. 20). And her husband is a prominent judge (v. 23).

DAY 73: PROVERBS 31:13–15

STEP ONE: **Read** aloud the text at least five times.

דָּרְשָׁה צֶמֶר וּפִשְׁתֶּים וַתַּעַשׂ בְּחֵפֶץ כַּפֶּיהָ:¹³

¹⁴הָיְתָה כָּאֳנִיּוֹת סוֹחֵר מִמֶּרְחָק תָּבִיא לַחְמָהּ:

¹⁵וַתָּקָם | בְּעוֹד לַיְלָה וַתִּתֵּן טֶרֶף לְבֵיתָהּ וְחֹק לְנַעֲרֹתֶיהָ:

STEP TWO: **Parse** the following verbs.

	Stem	Conj.	Pers.	Gend.	Numb.	Root	Trans.
(1) דָּרְשָׁה							
(2) וַתַּעַשׂ							
(3) תָּבִיא							
(4) וַתָּקָם							
(5) וַתִּתֵּן							

STEP THREE: **Translate** the text into understandable English.

_____

_____

VOCABULARY

דרש Qal: seek, look for; inquire about, investigate

צֶמֶר wool

פֵּשֶׁת linen, flax

חֵפֶץ delight, pleasure; wish

כַּף palm; hand (DU/PL + 3FS SF כַּפֶּיהָ)

אֳנִיָּה ship

סחר Qal: travel about; trade

מֶרְחָק distance; expanse

טֶרֶף food

חֹק instruction

נַעֲרָה young girl; maidservant

STEP FOUR: **Notice** significant exegetical insights.

- וַתַּעַשׂ . . . דָּרְשָׁה: The suffix conjugation followed by a *wayyiqtol* form creates a short sequence. The valiant wife acquires resources and works with them. Her creative endeavors involve צֶמֶר ("wool") and פֵּשֶׁת ("linen, flax"). These are regularly mentioned together (Lev. 13:47; Hosea 2:7, 11), traded as commodities (2 Kings 3:4; Ezek. 27:18), and mostly used as fabrics (Isa. 51:8), but not both in the same garment (Deut. 22:11; Ezek. 44:17). The noble task of garment production is the focus of verses 19, 21, 22, 24, and 25. Her joy in such work points to an exceptional person who finds contentment in commonplace activities and tasks (1 Tim. 6:6).

- וַתִּתֵּן טֶרֶף לְבֵיתָהּ וְחֹק לְנַעֲרֹתֶיהָ: The valiant wife is commended for managing her household. The final couplet involves arising early and providing food and direction for members of the family and staff. The verb is implicitly echoed (i.e., gapped) in the second half with a different object and indirect object. She gives food (טֶרֶף) to her house (לְבֵיתָהּ), and she gives instruction (חֹק) to her maidservants (לְנַעֲרֹתֶיהָ). Each activity recurs elsewhere in the acrostic. Foodstuffs are mentioned in the previous line (לַחְמָהּ). And supervision of the household is recapitulated in verse 27.

FOR THE JOURNEY

The valiant wife may be compared with other characters in Proverbs. Her descriptions contrast with the negative representations of the wicked and the foolish. Positively, she engages her context with the wisdom of the ages and the fear of the Lord.

She is the anti-sluggard (Prov. 6:6–11), the anti-sinner (1:10–19), and the anti-fool (10:1–24). She labors diligently to provide food. She engages others with honesty. Her wisdom and work bring life to those closest to her. In sum, she avoids walking the path of Woman Folly (5:20; 7:6–27; 9:13–18).

The capable wife personifies Woman Wisdom. She listens to prudent counsel, and her instructions are sensible (1:20–33). She brings pleasure and peace (3:13–18). She is valued beyond great wealth (8:1–21). She pursues life and understanding (9:1–12). Her wisdom benefits all those who dwell in her house and those who know her!

ANSWER KEY

1. *Parse:* (1) דָּרְשָׁה (Qal sc 3fs דרש "seek"). (2) וַתַּעַשׂ (Qal *wayyiqtol* 3fs עשׂה "make"). (3) תָּבִיא (Hiphil pc 3fs בוא "bring in"). (4) וַתָּקָם (Qal *wayyiqtol* 3fs קום "rise"). (5) וַתִּתֵּן (Qal *wayyiqtol* 3fs נתן "give").

2. *Translate:* "She seeks out fleece and flax fabric and then works with eager hands. / She is like the merchant vessels; she procures her food from far away. / She arises when it is still night, and then she provides sustenance for her household and instruction to her servants."

DAY 74: PROVERBS 31:16–17

STEP ONE: **Read** aloud the text at least five times.

¹⁶זָמְמָה שָׂדֶה וַתִּקָּחֵהוּ   מִפְּרִי כַפֶּיהָ נָטַע כָּרֶם׃

¹⁷חָגְרָה בְעוֹז מָתְנֶיהָ   וַתְּאַמֵּץ זְרוֹעֹתֶיהָ׃

STEP TWO: **Parse** the following verbs.

	Stem	Conj.	Pers.	Gend.	Numb.	Root	Trans.
(1) זָמְמָה							
(2) וַתִּקָּחֵהוּ							
(3) נָטַע							
(4) חָגְרָה							
(5) וַתְּאַמֵּץ							

STEP THREE: **Translate** the text into understandable English.

_____

_____

_____

VOCABULARY

זמם   Qal: purpose; plan

פְּרִי   fruit, produce

כַּף   palm; hand

נטע   Qal: plant (*Qere*: נָטְעָה)

כֶּרֶם   vineyard

חגר   Qal: gird (on)

עֹז   strength, might

מָתְנַיִם   loins

אמץ   Piel: make firm; strengthen

זְרוֹעַ   arm, forearm; shoulder

JOURNEY 3 · EXPANDING

STEP FOUR: **Notice** significant exegetical insights.

- זָמְמָה שָׂדֶה וַתִּקָּחֵהוּ . . . נָטְעָה כָּרֶם: Similar to the syntax of verse 13, the initial suffix conjugation is followed by a *wayyiqtol* and creates a short sequence. The valiant wife appraises a field. She judges its potential for agronomic production. Once she finds a suitable property, then she acquires it. She also establishes a winery and becomes a vinedresser. These economic activities reflect long-term investments and land management. She works for the good of her family and the peace of her community (cf. Jer. 29:4–7).

- חָגְרָה בְעוֹז מָתְנֶיהָ: The language shifts from her economic undertakings to her emotional and physical attributes. One may dress for various activities: battle (1 Sam. 25:13), bereavement (Isa. 32:11; Joel 1:8), lament (Lam. 2:10; Joel 1:13), surrender (2 Sam. 22:46; 1 Kings 20:32), triumph (Ps. 45:4), or joyous celebration (Ps. 65:13). Fortitude (i.e., עֹז) metaphorically describes the wife's attire. The following image involves the strengthening of her arms (וַתְּאַמֵּץ זְרֹעוֹתֶיהָ). Similar characteristics represent those who are steadfast and dependent on God's redemption (Isa. 35:3–4). These traits reflect spiritual courage and endurance (1 Cor. 9:24–27). The unifying characteristic is resolute valor. This notion connects to her main description as "a woman of strength" (Prov. 31:10).

FOR THE JOURNEY

Kingdom work involves activities that some may deem menial or even mundane. The Scriptures, however, are replete with examples extolling people who serve faithfully in the most ordinary tasks for God's glory (Col. 3:23). The valiant wife is praised for her productivity and agrarian activities. She acquires land and improves it. Further, she cultivates personal, spiritual, and emotional qualities. She purposes to develop the character and strength needed to live a wise life. None of her efforts are trivial.

The wife's vocation mirrors that of God's work in the world. She is a surveyor, an investor, and a developer. In these domains, she actively participates in God's kingdom. God planned and planted a garden in the east. He nurtured the growth of pleasing fruit (Gen. 2:8–9). His cultivation extends beyond Eden to the land of promise (Deut. 11:9–12). God gives his people a promised land abounding with bountiful orchards (Num. 13:23, 27). This land he provisions with cities, houses, cisterns, olive groves, and vineyards (Deut. 6:10–12; Josh. 24:13). God develops his vineyard, not sparing anything, yet his people yield only odious fruit (Isa. 5:1–4). But all is not lost. He will again sing a creation song and nurture a desirable vineyard on his holy mountain (27:2). This divine realm will provide an enduring home characterized by contented labor and satisfying vintages—the good life (65:17–25).

ANSWER KEY

1. *Parse:* (1) זָמְמָה (Qal sc 3fs זמם "plan"). (2) וַתִּקָּחֵהוּ (Qal *wayyiqtol* 3fs לקח "take" + 3ms sf). (3) נָטְעָה (Qal sc 3fs נטע "plant"). (4) חָגְרָה (Qal sc 3fs חגר "gird"). (5) וַתְּאַמֵּץ (Piel *wayyiqtol* 3fs אמץ "strengthen").

2. *Translate:* "She appraises a field and purchases it; she plants a vineyard with the fruit of her hands. / She girds her loins with resilience and strengthens her arms."

DAY 75: PROVERBS 31:18–19

STEP ONE: **Read** aloud the text at least five times.

¹⁸טָעֲמָה כִּי־טוֹב סַחְרָהּ   לֹא־יִכְבֶּה בַלַּיְלָ נֵרָהּ׃

¹⁹יָדֶיהָ שִׁלְּחָה בַכִּישׁוֹר   וְכַפֶּיהָ תָּמְכוּ פָלֶךְ׃

STEP TWO: **Parse** the following verbs.

	Stem	Conj.	Pers.	Gend.	Numb.	Root	Trans.
(1) טָעֲמָה							
(2) יִכְבֶּה							
(3) שִׁלְּחָה							

STEP THREE: **Translate** the text into understandable English.

_____

_____

VOCABULARY

טעם   Qal: taste; perceive

סָחַר   profit; gain (+ 3FS SF סַחְרָהּ)

כבה   Qal: be extinguished, go out

בַלַּיְלָ   at night (*Qere:* בַלַּיְלָה)

נֵר   lamp

כִּישׁוֹר   distaff

כַּף   palm; sole; bowl

תמך   Qal: grasp

פֶּלֶךְ   spindle whorl

STEP FOUR: **Notice** significant exegetical insights.

- טוֹב סַחְרָהּ: It is not entirely clear what kind of "gain" is in view. The term denotes general merchandise (1 Kings 10:15; Isa. 45:14) or revenue from the sale of products (Prov. 3:14; Isa. 23:3). The cognate verb points to trade, exemplified in the maritime commerce of the Phoenicians (Ezek. 27:12–36). In Isa. 23:17–18, Yahweh claims Tyre's profit for his own purposes. Their fine clothing and food are transferred to those dwelling in God's presence. In the context of Prov. 31, the goods could be lamp oil, textiles, or clothes. Regardless, it is evident that the profit was the result of the woman's endeavors. Her household, unlike the wicked Tyrians, benefits from these commodities.

- פֶּלֶךְ . . . בַּכִּישׁוֹר: These two implements are used to spin wool and flax into yarn, which is used to make fabrics (Deut. 22:11; Isa. 19:9–10; Hosea 2:11). These terms combine with several other descriptions of garment production in this chapter (vv. 13, 19, 21, 22, 24, and 25). It would not be inappropriate to suppose that the valiant wife is a prosperous businessperson. Clothing and trade are strongly linked in the ancient world. Apparel could be used as collateral (Prov. 20:16), abatement (Judg. 8:26), payment (2 Kings 5:26), and even treasured loot (1 Sam. 27:9).

FOR THE JOURNEY

The poem describes a woman who pursues and imitates Yahweh. Her focus is not on what is empty and ephemeral but on the needs of others and on providing for her household. She is industrious and selfless. Her efforts are not motivated by a desire for popularity and praise but reflect the wisdom and knowledge of the Lord.

Her vocation reflects God's work. She tastes and sees the goodness of Yahweh, taking refuge in him (Ps. 34:9). She lacks nothing and provides all that her family needs (Ps. 34:10–11). She prepares and burns her lamp continuously (Lev. 24:2–4). Her house provides light to live by (Ps. 119:105; Prov. 13:9; 20:27; 24:20). She dresses those under her charge in resplendent garments (Gen. 3:21; Rev. 3:18).

The valiant wife exemplifies faithfulness to Yahweh. She seeks wisdom by fearing God (cf. Prov. 1:7, 29; 2:5; 8:13; 9:10; 10:27). She possesses knowledge and pursues understanding, and her life benefits from this pursuit.

1. *Parse:* (1) טָעֲמָה (Qal SC 3FS טעם "perceive"). (2) יִכְבֶּה (Qal PC 3MS כבה "be extinguished"). (3) שִׁלְּחָה (Piel SC 3FS שלח "send out").

2. *Translate:* "She perceives that her revenue is good. Her lamp does not go out in the night. / She puts her hands to the distaff, and her hands take hold of the spindle."

DAY 76: PROVERBS 31:20–21

STEP ONE: **Read** aloud the text at least five times.

²⁰כַּפָּהּ פָּרְשָׂה לֶעָנִי וְיָדֶיהָ שִׁלְּחָה לָאֶבְיוֹן:

²¹לֹא־תִירָא לְבֵיתָהּ מִשָּׁלֶג כִּי כָל־בֵּיתָהּ לָבֻשׁ שָׁנִים:

STEP TWO: **Parse** the following verbs.

	Stem	Conj.	Pers.	Gend.	Numb.	Root	Trans.
(1) פָּרְשָׂה							
(2) שִׁלְּחָה							
(3) תִירָא							

STEP THREE: **Translate** the text into understandable English.

VOCABULARY

כַּף palm; sole (sg + 3fs sf כַּפָּהּ)

פרשׂ Qal: spread (out); stretch out

עָנִי needy; afflicted; humble

אֶבְיוֹן poor, impoverished

שֶׁלֶג snow

לְבוּשׁ clothing; garment

שָׁנִי scarlet

STEP FOUR: **Notice** significant exegetical insights.

- יָדֶיהָ שִׁלְּחָה . . . וְכַפֶּיהָ . . . כַּפָּהּ . . . וְיָדֶיהָ שִׁלְּחָה: A series of four clauses with similar initial nouns begins verse 19 and continues through verse 20. The similar vocabulary and clause structure connect to form a simple [AB–B'A'] chiasm. The first verse describes garment production, and the second verse involves generosity to those in need. These activities describe what the affluent woman purposes to do with her hands. Isaiah 58 lists similar behaviors that are connected to proper religious observance. Authentic fasting requires living righteously and caring for others. The prophet warns that one may not merely be contrite without acting to set the oppressed free and help the needy (vv. 5–10). Such pious assistance includes feeding the hungry, lodging the unhoused, and clothing the naked (v. 7; cf. Matt. 25:35–36). Israel is told that Yahweh is pleased with and responds to acts of religious faithfulness joined with societal justice.

- לֹא־תִירָא לְבֵיתָהּ מִשָּׁלֶג כִּי כָל־בֵּיתָהּ לָבֻשׁ שָׁנִים: The woman does not fear external threats because she fears Yahweh (Prov. 31:30). She provides for the needs of her own household (Isa. 58:7). Her confidence is grounded in the eternal and not the ephemeral.

- מִשָּׁלֶג: The preposition designates why the household may be under threat causing anxiety and distress. Even though snow was unusual in the kingdom of Judah, it was not unheard of, and the extreme cold necessitated special provisions of food and clothing. The valiant wife relies on God's safekeeping. She knows that Yahweh commands even the worst meteorological phenomenon (Job 37:6–7; Pss. 147:16; 148:8). Yet she is prepared and ready for the hazards of inclement weather.

FOR THE JOURNEY

Yahweh cares for the poor. He is a God who rescues the afflicted (Pss. 35:10; 72:12; 107:41; 113:7; 132:15). Throughout the Scriptures, he acts on behalf of the needy, particularly when their poverty is a result of oppressive actors or circumstances beyond their control. God does not take the side of the oppressor. And he does not show favoritism to the wealthy and successful (Job 34:19; James 2:2–3). Yahweh intends for his people to care for the poor. The disadvantaged are given favorable status with regard to their debts (Deut. 15:7–11). The righteous are to "open their hands" to the poor and needy in their land (v. 11).

In imitation of God, the prophets designate the care of the poor as the mark of true religion. Contrasting with the valiant wife, Amos declares a recompense for the Samarian women who profit from the poor and oppress the needy (Amos 4:1). Israel is likewise judged for taking bribes and depriving the poor of justice (5:12). Worshipers who cast aside the impoverished will be silenced (8:3–6). They embody the sin of Sodom since they are secure and do not use their privileged status to strengthen others (Ezek. 16:49).

The one honoring the Creator demonstrates kindness to the needy (Prov. 14:31). Lemuel's mother urges her son to act justly and to plead the cause of the poor and needy (Prov. 31:9). Her advice is embodied by the valiant wife. She works not just for her family's interests but also for the benefit of the less fortunate. She participates in the care of the poor.

ANSWER KEY

1. *Parse:* (1) פָּרְשָׂה (Qal sc 3fs פרש "spread"). (2) שִׁלְּחָה (Piel sc 3fs שלח "send out"). (3) תִירָא (Qal pc 3fs ירא "fear").

2. *Translate:* "She lends a helping hand to the poor, and she opens her hands to the needy. / She does not fear for her house owing to the snow because her entire household is clothed with scarlet."

DAY 77: PROVERBS 31:22–23

STEP ONE: **Read** aloud the text at least five times.

²²מַרְבַדִּים עָשְׂתָה־לָּהּ   שֵׁשׁ וְאַרְגָּמָן לְבוּשָׁהּ׃

²³נוֹדָע בַּשְּׁעָרִים בַּעְלָהּ   בְּשִׁבְתּוֹ עִם־זִקְנֵי־אָרֶץ׃

STEP TWO: **Parse** the following verbs.

	Stem	Conj.	Pers.	Gend.	Numb.	Root	Trans.
(1) עָשְׂתָה							
(2) נוֹדָע							
(3) בְּשִׁבְתּוֹ							

STEP THREE: **Translate** the text into understandable English.

> ### VOCABULARY
>
> מַרְבָד   cover
> שֵׁשׁ   linen
> אַרְגָּמָן   red-purple wool
> לְבוּשׁ   clothing
> בַּעַל   lord; husband
> זָקֵן   elder (PL CSTR זִקְנֵי)

STEP FOUR: **Notice** significant exegetical insights.

- לָּהּ: The prepositional phrase ("for her") is likely not a reflexive. That notion would more commonly be expressed as לְנַפְשָׁהּ ("for herself"). Instead, it functions as a possessive, attributing the ownership of the covers (מַרְבַדִּים). It is akin to the pronominal suffix, as found with the semantically similar noun at the end of the line (לְבוּשָׁהּ "her clothing"). This line continues the capacious references to garment production in this poem. Her magnanimity, industry, and fear of God connect with the description of Lydia of Thyatira (Acts 16:14–15).

- נוֹדָע בַּשְּׁעָרִים בַּעְלָהּ: The Niphal verb does not express an agent. Saying that the valiant wife's husband is known speaks of his renown and reputation among his people. Her noble character is his. As explained in the following phrase (בְּשִׁבְתּוֹ עִם־זִקְנֵי־אָרֶץ), the circumstance of his notoriety involves the council of elders (cf. Deut. 25:7; Josh. 20:4). The city gates are the location of justice, where court was held (Ruth 4:1–12; 2 Sam. 15:2–6).

FOR THE JOURNEY

Verse 23 expresses the central notion of the poem. The valiant wife is celebrated for her righteous life, and her husband holds a place of respect and public honor. Her praiseworthiness is not restricted merely to her positive traits or actions but incorporates that of her husband, and his elevated status accompanies her aptitude.

The husband is mentioned in relation to his wife in only two other places. Verses 11–12 describe his confidence in her abilities to provide for the family. Her capable management produces "good and not evil" (טוֹב וְלֹא־רָע). Their life together conforms to the path of light and righteousness rather than the way of darkness and wickedness (Prov. 4:18–19). This trust relates to the lavish praise he gives his wife (Prov. 31:28). She resembles Ruth, who is celebrated for her deeds (Ruth 3:11), and he is like Boaz sitting among the elders (Ruth 4:1).

Her husband and children commend her directly, saying, "Your fear of God and your accomplishments outshine all others!" (see Prov. 31:29). Everyone knows about her and respects her wisdom (v. 31).

ANSWER KEY

1. *Parse:* (1) עָשְׂתָה (Qal SC 3FS עשׂה "make"). (2) נוֹדָע (Niphal PTCL MS ידע "known"). (3) בְּשִׁבְתּוֹ (PREP + Qal INF CSTR ישׁב "sit" + 3MS SF).

2. *Translate:* "She makes her coverings of linen and her clothing of fine purple fabric. / Her husband is known in the gates, where he sits in the company of the elders of the land."

DAY 78: PROVERBS 31:24–25

STEP ONE: **Read** aloud the text at least five times.

²⁴סָדִין עָשְׂתָה וַתִּמְכֹּר וַחֲגוֹר נָתְנָה לַכְּנַעֲנִי:

²⁵עֹז־וְהָדָר לְבוּשָׁהּ וַתִּשְׂחַק לְיוֹם אַחֲרוֹן:

STEP TWO: **Parse** the following verbs.

	Stem	Conj.	Pers.	Gend.	Numb.	Root	Trans.
(1) עָשְׂתָה							
(2) וַתִּמְכֹּר							
(3) נָתְנָה							
(4) וַתִּשְׂחַק							

STEP THREE: **Translate** the text into understandable English.

_____

_____

VOCABULARY

סָדִין   linen cloak

מכר   Qal: sell

חֲגוֹר   belt, girdle

כְּנַעֲנִי   Canaanite (i.e., seafaring merchants)

עֹז   strength, might

הָדָר   splendor; honor

לבוּשׁ   clothing

שׂחק   Qal: laugh (≈ צחק)

אַחֲרוֹן   future

STEP FOUR: **Notice** significant exegetical insights.

- עָשְׂתָה וַתִּמְכֹּר: The suffix conjugation is followed by a *wayyiqtol* verb. This combination is comparable to the syntax of verses 13 and 16. It creates a short narrative consisting of two clauses. The valiant wife pursues textile materials and creates clothes (v. 13), and she appraises acreage and acquires it (v. 16). Returning here to her dexterity with fabric, she fashions garments and then exports them. Such garments could be of great quality and worth (Judg. 14:12; 1 Sam. 18:4; 2 Sam. 1:24). This archetypal woman is a resource broker, an investor, an agriculturalist, a seamstress, and an adept trader. Her skill and industry have no bounds!

- וַחֲגוֹר נָתְנָה: The second half of the line expands the merchandise being sold and specifies the buyers as "Canaanite merchants" (כְּנַעֲנִי). The initial noun develops her wardrobe repertoire. She is not limited to merely nice cloaks; she supplies sashes and belts as well. The term "girdle" (חֲגוֹר) is perhaps a callback to the description of the valiant wife's fortitude that metaphorically girds her waist (חָגְרָה בְעוֹז מָתְנֶיהָ, v. 17). The concept of "strength" (עֹז) as her clothing is then recapitulated in the following verse (עֹז־וְהָדָר לְבוּשָׁה, v. 25).

FOR THE JOURNEY

Laughter conveys various emotive responses. Triumph breeds mirth, even as others face great loss (Lam. 1:7). Yahweh is impassioned to chuckle at humanity's otiose strategies (Ps. 2:4). He derides conspiratorial evil, knowing that his good plan ultimately succeeds (Ps. 37:13). Wisdom likewise delights in God's ways (Prov. 8:30). She can only snicker at those who do not heed her warnings (Prov. 1:26) and those who rely on their own strength (Ps. 147:10). The righteous laugh at the tough guy boasting in evil, destruction, and treachery (Ps. 52:3–9). They celebrate when God's plan comes to pass (2 Sam. 6:5; 1 Chron. 13:8).

The valiant wife joins this jovial jubilee. She does not fear the future (Isa. 8:23) but welcomes the day of Yahweh's coming judgment (Isa. 30:8). She has clothed herself with a life based on the wisdom of God. She has only dignified righteousness. Her hope is completely found in her God. All her activities have been a faithful response to him. She will not be put to shame.

ANSWER KEY

1. *Parse:* (1) עָשְׂתָה (Qal sc 3fs עשׂה "make"). (2) וַתִּמְכֹּר (Qal *wayyiqtol* 3fs מכר "sell"). (3) נָתְנָה (Qal sc 3fs נתן "give"). (4) וַתִּשְׂחַק (Qal *wayyiqtol* 3fs שׂחק "laugh").
2. *Translate:* "She makes and sells linen apparel, and she supplies belts to merchants. / Strength and splendor are her clothing, and she laughs at the future."

DAY 79: PROVERBS 31:26–27

STEP ONE: Read aloud the text at least five times.

²⁶פִּיהָ פָּתְחָה בְחָכְמָה   וְתוֹרַת־חֶסֶד עַל־לְשׁוֹנָהּ׃

²⁷צוֹפִיָּה הֲלִיכוֹת בֵּיתָהּ   וְלֶחֶם עַצְלוּת לֹא תֹאכֵל׃

STEP TWO: Parse the following verbs.

	Stem	Conj.	Pers.	Gend.	Numb.	Root	Trans.
(1) פָּתְחָה							
(2) צוֹפִיָּה							
(3) תֹאכֵל							

STEP THREE: Translate the text into understandable English.

> **VOCABULARY**
>
> פֶּה   mouth; opening (+ 3FS SF פִּיהָ)
> פתח   Qal: open
> חָכְמָה   wisdom
> לָשׁוֹן   tongue; language
> צפה   Qal: keep watch; oversee
> הֲלִיכָה   going (on), way
> עַצְלוּת   idleness

STEP FOUR: Notice significant exegetical insights.

- פִּיהָ פָּתְחָה בְחָכְמָה . . . עַל־לְשׁוֹנָהּ: The idiom "open one's mouth" is used for eating (Ezek. 3:2) and speaking (Ps. 38:14). Words are articulated "upon one's tongue" (2 Sam. 23:2). The wicked lie by opening their mouths (Ps. 109:2) and having destructive words on their tongues (Prov. 17:4). The corresponding body parts are employed in parallel in contrast (Prov. 10:31) and

243

in concert (Ps. 37:30). Regarding wisdom, the mouth must open to pass along ancient insight (Ps. 78:1–4, esp. v. 2). King Lemuel's mother reiterates the need for her princely pupil to speak out in defense of the powerless (Prov. 31:8–9). Embodying this advice, the valiant wife instructs openly.

- תּוֹרַת־חֶסֶד: This expression is unique in the Scriptures. The book of Proverbs, however, addresses both "instruction" and "loving-kindness" as components of the wise life. Echoing the beginning of the book, the mother's teaching intones wisdom (Prov. 1:8; 6:20), which brings happiness (29:18). Such training is a light for one's path (6:23) and a way to life (7:2; 13:14). In this way, the content of the valiant wife's instruction is covenant faithfulness (see also the father's teaching in 3:1–3); חֶסֶד and אֱמֶת motivate turning from evil (16:6). God abounds in loving-kindness (Num. 14:18; Jer. 31:3), and it guides his people (Exod. 15:13). Because of it, he forgives and shows favor (Ps. 25:7). Following the example of the prophets, the wife communicates God's faithfulness (Ps. 89:2; Isa. 63:7; Mic. 7:20). She witnesses the truth.

FOR THE JOURNEY

Wisdom encompasses the totality of one's person. All body parts play their proper role. Lips, tongue, eyes, and mouth participate. When each functions according to God's purposed order, life is organized sagaciously. The valiant wife understands the purpose and utility of all God grants. She employs each to judicious ends.

The supervision of her household requires her full faculties. Her mouth and tongue instruct and guide with wisdom and faithfulness. She understands the world as God created it and is a teacher of righteousness. Her eyes carefully guard the activities and habits of her family. She forestalls failures and foresees feats. Like a sentry, she observes the practices of the household and notes potential problems.

Returning to the mouth and its other common function, the woman does not consume the fruit of apathy and inactivity. She is not satisfied with idleness but contented in her labor (Prov. 13:4). She learns from the positive example of the ant (6:6–11) and the negative example of the sluggard (24:30–34; 26:13–16). She knows the opportune times to plant and harvest (20:4). Her diet is industry and diligence, and her life is uprightness (15:19).

Whatever she sets her heart and hand to prospers.

ANSWER KEY

1. *Parse:* (1) פָּתְחָה (Qal sc 3fs פתח "open"). (2) צוֹפִיָּה (Qal act ptcl fs צפה "oversee"). (3) תֹאכֵל (Qal pc 3fs אכל "eat")

2. *Translate:* "She opens her mouth with wisdom, and the instruction of loving-kindness is upon her tongue. / Keeping watch over the habits of her household, she does not eat a diet of delay."

DAY 80: PROVERBS 31:28–29

STEP ONE: **Read** aloud the text at least five times.

²⁸קָ֣מוּ בָ֭נֶיהָ וַֽיְאַשְּׁר֑וּהָ   בַּ֝עְלָ֗הּ וַֽיְהַלְלָֽהּ׃

²⁹רַבּ֣וֹת בָּנ֖וֹת עָ֣שׂוּ חָ֑יִל   וְ֝אַ֗תְּ עָלִ֥ית עַל־כֻּלָּֽנָה׃

STEP TWO: **Parse** the following verbs.

	Stem	Conj.	Pers.	Gend.	Numb.	Root	Trans.
(1) וַיְאַשְּׁר֑וּהָ							
(2) וַיְהַלְלָֽהּ							
(3) עָלִית							

STEP THREE: **Translate** the text into understandable English.

_____

_____

VOCABULARY

אשר   Piel: laud, make happy

בַּעַל   lord; husband

הלל   Piel: praise

אַתְּ   you (FS)

כֹּל   all, every (+ 3FP SF כֻּלָּנָה "all of them")

STEP FOUR: **Notice** significant exegetical insights.

- קָ֣מוּ בָ֭נֶיהָ וַֽיְאַשְּׁר֑וּהָ [קָם] בַּ֝עְלָ֗הּ וַֽיְהַלְלָֽהּ: The second half of the line closely matches the first half of the line. The actors, "her children" and "her husband," both arise and express their appreciation to her. Every syntactic component aligns between the two lines except the initial verb. That concept is implicit in the second half. This poetic feature is often called gapping.

- קָ֫מוּ: Perhaps less clear is what the initial verb (קוּם) means. It generally denotes standing or movement from an initial position. In this context, it may denote arising from sleep (Prov. 6:9). Corresponding to verse 15 of the poem, her husband and children awake to appreciate her early-morning efforts. The act of rising may instead signal a public testimony to her valiant labors (Deut. 19:15). Perhaps similarly, the verb can point to the success of her plans (Prov. 15:22; 19:21). That is to say, the members of the family stand as a demonstration of her wise efforts on their behalf. They succeed because of her.

FOR THE JOURNEY

The husband and children praise the valiant wife and mother, and they laud her accomplishments. Their esteem is represented in the succinct pronouncement of verse 29. They compare her to other exemplary wives, mothers, and daughters. They commend her, saying, "You outdo all others!" What high and merited praise! One may hear its echo in the words of the master: "Well done, my virtuous and trustworthy servant!" (Matt. 25:21).

The comparison to the character of Ruth is significant. Orpah and Ruth are both valiant daughters (Ruth 1:11–13). They support Naomi even in the despair of her widowhood and their own (vv. 2, 5). The Moabite sisters-in-law leave their homeland (vv. 6–7), but their mother-in-law persuades Orpah to turn back (v. 14). Ruth, however, ignores the hopelessness of the circumstances and welcomes her uncertain future (vv. 15–18). In this way, she is the more excellent daughter (2:22; 3:1, 16, 18; 4:15).

The Bethlehemite population applauds Ruth's strength. Boaz praises her faithfulness (2:11) and treats her as a daughter of Israel (2:8; 3:10–11). The elders bless her to be as fruitful as the celebrated matriarchs of old, Rachel and Leah (4:11). They hope for her seed to populate the house of Judah (v. 12). And they call upon Yahweh to give strength (עֲשֵׂה־חַיִל) and renown (v. 11).

ANSWER KEY

1. *Parse:* (1) וַיְאַשְּׁרוּהָ (Piel *wayyiqtol* 3MP אשׁר "bless" + 3FS SF). (2) וַיְהַלְלָה (Piel *wayyiqtol* 3MS הלל "praise" + 3FS SF). (3) עָלִית (Qal SC 2FS עלה "rise").

2. *Translate:* "Her children rise to bless her; her husband applauds her: / 'Many women act valiantly, but you surpass all others.'"

DAY 81: PROVERBS 31:30–31

STEP ONE: **Read** aloud the text at least five times.

³⁰שֶׁקֶר הַחֵן וְהֶבֶל הַיֹּפִי   אִשָּׁה יִרְאַת־יְהוָה הִיא תִתְהַלָּל:

³¹תְּנוּ־לָהּ מִפְּרִי יָדֶיהָ   וִיהַלְלוּהָ בַשְּׁעָרִים מַעֲשֶׂיהָ:

STEP TWO: **Parse** the following verbs.

	Stem	Conj.	Pers.	Gend.	Numb.	Root	Trans.
(1) תִתְהַלָּל							
(2) תְּנוּ							
(3) וִיהַלְלוּהָ							

STEP THREE: **Translate** the text into understandable English.

_____

_____

> **VOCABULARY**
>
> שֶׁקֶר   deception, deceit; disappointment
>
> חֵן   grace, favor
>
> הֶבֶל   vanity; breath
>
> יְפִי   beauty (pausal: יֹּפִי)
>
> יִרְאָה   fear
>
> הלל   Piel: praise; Hitpael: be praised
>
> פְּרִי   fruit, produce; offspring

STEP FOUR: **Notice** significant exegetical insights.

- שֶׁקֶר הַחֵן וְהֶבֶל הַיֹּפִי: Two short, two-word clauses begin verse 30. They describe the abstract concepts of "grace" and "beauty" positively as qualities of a woman (Esther 1:11; Prov. 11:16). In these verses, however, they are portrayed negatively as "falsehood" and "vanity." The prophets reserve this harsh pairing to describe idolatry (Jer. 16:19; Zech. 10:2). In Proverbs, these descriptions amount to death (Prov. 21:6). Lemuel's mother reminds the king of the twofold nature of charisma and appeal. One may be an attractive charming fool or a charming attractive sage. The outward features of charm and attraction are indistinguishable even with individuals of diametrically opposite disposition and character. The true measure of a valiant wife is not found in physical appearance but in whether she fears Yahweh (31:30). A wise woman will receive proper and enduring acclaim.

- מִפְּרִי יָדֶיהָ: This expression is parallel to "her works" (מַעֲשֶׂיהָ) in the second half of the line. These accomplishments have been described throughout the poem as valiant acts of great worth (Prov. 31:10, 28). They include her successful ventures in textiles (v. 13), fabrics (vv. 19, 22), trade (v. 24), management (vv. 15, 21, 26), land acquisition and agriculture (v. 16), charity (v. 20), and wise counsel (v. 26). All these works join with the entire household to laud her (vv. 28–29).

FOR THE JOURNEY

Just as her husband is known in the gates (Prov. 31:23), so too are the achievements of the valiant wife (v. 31). The husband has an upright reputation among the community and sits with the elders. These behaviors point to his noble character and wise counsel as he engages with those outside of his household (Col. 4:5–6). At the center of the poem is the notion that the valiant wife strengthens and advances her husband's position. She is a selfless partner (Gen. 2:18, 20).

The final verse appears to be a response to the household's exclamation of praise. She is unrivaled, and her deeds surpass all other women (Prov. 31:29). Her children are grateful for her care (vv. 15, 18, 21, 27), and her husband lauds her successes and uprightness (vv. 11–12, 28). Yet, her acclaim transcends domestic concerns. Her community benefits from her wise capabilities, her wares are esteemed for their excellence, and she profits from her work. She is known and admired far and wide. The fruit of her labors calls out in praise.

Such a valiant and virtuous wife is of exceeding distinction. She is the embodiment of wisdom (1:20–33; 8:1–21; 9:1–6). The one who finds her truly finds an abundant life!

1. *Parse:* (1) תִּתְהַלָּל (Hitpael PC 3FS הלל "be praised"). (2) תְּנוּ (Qal IMV MP נתן "give"). (3) וִיהַלְלוּהָ (CJ + Piel PC 3MP הלל "praise" + 3FS SF).

2. *Translate:* "Charm is a charade, beauty beguiling, but a God-fearing wife obtains ovation. / Give her the fruit of her hands, so that her accomplishments will praise her in the gates."

ROUTE 11

Psalm 1:1–6

STEP ONE: **Read** aloud the text at least five times.

אַשְׁרֵי־הָאִישׁ   אֲשֶׁר ׀ לֹא הָלַךְֿ בַּעֲצַת רְשָׁעִים
וּבְדֶרֶךְ חַטָּאִים לֹא עָמָד   וּבְמוֹשַׁב לֵצִים לֹא יָשָׁב׃

STEP TWO: **Translate** the text into understandable English.

> **VOCABULARY**
>
> אַשְׁרֵי   blessed, happy
> עֵצָה   counsel, advice (cstr עֲצַת)
> חַטָּא   sinner
> מוֹשָׁב   seat; dwelling; assembly
> לֵץ   scoffer, mocker

STEP THREE: **Notice** significant exegetical insights.

- **הָאִישׁ אֲשֶׁר**: The blessed man is described using three connected clauses. While the relative particle (אֲשֶׁר) is not repeated with the latter two clauses, the second line creates a correlative series with initial conjunctions. The first clause is structured as a verb followed by a prepositional phrase. The second line reverses this arrangement. Both clauses contain a prepositional phrase followed by a negative verb. Yet the grammatical correspondences and semantic expansion link all three. The morphosyntactic similarities include a negated 3MS suffix conjugation verb, a בְּ preposition, and a construct phrase consisting of a singular noun and a plural noun. These structuring features help to provide a multispectral image of how the happy individual operates in a world filled with unhappy lives.

- **לֹא הָלַךְ . . . לֹא עָמָד . . . לֹא יָשָׁב**: *Walk. Stand. Sit.* These basic activities comprise much of life. The blessed man, however, distinguishes between the circumstances of appropriate action and of steadfast non-action. Success comes as much, if not more, from knowing when *not* to act as it does from knowing when to act (Isa. 56:2). Wisdom rarely enforces absolute rules on common actions (see Prov. 26:4–5). Yet conditions and realistic limits enable character. A happy individual must discern and develop a prudent intelligence quotient. Such a judicious life produces benevolence—righteousness, justice, success, and equity (Prov. 1:2–7).

- **בַּעֲצַת רְשָׁעִים . . . וּבְדֶרֶךְ חַטָּאִים . . . וּבְמוֹשַׁב לֵצִים**: The happy person avoids evil council, the sinful way of life, and scornful company. The wide-ranging warning is to avoid "sinners" (Prov. 1:8–19; also see 13:21; 23:17). These individuals actively oppose the will of God (Isa. 1:28) and seek the lives of others (1 Sam. 15:18). They are under judgment (Isa. 13:9). The negated portrayals consequently produce a call to one of two divergent paths (Matt. 7:13–14).

FOR THE JOURNEY

What constitutes a happy and blessed person? It is tempting to imagine the blessed life as positive circumstances, pleasant feelings, or amassing wealth and influence. Perhaps your vision of a blessed life is more modest. Healthy lives, gathered family, and a successful vocation could make your happy list.

The Scriptures speak often of the blessed individual, but such a life is described in much different terms. Rather than focusing on external blessings or certain achievements, the happy person is portrayed as the one who is actively pursuing a particular kind of life, one characterized as finding wisdom (Prov. 3:13).

Wisdom is described in detail and with extensive ancient examples in Proverbs, Job, and Psalms. Finding wisdom is much more than knowing information; it is a way of life that pursues knowledge, morality, and spirituality as fashioned by God in the fabric of reality. The blessed life fears God (Prov. 28:14; Ps. 112:1) and takes refuge in him (Ps. 34:9). It praises, worships, and trusts in Yahweh (40:5; 84:5–6, 13). Such a person seeks to live without sin (32:2) and to walk a blameless path (119:1). The disciple of God and the pupil of Torah are hallmarks of blessing (Job 5:17; Ps. 94:12). The happy and blessed person finds God's favor by listening habitually to him (Prov. 8:34–35).

ANSWER KEY

1. *Translate:* "Blessed is the man who does not walk according to the guidance of wrongdoers, / does not linger on the way of offenders, and does not abide in the company of mockers."

DAY 83: PSALM 1:2

STEP ONE: **Read** aloud verses 1–2 at least five times.

¹אַשְׁרֵי־הָאִישׁ אֲשֶׁר | לֹא הָלַךְ בַּעֲצַת רְשָׁעִים

וּבְדֶרֶךְ חַטָּאִים לֹא עָמָד וּבְמוֹשַׁב לֵצִים לֹא יָשָׁב:

²כִּי אִם בְּתוֹרַת יְהוָה חֶפְצוֹ וּבְתוֹרָתוֹ יֶהְגֶּה יוֹמָם וָלָיְלָה:

STEP TWO: **Parse** the following verb.

	Stem	Conj.	Pers.	Gend.	Numb.	Root	Trans.
(1) יֶהְגֶּה							

STEP THREE: **Translate** verse 2 into understandable English.

VOCABULARY

חֵפֶץ   delight; pleasure; wish

הגה   Qal: growl; mutter, speak

יוֹמָם   daytime; by day

STEP FOUR: **Notice** significant exegetical insights.

- **כִּי אִם**: These introductory particles signal a strong contrast with the previous alternatives. True pleasure accompanies only the road less traveled, not the wide path leading to destruction (Luke 13:24–30). The wise person knows which path brings genuine delight.

- **בְּתוֹרַת יְהוָה . . . וּבְתוֹרָתוֹ**: The initial phrases of each clause specify an alternative way to walk, stand, and sit (v. 1). Yahweh offers contentment to the one finding the path outlined in his Torah. Psalm 112:1 similarly connects the man "fearing Yahweh" (יְרֵא אֶת־יְהוָה) and the one "delighting in his commands" (בְּמִצְוֹתָיו חָפֵץ). Wisdom and God's instructions are a two-sided coin with which one acquires true happiness (Prov. 8:32–34).

FOR THE JOURNEY

The final verb of verse 2 stands out as the first positive action under-taken by the person seeking happiness. The prefix conjugation (יֶהְגֶּה) is modified with the temporal phrase "by day and night" (יוֹמָם וָלַיְלָה, see Josh. 1:8). This expression suggests that delight requires repetition and recurrence. The blessed life demands persistent upkeep.

What specific activity needs repeating? The semantics of הגה de-serve a close look. The verb is found alongside notions of remember-ing (זכר, Pss. 63:7; 143:5), meditating (שיח, 77:13; 143:5), praising (הלל, 35:28), and various verbs of speaking (37:30; Isa. 59:13). Most English translations use "meditate" as a one-word gloss. The Message employs an ingestion metaphor: "You chew on Scripture day and night." These interpretations are a helpful starting point to understand the He-brew term as a function of persistent action, connecting to the practice of pondering Scripture, which has a long tradition in the church and synagogue.

Yet the Hebrew expression moves beyond ruminating thoughts or even studying the Word of God. The verb assumes voiced repetition. Other uses describe the vocal activity of lions (Isa. 31:4) and of doves (38:14; 59:11). What is shared between these animals is their noisy constancy. Whether relentless grunts, growls, and purrs or incessant chirrups, trills, and warbles, both creatures devote themselves to some-thing like meditative muttering.

In like manner, true delight is found in persistent uttering and relent-less oral ruminating on Yahweh's revelation (Deut. 6:6–7).

DAY 84: PSALM 1:3

STEP ONE: **Read** aloud verses 1–3 at least five times.

אַשְׁרֵי־הָאִישׁ¹   אֲשֶׁר ׀ לֹא הָלַךְ בַּעֲצַת רְשָׁעִים

וּבְדֶרֶךְ חַטָּאִים לֹא עָמָד   וּבְמוֹשַׁב לֵצִים לֹא יָשָׁב׃

²כִּי אִם בְּתוֹרַת יְהוָה חֶפְצוֹ   וּבְתוֹרָתוֹ יֶהְגֶּה יוֹמָם וָלָיְלָה׃

³וְהָיָה כְּעֵץ שָׁתוּל עַל־פַּלְגֵי מָיִם   אֲשֶׁר פִּרְיוֹ ׀ יִתֵּן בְּעִתּוֹ

וְעָלֵהוּ לֹא־יִבּוֹל   וְכֹל אֲשֶׁר־יַעֲשֶׂה יַצְלִיחַ׃

STEP TWO: **Parse** the following verbs.

	Stem	Conj.	Pers.	Gend.	Numb.	Root	Trans.
(1) וְהָיָה							
(2) שָׁתוּל							
(3) יַצְלִיחַ							

STEP THREE: **Translate** verse 3 into understandable English.

_____

_____

VOCABULARY

שׁתל   Qal: plant; transplant

פֶּלֶג   channel

פְּרִי   fruit, produce; offspring

עֵת   time; occasion (+ 3MS SF עִתּוֹ)

עָלֶה   leaf, foliage (+ 3MS SF עָלֵהוּ)

נבל   Qal: decay; crumble

צלח   Hiphil: succeed; prosper

STEP FOUR: **Notice** significant exegetical insights.

- כְּעֵץ: The preposition sets up an extended comparison between the blessed man and a tree growing along a riverbed. Tree metaphors are employed commonly to describe countries (Isa. 10:33–34; Ezek. 31:2–10; Dan. 4:10–15), kings (Judg. 9:8–15; Isa. 11:1; 53:2), and the righteous (Isa. 61:3).

- אֲשֶׁר פִּרְיוֹ . . . וְעָלֵהוּ: Similar to the blessed man in verse 1, the tree is described by a relative clause. The focus is on its fruit and its foliage. Like the valiant wife, the wise life produces fruit and does not wither (Prov. 31:31). The deeds of the wicked, by contrast, are worthless (Jer. 11:18–19; Matt. 7:17–20; John 15:1–8).

FOR THE JOURNEY

Psalm 1:2–3 uses the vivid image of a healthy and flourishing fruit tree to describe the positive traits of the blessed person. This perfect embodiment of happiness ensures prosperity for those following Yahweh.

The non-metaphorical descriptions echo several key elements of Yahweh's commission of Joshua as Moses's successor. God urges Joshua to keep the Torah (הַתּוֹרָה, Josh. 1:7; הַתּוֹרָה הַזֶּה, 1:8) and to meditate (הגה) on it by day and by night (יוֹמָם וָלַיְלָה, 1:8). He further instructs him not to waver to the right or left (יָמִין וּשְׂמֹאול, Josh 1:7; also, Deut. 5:32; 17:11, 20; 28:14; Prov. 4:27). Instead, he must be careful to do (תִּשְׁמֹר לַעֲשׂוֹת) all that is written (Josh. 1:8; Deut. 4:6; 11:20–22; etc.). The promised result is that he will flourish (צלח) in this path and be wise (שכל, Josh. 1:8).

Many readers have noticed these connections and observed the substantial influence of the language of Deuteronomy on Ps. 1 and Josh. 1. In this way, the introductory verses of Ps. 1 serve to unite the three main divisions of the Hebrew Bible—the Torah, the Prophets, and the Writings.

ANSWER KEY

1. *Parse:* (1) וְהָיָה (Qal *waqātal* 3MS היה "be"). (2) שָׁתוּל (Qal PASS PTCL MS שתל "planted"). (3) יַצְלִיחַ (Hiphil PC 3MS צלח "succeed").

2. *Translate:* "He will be like a tree rooted beside watery streams which bears fruit in season / and whose foliage never falls. Whatever he does flourishes."

DAY 85: PSALM 1:4

STEP ONE: **Read** aloud verses 1–4 at least five times.

¹אַשְׁרֵי־הָאִישׁ   אֲשֶׁר ׀ לֹא הָלַךְ בַּעֲצַת רְשָׁעִים

וּבְדֶרֶךְ חַטָּאִים לֹא עָמָד   וּבְמוֹשַׁב לֵצִים לֹא יָשָׁב׃

²כִּי אִם בְּתוֹרַת יְהוָה חֶפְצוֹ   וּבְתוֹרָתוֹ יֶהְגֶּה יוֹמָם וָלָיְלָה׃

³וְהָיָה כְּעֵץ שָׁתוּל עַל־פַּלְגֵי מָיִם   אֲשֶׁר פִּרְיוֹ ׀ יִתֵּן בְּעִתּוֹ

וְעָלֵהוּ לֹא־יִבּוֹל   וְכֹל אֲשֶׁר־יַעֲשֶׂה יַצְלִיחַ׃

⁴לֹא־כֵן הָרְשָׁעִים   כִּי אִם־כַּמֹּץ אֲשֶׁר־תִּדְּפֶנּוּ רוּחַ׃

STEP TWO: **Parse** the following verb.

	Stem	Conj.	Pers.	Gend.	Numb.	Root	Trans.
(1) תִּדְּפֶנּוּ							

STEP THREE: **Translate** verse 4 into understandable English.

> **VOCABULARY**
>
> מֹץ   chaff
>
> נדף   Qal: scatter

STEP FOUR: **Notice** significant exegetical insights.

- **הָרְשָׁעִים**: The wicked stand in contrast to the blessed, righteous person. They are referred to in the plural (רְשָׁעִים), and the righteous one in the singular (צַדִּיק). This numerical dissimilarity is common (e.g., Prov. 10:6, 11; 12:10; 15:28). Jesus's discussion of wide and narrow gates may allude to a similar difference (Luke 13:23–27). The related passage in Matthew's Gospel specifies that the wide path is tread by many but the narrow one is found by few (Matt. 7:13–14).

- כִּי אִם: These particles indicate a strong contrast with the previous material (see v. 2). The blessed man is like a tree (v. 3), but the wicked are like chaff (v. 4). Chaff is also used to describe idolaters (Hosea 13:2–3) and those who challenge God's purposes (Ps. 35:4–5; Isa. 17:12–13; 29:5).

FOR THE JOURNEY

In the view of most modern people, changes in atmospheric pressure arise from natural and impersonal forces. Wind has no personal animating source. This assumption results in understanding the Hebrew lexeme רוּחַ with two distinct, non-overlapping meanings. The term is glossed as either "wind" or "spirit" based on contemporary usage. The former is impersonal and non-agentive, while the latter designates personal agency, especially God's.

These categories were not as neatly bifurcated by the ancients. רוּחַ is imbued with divine agency (Ps. 147:18), accompanies divine action (2 Sam. 22:11; Ezek. 1:4), and enlivens creation (Isa. 42:5; cf. Gen. 1:30; 2:7). Even the widely held belief that the wind conforms to divine command (Exod. 10:13–19; Ps. 107:25–28; Jon. 1:4; Matt. 8:27) is foreign to many readers today.

Psalm 35:5 provides another representative example. Following the call for the chaff-like evildoers to be chased away with the wind (רוּחַ), the parallel clause names the angel of Yahweh (מַלְאַךְ יְהוָה) as the pursuing agent and animating source (see also Isa. 17:13; 41:16). רוּחַ in Ps. 1:4 could be understood similarly. God does not endure wickedness forever (Gen. 18:25) but promises to act with justice through his animated forces (Isa. 29:5–6; Jer. 30:23).

ANSWER KEY

1. *Parse:* (1) תִּדְּפֶ֫נּוּ (Qal PC 3FS נדף "scatter" + 3MS SF).
2. *Translate:* "Not so the wicked. / Rather they are like chaff which the wind scatters."

DAY 86: PSALM 1:5

STEP ONE: **Read** aloud verses 1–5 at least five times.

¹אַשְׁרֵי־הָאִישׁ אֲשֶׁר ׀ לֹא הָלַךְ בַּעֲצַת רְשָׁעִים

וּבְדֶרֶךְ חַטָּאִים לֹא עָמָד וּבְמוֹשַׁב לֵצִים לֹא יָשָׁב:

²כִּי אִם בְּתוֹרַת יְהוָה חֶפְצוֹ וּבְתוֹרָתוֹ יֶהְגֶּה יוֹמָם וָלָיְלָה:

³וְהָיָה כְּעֵץ שָׁתוּל עַל־פַּלְגֵי מָיִם אֲשֶׁר פִּרְיוֹ ׀ יִתֵּן בְּעִתּוֹ

וְעָלֵהוּ לֹא־יִבּוֹל וְכֹל אֲשֶׁר־יַעֲשֶׂה יַצְלִיחַ:

⁴לֹא־כֵן הָרְשָׁעִים כִּי אִם־כַּמֹּץ אֲשֶׁר־תִּדְּפֶנּוּ רוּחַ:

⁵עַל־כֵּן ׀ לֹא־יָקֻמוּ רְשָׁעִים בַּמִּשְׁפָּט וְחַטָּאִים בַּעֲדַת צַדִּיקִים:

STEP TWO: **Parse** the following verb.

	Stem	Conj.	Pers.	Gend.	Numb.	Root	Trans.
(1) יָקֻמוּ							

STEP THREE: **Translate** verse 5 into understandable English.

_____

_____

> **VOCABULARY**
>
> חָטָא   sinful; sinner
>
> עֵדָה   assembly, congregation (CSTR עֲדַת)

STEP FOUR: **Notice** significant exegetical insights.

- לֹא־יָקֻמוּ: The negative verb phrase functions as the verb in both halves of this line. The subject is the plural noun, and the following prepositional phrase describes the location where the wicked or sinners will not stand. The assumption of the identical verb in the second clause is called gapping, and it is a common feature of biblical poetry.

• וְחַטָּאִים . . . רְשָׁעִים: These terms connect to previous verses. Both occur in verse 1, and "the wicked" is found in verses 4 and 6. Individually, these words convey specific meanings associated with doing evil or subverting God's norms. In this context, they are used together in a more general sense to indicate the opposite of the wise, blessed person.

FOR THE JOURNEY

The applications of wisdom pertain to both earthly and heavenly life. A wise person often finds success in worldly endeavors but more importantly discovers the path of following God. Conversely, those rejecting wisdom forsake spiritual competency and are doomed to earthly failure as well.

Psalm 1 describes these opposite outcomes now and in the life to come. The blessed individual is grounded and fruitful (v. 3), while the wicked and sinful do not endure (v. 5). Their failure to stand may be understood in a this-worldly sense and/or a heavenly sense. The idea of standing in an assembly and being judged can refer to communal arbitration (Ps. 130:3). Because they stand for anything, the wicked do not stand up to scrutiny (Prov. 21:15). In this way, "the judgment" can refer to an eventual human inspection and ruling. Their evil deeds will be publicly exposed by the "righteous assembly" (Exod. 18:13–26; Deut. 16:18–20).

Ultimately, earthly judgment proceeds from the character of Yahweh. God is described as enacting justice and righteousness in the earthly realm (Deut. 32:4; also Jer. 23:5). God is a just judge. He differentiates between the righteous and the wicked in judgment (Gen. 18:25). In this sense, the assembly of the righteous ones may be read as a divine congregation (Pss. 7:8; 82:1).

ANSWER KEY

1. *Parse:* (1) יָקֻמוּ (Qal PC 3MP קום).
2. *Translate:* "Therefore, the wicked will not stand in the judgment, / nor sinners in the congregation of the righteous."

DAY 87: PSALM 1:6

STEP ONE: **Read** aloud verses 1–6 at least five times.

¹אַשְׁרֵי־הָאִישׁ   אֲשֶׁר ׀ לֹא הָלַךְ בַּעֲצַת רְשָׁעִים

וּבְדֶרֶךְ חַטָּאִים לֹא עָמָד   וּבְמוֹשַׁב לֵצִים לֹא יָשָׁב:

²כִּי אִם בְּתוֹרַת יְהוָה חֶפְצוֹ   וּבְתוֹרָתוֹ יֶהְגֶּה יוֹמָם וָלָיְלָה:

³וְהָיָה כְּעֵץ שָׁתוּל עַל־פַּלְגֵי מָיִם   אֲשֶׁר פִּרְיוֹ ׀ יִתֵּן בְּעִתּוֹ

וְעָלֵהוּ לֹא־יִבּוֹל   וְכֹל אֲשֶׁר־יַעֲשֶׂה יַצְלִיחַ:

⁴לֹא־כֵן הָרְשָׁעִים   כִּי אִם־כַּמֹּץ אֲשֶׁר־תִּדְּפֶנּוּ רוּחַ:

⁵עַל־כֵּן ׀ לֹא־יָקֻמוּ רְשָׁעִים בַּמִּשְׁפָּט   וְחַטָּאִים בַּעֲדַת צַדִּיקִים:

⁶כִּי־יוֹדֵעַ יְהוָה דֶּרֶךְ צַדִּיקִים   וְדֶרֶךְ רְשָׁעִים תֹּאבֵד:

STEP TWO: **Parse** the following verb.

	Stem	Conj.	Pers.	Gend.	Numb.	Root	Trans.
(1) תֹּאבֵד							

STEP THREE: **Translate** verse 6 into understandable English.

_____

_____

> ### VOCABULARY
>
> אבד   Qal: perish; be destroyed

STEP FOUR: **Notice** significant exegetical insights.

- יוֹדֵעַ . . . תֹּאבֵד: The contrasting conjugations serve to highlight an important and easily overlooked element of wisdom. God's role is active, but it may be delayed. Yahweh "is knowing" (יוֹדֵעַ) the path of the righteous. He is fully aware of their circumstances. He takes an interest in their activities in his created world. Yet it may seem that he is not as active in his awareness of evil. Wrongdoers are prosperous and appear happy (Job 21:7). They may even be persecuting and oppressing the righteous, making the upright path more difficult. The prefix conjugation holds a key to the wise life. The verb is coming to pass. Those on the path of the wicked are destined to destruction. They will perish if they continue. God will set things right. He promises justice, but such a resolution may be delayed or occur in a manner not visible to the righteous.

- וְדֶרֶךְ רְשָׁעִים תֹּאבֵד: The second clause provides a sharp contrast with the first clause. The initial clause follows the basic word order of verb followed by the subject (יוֹדֵעַ יְהוָה) and then the object (דֶּרֶךְ צַדִּיקִים). The parallel clause begins with the subject and employs a similar phrase as the previous object (וְדֶרֶךְ רְשָׁעִים). But צַדִּיקִים and רְשָׁעִים are antonyms. The antithetical relationship leads one to interpret the conjunction as contrastive, like English *but*, *however*, or *nonetheless*.

FOR THE JOURNEY

Life conforms to one of two divergent journeys. The wicked follow the path of destruction and perishing. The blessed follow the path of righteousness and prosperity. The final line of the psalm returns to this opening theme, but it includes the first explicit statement on the role of God in the blessed life.

Yahweh "knows" (ידע) the way of the righteous. On the one hand, his activity could imply that he is informed about where the righteous route lies. He distinguishes the pathway and even provides a map. While various didactic passages appeal to this inference (Exod. 18:20; Deut. 5:33), the present context seems to offer a better understanding in light of the semantics of the verb in the second half of the line. Together these two notions create opposite meanings in line with the contrasting paths of the righteous and the wicked. That is, "know" (ידע) contrasts with "perish" (אבד). The meaning is not exclusively focused on knowledge, information, or expertise but emphasizes familiarity ("pay attention to, be acquainted with") and care ("be concerned about, watch over"). Yahweh watches over the blessed life.

1. *Parse:* (1) תֹּאבֵד (Qal PC 3FS אבד "perish").
2. *Translate:* "For Yahweh watches over the way of the righteous, / but the way of the wicked shall perish."

ROUTE 12

Psalm 23:1–6

STEP ONE: **Read** aloud the text at least five times.

¹מִזְמוֹר לְדָוִד   יְהוָה רֹעִי לֹא אֶחְסָר:

²בִּנְאוֹת דֶּשֶׁא יַרְבִּיצֵנִי   עַל־מֵי מְנֻחוֹת יְנַהֲלֵנִי:

STEP TWO: **Parse** the following verbs.

	Stem	Conj.	Pers.	Gend.	Numb.	Root	Trans.
(1) רֹעִי							
(2) אֶחְסָר							
(3) יַרְבִּיצֵנִי							
(4) יְנַהֲלֵנִי							

STEP THREE: **Translate** the text into understandable English.

_____

_____

VOCABULARY

מִזְמוֹר   psalm; melody

רעה   Qal: shepherd, graze; pasture; feed

חסר   Qal: decrease; lack; be in need of

נָוֶה   dwelling place; grazing place (PL CSTR נְאוֹת)

דֶּשֶׁא   grass

רבץ   Hiphil: make lie down

מַיִם   water (CSTR מֵי)

מְנוּחָה   rest; resting place

נהל   Piel: lead, guide; provide

STEP FOUR: **Notice** significant exegetical insights.

- מִזְמוֹר לְדָוִד: The initial two words stand outside of the poem. Eight psalms begin with an identical phrase (Pss. 3; 15; 23; 29; 38; 63; 141; 143), and twenty more contain it as part of the opening verse. These introductory words are typically referred to as the superscription, which functions as a kind of subtitle or identifier. Most English translations include the superscription before verse 1, but in Hebrew it is enumerated and accented as part of the first verse.

- רֹעִי: This participle could be nominal or verbal. The nominal interpretation yields "my shepherd," an agent noun with the possessive suffix. The verbal sense would indicate an active, ongoing action with the object being the speaker: "Yahweh is shepherding me." The prophets frequently employ this metaphor to describe Yahweh as shepherding his people (Hosea 4:16; Zech. 11:7; see also Jer. 23; Ezek. 34).

FOR THE JOURNEY

Tending livestock is a common vocation around the world. While different environments and animals present distinct challenges, the basic responsibilities are generally the same. Shepherds guide various kinds of livestock to the necessities of life. They provide food and water. They seek out the lost, heal the wounded, and rescue those in trouble.

Psalm 23:1–4 employs the practice of shepherding to describe Yahweh's active care of his people.

Throughout the Hebrew Bible, the shepherd metaphor also describes the activities of Israel's rulers, particularly the king. Moses appointed his successor to lead Yahweh's community so that they would not be "like sheep without a shepherd" (Num. 27:15–17; cf. 1 Kings 22:17; Ezek. 34:5). David plays this role of shepherd, and as a result the people anoint him as king (2 Sam. 5:1–2). Israel's monarchy is an extension of Yahweh's kingship over Israel (Jer. 31:10) and the entire world (Mic. 5:4).

In the NT, Jesus takes up this shepherd-king metaphor. He claims to be the good shepherd (John 10:1–18). He leads and looks after his people (Matt. 9:35–36). He seeks and saves the lost. He even gives his life for them (Matt. 20:28). They lack nothing in his care.

DAY 89: PSALM 23:3–4

STEP ONE: **Read** aloud verses 1–4 at least five times.

¹מִזְמוֹר לְדָוִד יְהוָה רֹעִי לֹא אֶחְסָר:

²בִּנְאוֹת דֶּשֶׁא יַרְבִּיצֵנִי עַל־מֵי מְנֻחוֹת יְנַהֲלֵנִי:

³נַפְשִׁי יְשׁוֹבֵב יַנְחֵנִי בְמַעְגְּלֵי־צֶדֶק לְמַעַן שְׁמוֹ:

⁴גַּם כִּי־אֵלֵךְ בְּגֵיא צַלְמָוֶת

לֹא־אִירָא רָע כִּי־אַתָּה עִמָּדִי

שִׁבְטְךָ וּמִשְׁעַנְתֶּךָ הֵמָּה יְנַחֲמֻנִי:

STEP TWO: **Parse** the following verbs.

	Stem	Conj.	Pers.	Gend.	Numb.	Root	Trans.
(1) יְשׁוֹבֵב							
(2) יַנְחֵנִי							
(3) אֵלֵךְ							
(4) אִירָא							
(5) יְנַחֲמֻנִי							

STEP THREE: **Translate** verses 3–4 into understandable English.

_____

_____

VOCABULARY

נחה Hiphil: lead, conduct	שֵׁבֶט rod, staff, scepter; tribe
מַעְגָּל path, course	מִשְׁעֶנֶת staff
צֶדֶק righteous, righteousness	נחם Piel: comfort
גַּיְא valley (CSTR גֵּיא)	
צַלְמָוֶת darkness, gloom (see "For the Journey" below)	
עִם at; with; beside; against (+ 1CS SF עִמָּדִי or עִמִּי)	

STEP FOUR: **Notice** significant exegetical insights.

- **לְמַעַן שְׁמוֹ**: Yahweh leads his people like a shepherd "on account of his name." This reason may not be altogether transparent. What is it about the name of Yahweh that restores and provides guidance? Other instances give some sense as to the connection. Such an invocation signals forgiveness and the renewal of the covenant (Jer. 14:21). Ezekiel connects the name with the redemption from Egypt, in particular Yahweh's forgiveness of the people in the wilderness rebellion (Ezek. 20:9, 14, 22). In this way, the giving of the name is identified with the giving of the covenant (v. 44). The prophets say the name mitigates judgment (Isa. 48:9) and leads to the forgiveness of sin and rebellion against God (Jer. 14:7). Solomon invokes the name as an acknowledgment of Yahweh's great acts of redemption and response in worship (1 Kings 8:41). In the Psalms, the worshiper invokes God's name for individual forgiveness (Ps. 25:11). God guides and protects (31:4), he rescues (79:9), saves (106:8), and he deals faithfully, all for the sake of his name (109:21).

FOR THE JOURNEY

The fearsome darkness (צַלְמָוֶת) appears to be a compound of the Hebrew terms for "shadow" (צֵל) and "death" (מָוֶת). The Coverdale Bible (1535) exquisitely and famously renders it as "the valley of the shadow of death." Such an understanding reflects early Jewish and Christian interpretations as well.

More recently, scholars connect the term to a common Semitic root *ṣlm* meaning "be(come) dark, black" and its associated nouns in Arabic, Akkadian, and Ethiopic. This alternative interpretation involves suggesting that the term was originally a plural (צְלָמוֹת) or abstract noun (צַלְמוּת) that was forgotten, resulting in the form being read as a compound of two more familiar words in the Tiberian tradition. Notice that in the original unpointed text, the spelling צלמות would have been indistinguishable. However, neither of the proposed "original" forms occurs elsewhere in the Bible or in later Hebrew texts.

Regardless, the semantics of the word can be explored apart from the etymological realties. צלמות is used eighteen times in BH. Frequently, parallel terms convey the concept of darkness (Ps. 107:10; Jer. 13:16; Amos 5:8) or dark clouds (Job 3:5). "Day" and "light" are contrasting words (Job 3:5; Isa 9:1; Jer. 13.16; Amos 5:8). Other contexts suggest metaphorical darkness of mind (Job 12:22) and the place of death (Job 10:21–22; Ps. 44:20). Perhaps the most pervasive idea is that of judgment or doom (Job 3:5; 10:21–22; Jer. 13:16). Yahweh is the only escape from this form of gloom and hopelessness, as he was for the people in the darkness of the exodus (Ps. 107:10–14; Jer. 2:6).

ANSWER KEY

1. *Parse:* (1) יְשׁוֹבֵב (Polel PC 3MS שׁוב "restore"). (2) יַנְחֵנִי (Hiphil PC 3MS נחה "guide" + 1CS SF). (3) אֵלֵךְ (Qal PC 1CS הלך "walk"). (4) אִירָא (Qal PC 1CS ירא "fear"). (5) יְנַחֲמֻנִי (Piel PC 3MP נחם "comfort" + 1CS SF).

2. *Translate:* "He restores my life; he guides me in just paths for the sake of his name. / Even when I walk through a valley of dark doom, I will not fear evil, for you are with me; your rod and your staff comfort me."

DAY 90: PSALM 23:5–6

STEP ONE: **Read** aloud verses 1–6 at least five times.

¹מִזְמוֹר לְדָוִד   יְהוָה רֹעִי לֹא אֶחְסָר׃

²בִּנְאוֹת דֶּשֶׁא יַרְבִּיצֵנִי   עַל־מֵי מְנֻחוֹת יְנַהֲלֵנִי׃

³נַפְשִׁי יְשׁוֹבֵב יַנְחֵנִי בְמַעְגְּלֵי־צֶדֶק   לְמַעַן שְׁמוֹ׃

⁴גַּם כִּי־אֵלֵךְ   בְּגֵיא צַלְמָוֶת

לֹא־אִירָא רָע   כִּי־אַתָּה עִמָּדִי

שִׁבְטְךָ וּמִשְׁעַנְתֶּךָ   הֵמָּה יְנַחֲמֻנִי׃

⁵תַּעֲרֹךְ לְפָנַי ׀ שֻׁלְחָן   נֶגֶד צֹרְרָי

דִּשַּׁנְתָּ בַשֶּׁמֶן רֹאשִׁי   כּוֹסִי רְוָיָה׃

⁶אַךְ ׀ טוֹב וָחֶסֶד יִרְדְּפוּנִי   כָּל־יְמֵי חַיָּי

וְשַׁבְתִּי בְּבֵית־יְהוָה   לְאֹרֶךְ יָמִים׃

STEP TWO: **Parse** the following verbs.

	Stem	Conj.	Pers.	Gend.	Numb.	Root	Trans.
(1) תַּעֲרֹךְ							
(2) צֹרְרָי							
(3) דִּשַּׁנְתָּ							
(4) יִרְדְּפוּנִי							
(5) וְשַׁבְתִּי							

STEP THREE: **Translate** verses 5–6 into understandable English.

_____

_____

VOCABULARY

עָרַךְ	Qal: arrange; set in order	כּוֹס	cup
שֻׁלְחָן	table	רְוָיָה	saturation
נֶגֶד	before; front; opposite	אַךְ	surely; only; however
צָרַר	Qal: attack	רָדַף	Qal: pursue
דָּשֵׁן	Piel: anoint; drench	אֹרֶךְ	length
שֶׁמֶן	fat, oil		

STEP FOUR: **Notice** significant exegetical insights.

- טוֹב וָחֶסֶד: These terms convey the essence of the final wish. God hears the prayers of his people. He hears their cry. And he responds with goodness and love (Ps. 86:5). In Prov. 14:22 the words are set in opposition to those seeking evil.

FOR THE JOURNEY

These final verses utilize several multifaceted metaphors to depict God's faithfulness and call for hope in Yahweh's enduring deliverance.

The table, oil, and cup can have ritualistic or commonplace purposes. The table (שֻׁלְחָן) could be a place for sacrifice (Ezek. 41:22) or royal provision (1 Kings 2:7). It can play a ceremonial role (Exod. 40:4) or a more mundane one of eating a meal (Ps. 78:19; Prov. 9:2; Isa. 21:5). Applying oil to one's head (בַשֶּׁמֶן רֹאשִׁי) marks the commencement of priests (Exod. 29:7; Lev. 8:12; Ps. 133:2) and kings (1 Sam. 10:1; 2 Kings 9:3). Oil can also have restorative purposes (Isa. 1:6). In the Psalms, the cup (כּוֹסִי) symbolizes blessing (16:5), salvation (116:13), and destruction for the wicked (75:9).

These metaphors elicit God's actions in the world on behalf of his anointed and are contrasted with the derision of his enemies. God has provided provision, restoration, and salvation even in the face of fearsome adversaries. Now the psalmist hopes that the blessings of covenant loyalty and nearness will cast a long shadow over his entire life. Surely Yahweh is not finished with his work. The Shepherd-King will continue to set the table with all manner of riches for those who desire to dwell in his eternal house!

JOURNEY 3 · EXPANDING

1. *Parse:* (1) תַּעֲרֹךְ (Qal PC 2MS ערך "arrange"). (2) צֹרְרָי (Qal ACT PTCL MP צרר "attack" + 1CS SF). (3) דִּשַּׁנְתָּ (Piel SC 2MS דשן "enrich"). (4) יִרְדְּפוּנִי (Qal PC 3MP רדף "pursue" + 1CS SF). (5) וְשַׁבְתִּי (Qal *wəqātal* 1CS שוב "return" or amend to יָשַׁבְתִּי Qal SC 1CS ישב "dwell").

2. *Translate:* "You arrange a table before me in full view of my attackers. / You anoint my head with oil; my cup is full. / May only goodness and covenant faithfulness pursue me all the days of my life, / and then may I dwell in the house of Yahweh for a long time."

Appendix

SUPPLEMENTAL VOCABULARY

Words in the Readings That Occur
More Than 200 Times in the Old Testament

אָב		father	N MS
	אָבִיךָ		+ 2MS SF
	אֲבִיהֶן		+ 3FP SF
	אָבֹת		PL ABS
	אֲבֹתֶיךָ		+ 2MS SF
	אֲבוֹתֵיכֶם		+ 2MP SF
	אֲבוֹתֵינוּ		+ 1CP SF
אֶבֶן		stone, rock	N FS
אָדָם		man, person; humanity	N MS
אָדוֹן		lord, master; husband	N MS
	אֲדֹנָי		PL + 1CS SF (= the Lord)
אֲדָמָה		earth, land	N FS
אהב		Qal: love, like	VB
אֹהֶל		tent	N MS
אָח		brother; fellow	N MS
	אֶחָיו		PL + 3MS SF

אֶחָד	one; a(n)	NUM/ADJ MS ABS
	אַחַד	MS CSTR
	אַחַת	FS CSTR
אַחַר (or אַחֲרֵי)	behind; after, afterward	PREP
	אַחֲרֶיךָ	+ 2MS SF
	אַחֲרַיִךְ	+ 2FS SF
אֹיֵב	enemy	N MS
	אֹיְבֶיךָ	PL + 2MS SF
אַיִן	there is not; not, no	PTC
	אֵין	CSTR
אִישׁ	man, human; husband	N MS
	אִישָׁהּ	+ 3FS SF
	אֲנָשִׁים	PL ABS
אכל	Qal: eat, consume	VB
אַל	no, not	NEG
אֵל	god, deity	N MS
אֶל	toward; against; according to; concerning	PREP
	אֵלֶיהָ	+ 3FS SF
	אֵלַי	+ 1CS SF
	אֲלֵיהֶן	+ 3FP SF
אֵלֶּה	these	DEM
אֱלֹהִים	God, god(s), deity	N MP
	אֱלֹהֵי	CSTR
	אֱלֹהֶיהָ	+ 3FS SF
	אֱלֹהֶיךָ	+ 2MS SF
	אֱלֹהַיִךְ	+ 2FS SF
	אֱלֹהַי	+ 1CS SF

	אֱלֹהֵיכֶם	+ 2MP SF	
	אֱלֹהֵינוּ	+ 1CP SF	
אֶלֶף	thousand	N MS	
	אֲלָפִים	PL ABS	
אִם	if, if only; not; whether; unless	CJ	
אֵם	mother	N FS	
	אִמָּהּ	+ 3FS SF	
	אִמְּךָ	+ 2MS SF	
אַמָּה	cubit; forearm	N FS	
	אַמּוֹת	PL CSTR	
אמר	Qal: say	VB	
אֲנִי	I	PRO	
אָנֹכִי	I	PRO	
אֶרֶץ	earth, land, ground	N FS	
	אָרֶץ	(in pause)	
	אַרְצָם	+ 3MP SF	
אִשָּׁה	woman; wife	N FS	
	אֵשֶׁת	CSTR	
	אִשְׁתּוֹ	+ 3MS SF	
	נָשִׁים	PL ABS	
אֲשֶׁר	who, which, that	REL	
אֵת	definite direct-object marker	PTC	
	אֹתוֹ (or אוֹתוֹ)	+ 3MS SF	
	אֹתָם	+ 3MP SF	
	אֶתְכֶם	+ 2MP SF	
	אֹתָנוּ	+ 1CP SF	
אֵת	with, beside	PREP	
	אִתָּהּ	+ 3FS SF	

	אִתָּךְ	+ 2FS SF
אַתָּה	you (MS)	PRO
אַתֶּם	you (MP)	PRO
בְּ (בַּ, בָּ, בֶּ, בֵּ, בֶּ)	in, on, at; with; through; among; when; in exchange for	PREP
	בּוֹ	+ 3MS SF
	בָּהּ	+ 3FS SF
	בִּי	+ 1CS SF
	בָּם	+ 3MP SF
	בָּכֶם	+ 2MP SF
	בָּנוּ	+ 1CP SF
בּוֹא	Qal: enter, come in; Hiphil: bring in, lead in	VB
בֵּין	between	PREP
	בֵּין	CSTR
	בֵּינֵךְ	+ 2FS SF
	בֵּינִי	+ 1CS SF
בַּיִת	house; family	N MS
	בֵּית	CSTR
	בֵּיתָהּ	+ 3FS SF
	בֵּיתְךָ (in pause בֵּיתֶךָ)	+ 2MS SF
	בֵּיתִי	+ 1CS SF
	בָּתִּים	PL CSTR
בֵּן	son	N MS
	בֶּן־	CSTR
	בִּנְךָ	+ 2MS SF
	בָּנִים	PL ABS
	בְּנֵי	PL CSTR

	בָּנָיו	+ 3MS SF
	בָּנֶיהָ	+ 3FS SF
	בָּנֶיךָ	+ 2MS SF
בנה	Qal: build	VB
בֹּקֶר	morning	N MS
בקש	Piel: seek; require; consult; Pual: be sought	VB
בְּרִית	covenant; contract	N FS
	בְּרִיתוֹ	+ 3MS SF
ברך	Piel: bless; praise	VB
בַּת	daughter	N FS
	בִּתּוֹ	+ 3MS SF
	בִּתְּךָ	+ 2MS SF
	בָּנוֹת	PL ABS
	בְּנֹתָיו	+ 3MS SF
	בְּנֹתַי	+ 1CS SF
גָּדוֹל	great	ADJ MS
	גְּדֹלִים	MP ABS
	גְּדוֹלָה	FS ABS
	גְּדֹלוֹת	FP ABS
גַּם	also, even	ADV
דבר	Piel: speak	VB
דָּבָר	word, speech, thing	N MS
	דְּבַר	CSTR
	דְּבָרִים	PL ABS
דָּוִד	David	PN
דֶּרֶךְ	way, road, journey; custom, manner	N MS/FS

הַ (הָ, הֶ)	DEF ART	PTC
הֲ (הַ, הֶ)	interrogative	PTC
הוּא	he	PRO
הִיא	she	PRO
היה	Qal: be; become; happen; occur	VB
הלך	Qal: go, come; walk; behave; Hiphil: bring; lead; Hitpael: walk about	VB
הֵם (הֵמָּה)	they (MP)	PRO
הִנֵּה	behold! lo!	interjection
הִנְנִי		+ 1CS SF
וְ (וּ, וַ, וֵ, וִ, וָ)	and, also; but; so; then	CJ
זֹאת	this; here	DEM FS
זֶה	this; here	DEM MS
זכר	Qal: remember	VB
זֶרַע	seed, offspring; sowing	N MS
זָרַע		(in pause)
זַרְעוֹ		+ 3MS SF
זַרְעֲךָ		+ 2MS SF
חַטָּאת	sin; sin offering	N FS
חַטָּאתְךָ		+ 2MS SF
חַטֹּאותֵיכֶם		PL + 2MP SF
חַיִּים	life, lifetime	N MP
חַיֶּיהָ		+ 3FS SF
חַיֶּיךָ		+ 2MS SF
חַיַּי		+ 1CS SF
חַיִל	strength; wealth; army	N MS
חָיִל		(in pause)

חֶסֶד	faithfulness, loyalty; kindness, goodness	N MS
חַסְדִּי		+ 1CS SF
טוֹב	good; desirable; usable; kind	N MS
יָד	hand	N FS
יַד		CSTR
יָדוֹ		+ 3MS SF
יָדְךָ		+ 2MS SF
יָדֶיהָ		PL + 3FS SF
ידע	Qal: know; Niphal: be known; Pual: be known	VB
יְהוּדָה	Judah	PN
יהוה	Yahweh	PN
יְהוֹשׁוּעַ	Joshua	PN
יוֹם	day, daylight; lifetime; year	N MS
יָמִים		PL ABS
יְמֵי		PL CSTR
יָמֶיךָ		+ 2MS SF
ילד	Qal: bear, give birth	VB
יָם	sea	N MS
יַמִּים		PL ABS
יסף	Qal: add; Hiphil: increase, add	VB
יַעֲקֹב	Jacob	PN
יצא	Qal: go out, come out; Hiphil: lead out	VB
ירא	Qal: fear	VB
ירד	Qal: go down; descend	VB
ירשׁ	Qal: take possession of; inherit	VB
ישׁב	Qal: sit, dwell, remain, stay	VB
יִשְׂרָאֵל	Israel	PN

(כְ, כֵָ, כַָ) כְ	like, as, similar to; according to, about	PREP
כֹּה	thus; here; now	ADV
כֹּהֵן	priest	N MS
כּוּן	Niphal: be firm, be established; endure; Polel: establish, make firm; Polal: be established; Hiphil: prepare, accomplish	VB
כִּי	for, because, that; when; if; indeed	CJ
כֹּל (כָּל-)	all, every, entirety, whole	N MS
כֻּלָּנָה		+ 3FP SF
כלה	Qal: stop; be finished; perish; Piel: bring to an end, complete; Pual: be finished	VB
כֵּן	thus, so; then	ADV
כרת	Qal: cut off, cut down; Hiphil: exterminate	VB
כתב	Qal: write	VB
(לְ, לֵָ, לָ, לֶָ, לַ) לְ	to, toward; for; in regard to; of, about	PREP
לוֹ		+ 3MS SF
לָהּ		+ 3FS SF
לְךָ		+ 2MS SF
לָךְ		+ 2FS SF
לִי		+ 1CS SF
לָהֶם		+ 3MP SF
לָהֶן		+ 3FP SF
לָכֶם		+ 2MP SF
לָנוּ		+ 1CP SF
לֹא	no, not	NEG
לֵב	heart; mind; disposition; will	N MS

לֵבָב	heart; mind; disposition; will	N MS
לְבָבוֹ		+ 3MS SF
לְבָבְךָ		+ 2MS SF
לְבַבְכֶם		+ 2MP SF
לֵוִי	Levi	PN
לֶחֶם	food; bread	N MS
לָחֶם		(in pause)
לַחְמָהּ		+ 3FS SF
לַיְלָה	night	N MS
לָיְלָה		(in pause)
לְמַעַן	in order that; for the sake of; on account of	PREP/CJ
לִפְנֵי	before, in front of	PREP
לְפָנָיו		PREP + 3MS SF
לְפָנַי		PREP + 1CS SF
לקח	Qal: take, receive	VB
מְאֹד	muchness; strength, power; abundance; exceedingly, very	N/ADV
מְאֹדֶךָ		+ 2MS (in pause)
מָה (מַה־)	what? how?	INT
מוֹעֵד	appointed time; meeting, assembly place	N MS
מוֹעֲדִים		PL ABS
מות	Qal: die, perish	VB
מִזְבֵּחַ	altar	N MS
מִי	who?	INT
מַיִם	water	N MP
מֵי		CSTR
מלא	Qal: fill; be full; Niphal: be filled; be accomplished	VB

מֶלֶךְ	king	N MS
מִן	from; of; on account of; beside; above; than; since	PREP
מִמֶּנּוּ		+ 3MS SF
מִכֶּם		+ 2MP SF
מצא	Qal: find; obtain	VB
מִצְרַיִם	Egypt; Egyptians	PN
מִצְרִי		ADJ MS
מָקוֹם	place, locality	N MS
מֹשֶׁה	Moses	PN
מִשְׁפָּחָה	clan, family	N FS
מִשְׁפַּחַת		CSTR
מִשְׁפָּט	judgment; case; claim	N MS
מִשְׁפָּטִים		PL ABS
נגד	Hiphil: tell, announce, declare	VB
נַחֲלָה	possession; property; inheritance	N FS
נַחֲלָתוֹ		+ 3MS SF
נטה	Hiphil: stretch; extend	VB
נכה	Hiphil: strike, smite	VB
נַעַר	young man, lad; servant	N MS
נֶפֶשׁ	soul; life; person, living being; self; desire, passion	N FS
נַפְשְׁךָ		+ 2MS SF
נַפְשִׁי		+ 1CS SF
נצל	Hiphil: take away; rescue	VB
נשׂא	Qal: lift, carry; take; Niphal: be carried, be elevated	VB
נתן	Qal: give; set, put	VB
סור	Qal: turn aside; retreat; Hiphil: remove	VB

עָבַד	Qal: labor, work; serve; Hophal: be made to serve	VB
עֶבֶד	slave, servant	N MS
עַבְדּוֹ		+ 3MS SF
עַבְדְּךָ		+ 2MS SF
עַבְדִּי		+ 1CS SF
עֲבָדִים		PL ABS
עָבַר	Qal: pass over, cross; traverse	VB
עַד	until; during; upon	PREP
עוֹד	still, yet; again; besides; duration	ADV
עוֹלָם	long time; future	N MS
עָוֹן	iniquity; punishment, guilt; sin	N MS
עֲוֹן		CSTR
עֲוֹנֶךָ		+ 2MS SF
עָזַב	Qal: leave; forsake; loose	VB
עַיִן	eye; spring	N FS
עֵינָיו		PL + 3MS SF
עֵינֶיךָ		PL + 2MS SF
עֵינֵיכֶם		PL + 2MP SF
עֵינַי		PL + 1CS SF
עֵינֵינוּ		PL + 1CP SF
עִיר	city; district	N FS
עָרִים		PL ABS
עַל	on; toward; beside; against; according to; more than; before; because	PREP
עָלָיו		+ 3MS SF
עֲלֵיהֶן		+ 3FP SF
עָלֵינוּ		+ 1CP SF

עָלָה	Qal: go up, climb, ascend; Hiphil: lead up, bring up	VB
עַם	people; nation	N MS
עַמּוֹ		+ 3MS SF
עַמָּהּ		+ 3FS SF
עַמֵּךְ		+ 2FS SF
עַמִּי		+ 1CS SF
עַמִּים		PL ABS
עִם	with; toward	PREP
עִמָּהּ		+ 3FS SF
עִמְּךָ		+ 2MS SF
עִמָּכֶם		+ 2MP SF
עִמִּי (עִמָּדִי)		+ 1CS SF
עִמָּנוּ		+ 1CP SF
עָמַד	Qal: stand; take a stand; abide	VB
עָנָה	Qal: answer, reply, respond	VB
עֵץ	tree; timber, wood; forest	N MS
עָשָׂה	Qal: do; make, create; obtain; Niphal: be done; be made	VB
עֶשֶׂר	ten	NUM with F N
עֲשֶׂרֶת		CSTR with M N
עֵת	time; occasion	N MS/FS
עִתּוֹ		+ 3MS SF
עַתָּה	now	ADV
פֶּה	mouth; opening	N MS
פִּי		CSTR (identical to the 1CS SF form)
פִּיהָ		+ 3FS SF
פִּי		+ 1CS SF (identical to the CSTR form)

פָּנִים	face	N MP
	פְּנֵי (see also לִפְנֵי)	CSTR
	פָּנָיו (see also לְפָנָיו)	+ 3MS SF
	פָּנֶיךָ	+ 2MS SF
	פָּנַי (see also לְפָנַי)	+ 1CS SF
	פָּנֵינוּ	+ 1CP SF
פקד	Qal: assign a position; remember; investigate; muster; miss; punish; number	VB
פַּרְעֹה	Pharaoh	PN
צֹאן	small cattle; sheep and/or goats	N FS
	צֹאנָם	+ 3MP SF
צָבָא	army, troops; war, warfare	N MS/FS
	צְבָאָם	+ 3MP SF
	צְבָאוֹת	PL ABS
צַדִּיק	just, righteous	ADJ MS
	צַדִּיקִים	MP ABS
צוה	Piel: command	VB
קֹדֶשׁ	holiness, sacredness, apartness	N MS
קוֹל	sound, voice	N MS
	קוֹלוֹ	+ 3MS SF
	קוֹלָן	+ 3FP SF
קום	Qal: arise, stand; Hiphil: lift up, raise, erect, establish	VB
קרא	Qal: call, proclaim, read	VB
קֶרֶב	midst, among; inward part	PREP
	קִרְבְּכֶם	+ 2MP SF
	קִרְבָּם	+ 3MP SF

רָאָה	Qal: see; reveal; perceive, understand; select; Niphal: become visible, appear	VB
רֹאשׁ	head; top; chief; beginning	N MS
רֹאשִׁי		+ 1CS SF
רַב	great	ADJ MS
רַבִּים		MP ABS
רַבּוֹת		FP ABS
רֶגֶל	foot	N FS
רַגְלָיו		PL + 3MS SF
רוּחַ	spirit; breath; wind	N FS
רַע	evil, bad, depraved; poor	ADJ MS
רָע		(in pause)
רָשָׁע	wicked; guilty	ADJ MS
רְשָׁעִים		MP ABS
שָׂדֶה	field, pasture, land	N MS
שְׂדֵה		CSTR
שְׂדֵי		PL CSTR
שִׂים	Qal: put, place, set (up); arrange; establish	VB
שַׂר	ruler; prince; officer	N MS
שָׁאוּל	Saul	PN
שֶׁבַע	seven, group of seven	NUM with F N
שׁוּב	Qal: return, turn back; Hiphil: make return, bring back; Polel: bring back; restore	VB
שָׁכַב	Qal: lie (down), sleep	VB
שָׁלַח	Qal: send (out, away); stretch out; Piel: let go; send out	VB
שָׁלֹשׁ	three	NUM with F N
שְׁלֹשָׁה		ABS with M N

שָׁם	there; then	ADV
שָׁמָּה		+ directive *heh* ("to there")
שֵׁם	name	N MS
שְׁמוֹ		+ 3MS SF
שְׁמִי		+ 1CS SF
שָׁמַיִם	heaven, sky; heavens	N MP
שָׁמָיִם		(in pause)
שׁמע	Qal: hear, listen; obey	VB
שׁמר	Qal: keep, watch over, guard	VB
שָׁנָה	year	N FS
שְׁנַת		CSTR
שָׁנִים		PL ABS
שְׁנַיִם	two	NUM MP ABS
שְׁנֵי		MP CSTR
שְׁנֵיהֶם		+ 3MP SF
שְׁתַּיִם		FP ABS
שְׁתֵּי		FP CSTR
שְׁתֵּיהֶם		+ 3MP SF
שַׁעַר	gate	N MS
שְׁעָרִים		PL ABS
שְׁעָרֶיךָ		+ 2MS SF
שׁפט	Qal: judge, rule	VB
שֵׁשׁ	six	NUM with F N
שֵׁשֶׁת		CSTR with M N
תָּוֶךְ	midst	N MS
תּוֹךְ (+ PREP בְּתוֹךְ)		CSTR

תּוֹרָה	instruction; law	N FS
	תּוֹרַת	CSTR
	תּוֹרָתוֹ	+ 3MS SF
תַּ֫חַת	below, underneath; instead of	PREP
	תַּחְתָּיו	+ 3MS SF

AUTHOR INDEX

SCRIPTURE INDEX

25:22 212
25:28 112
27:9 233
31:12 222

2 Samuel

1:24 241
3:9 212
3:35 212
5:1–2 268
6:5 241
7 94
7:1 80, 88
7:2 79, 88
7:2–3 77
7:3 76
7:4 94
7:4–5 75–77
7:5 80, 80n1, 88
7:6 88
7:6–7 78–80
7:7 88
7:8 88, 118
7:8–9 81–83
7:10–11a 84–86
7:11 77, 80, 88
7:11b–13 87–89
7:12 89, 92
7:13 94
7:14–15 90–92
7:16–17 93–95
7:25 82
11:16 222
15:2–6 239
19:14 212
19:15 117
20:2 209
22:11 260
22:46 230
23:2 243
24:9 222

1 Kings

1:13 94
1:17 94
1:20 94

1:24 94
1:27 94
1:30 94
1:35 94
1:37 94
1:42 222
1:46 94
1:47 94
1:48 94
2:4 94
2:7 273
2:12 94
2:19 94
2:23 212
2:24 94
2:33 94
2:45 94
3:6 94
3:14 70
5:19 94
6:23–28 130
8:10 128
8:11–12 128
8:25 94
8:27 80
8:41 270
8:42 82
8:58 117
9:5 94
10:9 94
10:15 232
11:2 117
11:3 117
11:4 117
11:9 117
12:1 120
17:20 219
19:6 137
19:18 202
20:10 212
20:32 230
21:17 77
21:19 70
22:17 268
22:19 32, 127

2 Kings

1:17 166
3:4 227
4:27 219
5:1 222
5:15 210
5:26 233
6:19 164
6:31 212
8:1–2 190
9:3 273
11:18 16
15:2 127
16:10 16
17:34–39 39
17:37 39
18:4 130
22:15–20 142
23:25 47

1 Chronicles

1:29 35
2:12 197
2:19 193
2:35 182
2:50 193
4:4 193
5:2 206
5:24 82
6:3 151
12:31 82
13:8 241
14:17 82
23:13 130
26:7–8 222

2 Chronicles

3:17 222
4:3 16
5:7–8 130
13:10 47
18:18 32
21:17 196
26:3 127
26:16–23 127

New Testament